IN SEARC

IN SEARCH OF SITA

REVISITING MYTHOLOGY

Edited by

Malashri Lal

and

Namita Gokhale

YATRA BOOKS PENGUIN BOOKS

PENGUIN BOOKS
Published by the Penguin Group
Penguin Books India Pvt. Ltd, 11 Community Centre, Panchsheel Park,
New Delhi 110 017, India
Penguin Group (USA) Inc., 375 Hudson Street, New York, New York 10014, USA
Penguin Group (Canada), 90 Eglinton Avenue East, Suite 700, Toronto,
Ontario, M4P 2Y3, Canada (a division of Pearson Penguin Canada Inc.)
Penguin Books Ltd, 80 Strand, London WC2R 0RL, England
Penguin Ireland, 25 St Stephen's Green, Dublin 2, Ireland (a division of Penguin Books Ltd)
Penguin Group (Australia), 250 Camberwell Road, Camberwell, Victoria 3124, Australia
(a division of Pearson Australia Group Pty Ltd)
Penguin Group (NZ), 67 Apollo Drive, Rosedale, North Shore 0632, New Zealand
(a division of Pearson New Zealand Ltd)
Penguin Group (South Africa) (Pty) Ltd, 24 Sturdee Avenue, Rosebank,
Johannesburg 2196, South Africa

Penguin Books Ltd, Registered Offices: 80 Strand, London WC2R 0RL, England

First published by Penguin Books India and Yatra Books 2009

Pages 261–62 are an extension of the copyright page

All prints reproduced in this book are from the collection of Aman Nath

10 9 8 7 6 5 4 3 2 1

ISBN 9780143068181

Typeset in Adobe Garamond by SÜRYA, New Delhi
Printed at Thomson Press India Ltd.

'To all the incarnate goddesses and to Bellisima, the lady of the waters, at Bellagio.'

CONTENTS

IN DIALOGUE

VERSIONS

CREATIVE INTERPRETATIONS

ACKNOWLEDGEMENTS

THANK YOU TO so many people who discussed their perspectives on Sita with us—Kesav Desaraju, Paula Richman, Sukrita Paul Kumar, Sumanyu Satpathy, Shyamala Narayan and others.

We are grateful for valuable research assistance from Shvetal Vyas, Kanishka Gupta and Rina Tripathi. To Shubhda Khanna who helped bring this anthology to the final stages. To Neeta Gupta and Yatra Books for believing in this book. To Ravi Singh, R. Sivapriya and Debasri Rakshit for their help, encouragement and guidance.

Our gratitude to the Rockefeller Foundation for the fellowship at Bellagio which provided us time and space to work on Sita.

SITA: A PERSONAL JOURNEY

NAMITA GOKHALE

THIS SEARCH FOR Sita began near the botanical gardens in Peradiniya, Sri Lanka, on a day redolent with the breezes of spring. As I absorbed the lush landscape, the swaying palms, the feather-leaved bamboos, the Java willows, I thought I saw her, sitting on a rock, perhaps an apparition from a Raja Ravi Varma painting.

Sita, Janaki, Bhaumi, Bhumija, Bhukanya, daughter of the Earth. A flesh-and-blood presence, a young woman in distress. Was it myself that I saw there, sitting on that rock? For all of us Indian women carry some of her within us: Sita's strength and her vulnerability.

The name Sita derives from the Sanskrit word for 'furrow' or 'marks of the plough', and metaphors of the earth surround her birth. Janaki, the daughter of Janaka, was a strong young woman who could lift the Hara, Shiva's bow, with one arm while swabbing the floor with the other in her father's house.

Then why do I picture her weeping? When and why did she become a figure of weakness rather than strength? Sita, in our prevalent idiom, is weak, oppressed, a natural victim. Considering that Sri Rama's wife—Vaidehi, Sita, Ramaa, call her what you will—is the primary archetype for all Indian women, a role model pushed and perpetuated by a predominantly patriarchal society, it is no wonder that she is someone the modern emancipated consciousness prefers to banish into yet another exile.

But she does not exit so easily. Sita has been there, in the mass consciousness of our subcontinent, for very long now. She has been there since the beginning of our timeless history, in the different versions and recensions of the Ramayana, written or recited, and never forgotten. She lives on in all the Sitapurs and Sitamarhis of the nation, in the Janakpurs and Ramgarhs and Rampurs. She has been seen on celluloid, and on television; she has been elected to Parliament from Vadodara, in the person of Deepika Chikhalia, the actress who played her role in Ramanand Sagar's television serial titled *Ramayana*. She is there in song, in poetry, in the tears that Indian women have been shedding through generations as they tread the *lakshmana rekha*s that barricade their lives, as they are consumed by the flames of the penitential *agni pareeksha*s that their families regularly subject them to.

Is this why those hot, helpless tears do not leave my vision or memory?

Mythology in India is not just an academic or a historical subject, it is a vital and living topic of contemporary relevance. The complex social, political and religious attitudes of 'modern' India cannot be understood without an understanding of our myths and their impact on the collective faith of the people. The emotions that drove my quest to deconstruct the real woman behind the anguished formal portrait of Mrs Ramachandra Raghuvanshi were those of sympathy, empathy and curiosity about the fractured identities and expectations of most women in India today. When Dr Malashri Lal and I began work on the compilation of this anthology, we wished to present a composite picture of Sita, of a woman negotiating the public and private spaces in society—between kingship and exile, duty and assertion, loyalty and rejection.

The Ramayana is considered an *adikavya*, an epic in the realm of poetics, in contrast to the Mahabharata, which is described as *itihaas* or history. The sage Valmiki, to whom the definitive or classical version of the Ramayana is ascribed, was inspired to begin the epic poem after seeing a kraunch bird, in sight of its mate, killed by a cruel hunter. The dominant emotion invoked in the opening passages is that of compassion, and it is compassion, again, that is evoked in the seventh segment, the Uttara Kanda, where Sita, that brave single parent, bears and rears her twin sons. Her children, Lava and Kusha, are described by Valmiki in the matrilineal mode as Sita's sons—'*Maithili sutau, Sita putrau*'. Called '*suvrata dharmacharini*', or the abstemious and righteous one, Sita is never, in any interpretation, depicted as having deviated from her loyalty and integrity to her royal husband.

The Ramayana is a story about monogamous love, in contrast to the complex and passionate codes and polygamous practices of the Mahabharata. Rama's father, Dasharatha, had suffered the consequences of polygamy and the attendant succession crisis, but Sri Rama determinedly maintained his monogamous resolve and adhered to his '*ek patni vrata*'.

Kalidasa's *Raghuvamsha*, Bhavabhuti's *Uttara Ramacharita*, and all the variations and regional interpretations of this heroic poem, celebrate kinship and the affection and loyalty of brothers, and other social codes of crucial importance in a complex feudal society. Sita, portrayed as being utterly and unquestioningly in love with her husband, is always brave, always dutiful, and does everything in her power to preserve the fabric of this patriarchal universe. She indicates her anguish and exerts her autonomy by departing from this world after being asked to take the second test of fire, but only after having completed the full cycle of her perceived duties. In diasporic and local versions of the epic, however, the contours of the story remain more human and compelling. A handsome and loving couple, united by destiny, the gods, and love for each other, are sent into exile because of feminine manipulations and domestic discontent. The screenplay has all the box office elements of drama and suspense, and the lofty emotions of honour, duty and revenge are played out to a successful denouement.

The anticoda begins with the spoils of peace. When a washerman disgruntled with his wife starts slandering Sita, the anointed queen of Ayodhya, the rites of kingship dictate that the subject of the slander be censured by being banished to live in the forest, alone. The inequity of the situation and the cruelty of the indictment are dealt with quite differently in folk tradition and high art. While sophisticated moralists and classicists have many explanations and alibis for Rama's royal lapse (including some deeply obtuse metaphysical justifications), the folk songs and alternate traditions wax indignant and side with the victim.

This collection of essays attempts to accommodate different points of view. It is divided into sections covering 'Commentary', 'Dialogue', 'Sources' and 'Interpretations'. Lord Meghnad Desai, in 'Sita and

Some Better Women in the Epics', contrasts the women of the Mahabharata with those portrayed in the Ramayana. In 'Janaki: The Fire and the Earth', Tarun Vijay explains the nuances of the *maryada* that define Rama's moral position, presenting the picture from what might perhaps be Sri Rama's point of view. Interestingly, this thread is picked up again in Arshia Sattar's thoughtful retrospective gaze, as she re-examines the translation of the Ramayana she completed some ten years ago. 'I am shocked that it is he who draws me to him, compels me to try and understand his cruelty towards Sita and what it means for him to be king, perhaps even against his innermost wishes. I find myself more and more involved with Rama and am convinced that the way to a more complete understanding of the Ramayana, especially for contemporary women, has to be through an inclusion rather than a rejection of Rama and his questionable behaviour.'

Creative fiction on the subject of Sita takes many imaginative directions. Shashi Deshpande gives voice to Sita's emotions when she is abandoned in the forest, Vijay Lakshmi Chauhan weaves a modern story on the theme of jealousy. Mallika Sengupta retells the taut drama of the agni pareeksha. In her piece on Bhojpuri women's songs, Smita Tewari Jassal brings alive the vital folklore on the subject. Madhureeta Anand discusses the experience of scripting and shooting the film she has made on Sita, *Laying Janaki to Rest*, in contemporary terms. Sonal Mansingh, Indira Goswami and Madhu Kishwar share their views and insights on the Sita archetype. A few of the diverse traditions in which the Sita narrative is interpreted are included, as are creative personal interpretations of the Sita myth.

Reading and reacting to the mountains of material that the subject generated was a tiring but consciousness-enhancing task. It was the last piece which swung the whole thing into perspective for me. Keshav Desaraju had suggested that we look at the works of the late Kumudini, who humanized the epic by writing about Sita's imagined letters to her mother. Devotion and respect had distanced Sita from us, while academic interpretations had sterilized the subject. This imaginary daily life reminded me that, at some level, Sita was a human incarnation, tried and tested by extraordinary circumstances.

At a moment of change, when some people are holding on to, while others are letting go of, our past, I want to stress upon the continuity and flexibility of Indian culture and traditions. This book was conceived with love and respect by a practising Hindu: one who recognizes the strength of debate, dissent and questioning within our way of life.

Sita was not only an immortal daughter of the Earth or an incarnation of Lakshmi. She was also intensely human, although her vulnerabilities are lost in the accretions of myth and reverence. But Indian myth is never static, it is constantly in the process of reinterpreting and revalidating itself, and the society that it defines. Perhaps it is time to seek a new image of Sita—one who does not have to return to the Earth, but can resolutely reclaim it.

COMMENTARY

SITA AND SOME OTHER WOMEN FROM THE EPICS

MEGHNAD DESAI

SITA IS THE ideal woman, the faithful wife. Indeed, even her husband, Ramachandra is described as Siyavar, 'the groom of Sita'. Yet there are other women in both the Ramayana and the Mahabharata who need to be studied along with Sita to enable us to view her in a clearer light. In this brief essay, I wish to open out the space of discussing womanhood in the context of the many female characters in these two epics and ask if there are better ideals than Sita.

The Absent Heroine

Sita is iconic as the ideal wife. Rama, even though a *maryada purushottam,* is not an ideal husband. He is not regarded as such either in the many versions of the epic or in the popular imagination of Indians, as Madhu Kishwar discovered during her survey. Both men and women tend to consider Shiva as the ideal husband. Shiva loved his wife Sati intensely and was distraught by her death till Parvati lured him back to active life. Yet while Sita is an ideal wife, she is seen neither as an ideal consort nor as a parent, except when she abandons her young twelve-year-old boys and returns to her mother, Earth.

As a wife and indeed as a character in the Ramayana, Sita is strangely absent. Valmiki allows her very little space. She is barely mentioned in Bala Kanda, even when Rama wins her in the *swayamvar,* since Valmiki is more enamoured of the men in the story—

Vishwamitra, Janaka, Rama—than Sita (Bala Kanda, *sarg* 66). In Ayodhya Kanda, she figures in eleven sargs out of 119, and in Aranya Kanda, in fourteen sargs out of seventy-five. There is no reference to her at all in Kishkindha Kanda except by way of the lamentations of Rama, and we have to wait till Sundara Kanda for our heroine to make an appearance. Here she figures in thirty-one sargs out of sixty-eight. In Yuddha Kanda, she is mentioned in five sargs before she finally appears at the end of Rama's triumph only after he has had Ravana cremated by Vibhishana and conducted Vibhishana's coronation. Rama then asks Hanuman to take Vibhishana's permission to go and fetch Sita, since obviously, in Rama's view, she has now become Vibhishana's property, having previously been Ravana's. Thus, we come at last to Uttara Kanda, and here again she is short-changed. In total, Sita appears in seventy-six sargs out of 645, accounting for barely 10 per cent of the Valmiki Ramayana. I may have missed out one or two of her appearances, but the sheer absence of Sita throughout the Ramayana is noteworthy. Even her beauty is not described directly in her presence (as Kamban describes it) but in Rama's lamentations after her abduction.

Sita is, of course, the principal excuse for the conquest of Lanka and the defeat of Ravana, but not for herself, as Rama shows little interest in her qua person. Gandhiji saw Sita as a symbol for woman's struggle in a man's world precisely because her chastity holds off Ravana. Rama looks on as Lakshmana disfigures Surpanakha but then, he is maryada purushottam. The ideal man allows other women to be disfigured and, constantly suspicious of her chastity, neglects his own wife! Rama does not even have the courage to tell Sita to her face that he is sending her into exile, knowing that she is pregnant with his progeny. He asks Lakshmana to take on the duty of leaving her in the forest. We see nothing of Sita as a mother. We see her exiled and the next thing we get to know after fifty odd sargs is that the boys are twelve years old, and she bids them farewell and leaves the world. There is a puzzle here. Rama and Sita were married when they were quite young. The story of Sita lifting the Shiva *dhanushya*, which it takes 5000 servants to fetch for Rama to break (Bala Kanda, sarg 66), signifies the onset of puberty. Yet, if we are to take this literally, we have to ask what happened to this strong woman after marriage that she let herself be abducted by Ravana without a fight.

Even then, what is the conjugal life of Rama and Sita like? We have very few clues in the Valmiki Ramayana. In my Gujarati translation, there is an intriguing footnote to Ayodhya Kanda, sarg 20.[1] This is in relation to Sumitra's lament that she has spent only seventeen years since Rama's *upanayan*. The sarg contains a survey of expert opinion on how old Rama is when he has his upanayan and cites a verse saying that he is eleven when he has his *ekadashe rajanyam*. After some elaboration, the author/translator says that Rama gets married at the age of sixteen and then lives twelve years after his marriage in Dasharatha's palace, and at the age of twenty-eight he goes into exile for fourteen years, and returns to Ayodhya when he is forty-two. If this is true, then during the twelve years of marriage at home and thirteen years of exile (before Sita is abducted), Rama and Sita are happily married, and Valmiki says little about that. What is interesting is they have no children in these long years and Sita becomes a mother in her late thirties or perhaps even later. This implies that she is at least in control of her reproductive cycle, as she manages to delay her child-bearing until her husband is secure on a throne. This is one hidden strength she displays, as she does again, when finally, at the age of perhaps fifty, she abandons her family. Thus, a woman who seems to be a passive character in major portions of the Ramayana, following her husband through thick and thin, insistent in her demand for the *suvarnamrig*, finally emerges as a strong woman with a will of her own. However, that is not what she is worshipped for.

Other Women in the Ramayana

The character of Sita is in contrast with some strong characters in the Ramayana. There is, of course, Kaikeyi, who alone among the three queens of Dasharatha, has any personality. She was at his side as his charioteer on the battlefield and saved him when he was injured, as a result of which he granted her two wishes. As Manthara reminds her, Dasharatha still finds her attractive and would leap into the fire if she asked him to do so (Ayodhya Kanda, sarg 9). Manthara tells Kaikeyi that Dasharatha would not be able to withstand her anger and would agree to fulfil the two wishes he had granted her many years ago. She is thus ostensibly still attractive enough for Dasharatha to be enamoured of her. Kaikeyi also keeps her nerve through Dasharatha's lamentations once he finds himself trapped by his past promises. When he is incapable of telling Rama what he has done, once again it is Kaikeyi who has to convey the bad news to Rama. Villainous though she is cast to be, Kaikeyi is still a strong character.

A more interesting character than Kaikeyi is that of Manthara. She is not just a servant. As Valmiki mentions, we do not know what *kula* Manthara was born in (Ayodhya Kanda, sarg 7), but she was a *dasi* in Kaikeyi's parental home and had been with Kaikeyi since her childhood. Manthara's motives for seeking Rama's exile are not developed at all by Valmiki. Was she a *dasyu*, that is, one of the defeated people, and did she want revenge for her 'race'? She is clearly very persuasive, and causes havoc in Ayodhya though she has nothing to gain personally from her instigations.

Another notable female character in the Ramayana is that of Tara, the wife of Vali. The Vali–Sugriva story is a variant on the main theme of the Ramayana, that is, the legitimacy of succession. Rama has been displaced by his younger brother Bharata, thanks to Kaikeyi. Bharata refuses to ascend the throne and he preserves it for Rama, the legitimate heir. Vali is the older brother but Sugriva occupies his throne believing wrongly that Vali has died in battle. When Vali returns, he dismisses Sugriva. Sugriva then takes Rama's help to reclaim the throne. The injustice of the act and of Rama's secret help to Sugriva in killing Vali remains questionable. Tara is inconsolable that her brave husband has died. Vali was a sensuous man with a large *antahpur* (harem) but Tara was his principal queen. As he is dying, Vali tells Sugriva that Tara is capable of sharp analytical thinking in matters concerning *arthashastra* (Kishkindha Kanda, sarg 22) and he should listen to Tara. She is distraught at Vali's death but then is reconciled to the fact that her son Angad will be well looked after by Sugriva, who then takes over his brother's harem, including his principal queen Tara. When Lakshmana comes, full of anger at Sugriva for having forgotten the urgent task of rescuing Sita and finds him (Sugriva) absorbed in revelries, it is Tara, clever and conciliatory, who charms Lakshmana and deflects his anger (Kishkindha Kanda, sarg 33). Beautiful and sensuous, she laments the betrayal of her husband by his younger brother, but in her son's interest, marries the same brother. She is thus married to the throne, as it were.

Mandodari is the last of the women in the Ramayana whose

character contrasts with that of Sita. She only surfaces when Ravana is slain (Yuddha Kanda, sarg 111). She laments that though there were more beautiful women than Sita in his harem, he was blinded by Sita. As she says, Ravana could not see that in '*kula*, *rupa* or *dakshinya*', Sita was not better but perhaps only Mandodari's equal. How could her brave, learned, powerful husband be defeated by a man wandering in the forest?

Women in the Mahabharata

The Ramayana has women who are clever and sensuous—Kaikeyi, Tara and Mandodari. Yet it is only Sita, passive and helpless and faithful to a fault, who is identified as an iconic character. Indeed, Sita's behaviour is contrasted in subtle ways with that of the other women. Unlike Tara who marries her husband's younger brother, Sita affords Lakshmana no room for admiration except when she impugns his motives as he hesitates to respond to Marichi's false cries (Aranya Kanda, sarg 45). Lakshmana, of course, never lifts his eyes towards his sister-in-law. Thus, Rama and his brothers, comprising the new generation of the Raghus, set the pattern for ideal behaviour—monogamy and deep respect for the property rights of a husband over his wife unlike the *vanar* people wherein Tara can marry a second time. Rama's monogamy also contrasts with his father's, who no doubt paid dearly for his polygamy.

One can see why such control over women's choices was necessary when one sees how much more free the women of the Mahabharata are. Draupadi is a king's daughter and gets married to the five brothers masquerading as Brahmins and suffers as one with them while they seek their due share of land. She is polyandrous and has five sons, presumably by each of her five husbands. But there is a strict serial sexual code she follows. Angered by the sexual advances of the Kauravas, she is passionate in seeking revenge on Dushasana and Duryodhana. Her menstrual blood, which was streaming when Dushasana attempted to strip her in front of the entire court (she was *ekavastra rajasvala*) has to be repaid in the form of Dushasana's blood being drunk by Bheema. Duryodhana's thighs too have to be smashed since he had gestured to Draupadi to sit on them.

Society portrayed in the Mahabharata is sexually open and free with few legitimate sexual unions and many examples of unregulated conduct. From the outset, the book is replete with loose sexual attitudes. Shantanu lusts after Ganga. She marries him and then drowns their first eight daughters. Shantanu is then attracted towards Matsyagandha and forces his son Devadatta to take a vow of celibacy and renounce his claim to the throne. As Bhishma, Devadatta now has to find brides for his two stepbrothers, Chitrangada and Vichitravirya. So he abducts Amba, Ambika and Ambalika, of whom the latter two are willing to accept his command. Amba curses him and goes off to die after doing penance, till she is reborn as Shikhandin.

However, since Bhishma's stepbrothers are incapabale of producing progeny, Vyasa is asked to help. Yet neither Dhritarashtra nor Pandu, the children of these two illicit unions, can produce progeny either. Hence, it is Kunti who plays a pivotal role in the epic. Indeed, Kunti is for me the most powerful woman of the two epics. She is in complete control of her reproductive rights. She has four children by four different gods—Surya, Yama, Indra and Vayu. She abandons the first one as she is not married then and has the other three after marrying Pandu, for whom sex is proscribed by a divine curse. Kunti generously passes on two of her boons to her co-wife Madri so that she too can taste the joys of motherhood. Hence, Kunti is thoughtful and unselfish. It is Kunti's example that incites Gandhari to seek a boon which would give her a hundred sons! But again Dhritarashtra, incapacitated and blind, has nothing to do with their birth.

Kunti determines the key relationships in the Mahabharata. It is also she who enjoins her sons to share the prize that Arjuna has won—Draupadi. Her sons are capable of fathering their own progeny and indeed Arjuna also marries Subhadra and Ulupi besides Draupadi. While the five sons of the Pandavas die at the hands of Ashwathama, the succession comes through Abhimanyu—Arjuna's son by Subhadra. It is Abhimanyu's posthumous son by Uttara who succeeds to the throne when the Pandavas withdraw to the Himalayas. Kunti, now a great-grandmother, is still with them at that time.

Conclusion

The Mahabharata is thus no supporter of men's dominance or of the monogamous model of marriage. The epic has powerful women—

Ganga, Matsyagandha, Amba, Kunti, Draupadi—and they frequently get their men out of trouble (as Kaikeyi does in the Ramayana, but then she is a villain). By the time the Ramayana was written by Valmiki, patriarchy had registered its authority over women's bodies and over their reproductive rights. Rama considers Sita his property until he loses her to Ravana. Despite Sita's purity, Rama rejects her twice, doubting her fidelity. One cannot imagine anyone doing this to Draupadi and it is impossible to accuse Kunti of any infidelity except to her own self! Yet Sita is a silent heroine as she refuses to bear Rama any child till he secures his throne. She brings up her sons on her own as a single abandoned mother and finally returns to her mother's womb, thus establishing the autonomy of the female.

VALMIKI'S RAMAYANA

ARSHIA SATTAR

I) INTRODUCTION TO VALMIKI'S RAMAYANA

My abridged translation of Valmiki's Ramayana was published at the very end of 1996. When I got the first copies, I was awed by the gravitas the work had acquired by being transformed into a heavy, black-jacketed hardback book. I put it away in my bookshelf and never really opened it until seven years later in 2003, when I had to teach Ramayana as a part of a classical Indian literature course. Since then, in some way or another, I've been teaching from the text and around it on several occasions each year. And I've had to confront what I translated: what I put in and what I left out, what I chose to say and how I chose to say it. I have also had to consider what I might have done differently were I to do the same translation now.

In many ways, my own 'denial' of the Ramayana for all those years, between 1997 and 2003, was a reflection of what happened to many of us across the country and the world who love and work with Ramayana materials. Those were the years when the Hindu right was firmly entrenched in the national consciousness as well as in political power. This constellation of political parties, scholars, local politicians and men-on-the-street had appropriated Rama and his story, making it the basis of their antagonism to those they perceived as hostile to Hinduism and to the 'Indian' nation. What were we, those of us who worked with the Rama story and were of a liberal (if not always and entirely secular) bent of mind, to make of this? Was the story the

Hindu right had taken as their own the same story that we were telling? Was there something in the Rama story that lent itself to this kind of exclusionary cultural and nationalistic politics? Was our hero, the righteous but troubled prince of Ayodhya, really a vengeful warrior god? These confusions made us back off from the Ramayana, to collect our thoughts and reconsider our own relationship with the text and the story. Many of us retreated from the public sphere and the aggression of its Rama-related discourse.

Those years of silence seem to have ended. Despite the occasional incident (like the recent vandalism at Delhi University over a reference to a Santhali version of the story in a prescribed text), the Ramayana has returned in all its pluralistic glory. Robust classical and folk performances, some mainstream and others subversive, continued uninterrupted through these years but now there are contemporary additions to this space, making it even richer and more diverse, like the new television version made by Ramanand Sagar's sons, Ashok Banker's remarkable multi-volume recreation of the Rama story, and contemporary puppet performances that examine Rama's actions and thoughts.

It is in this context, the years of silence as well as the new flowering of 'three hundred Ramayana', that I have had to rethink my own Ramayana work and my relationship with the text that I translated. Were I to translate the same text now, it would probably be much the same in terms of tone and texture. The same events and conversations would be included, the same peripheral stories and lengthy descriptions of the battle excluded. I would probably make the Uttara Kanda, the Epilogue, longer so that the English is more representative of the Sanskrit text where the last kanda is enormous. I would also increase the length of that section so that readers unfamiliar with the original text would not think (as they might now) that the Uttara Kanda consists merely of Sita's banishment and its aftermath. What might differ would be the Introduction, parts of which are reproduced here.

Because of teaching from it and reading it over and over again in the past few years, I have developed a new intimacy with the text, one entirely different from the closeness that I had to it when I was translating. To my surprise at this rapproachment, I find my thoughts going more and more to Rama. As a card-carrying feminist, I am shocked that it is he who draws me to him, compels me to try and *understand* his cruelty towards Sita and what it means for him to be king, perhaps even against his innermost wishes. I find myself more and more involved with Rama and am convinced that the way to a more complete understanding of the Ramayana, especially for contemporary women, has to be through an inclusion rather than a rejection of Rama and his questionable behaviour.

The idea is not to justify Rama's actions (the more conservative tradition has done that for centuries resulting in enormous damage to women and marginalized groups) but to examine these acts in a more existential light—what is the self that Rama is creating as he reacts to his numerous trials and tribulations? And to what end is he creating that self?

In the parts of the Introduction reproduced here, I state that Rama's rejection of Sita is based in his adherence to *dharma*, the divinely sanctioned law that he must uphold as a righteous king. What I am exploring now is how Rama moved from being an exiled prince to becoming a righteous king—the physical and emotional journey that he makes between these two points holds, I believe, the key to Rama's transformation from besotted husband to mighty consort. In this journey the forest, where Rama dons the garb of an ascetic but carries the weapons of a warrior, is critical. It is here that he meets the peaceful sages who show him another way to be in the world. He also encounters *rakshasa*s who challenge him in different ways as do the monkeys with their way of life and their willingness to help him. The early skirmishes with the rakshasas and his deepening relationship with the monkeys force Rama to embrace the dharma of a *kshatriya* more and more fully. This dharma and his acceptance of it are fully realized when Rama has to fight a terrible war to reclaim his wife—for his honour as much as for his love.

It is the internal battles that Rama has to fight that interest me now, and there are many. Sadly, he loses the most important battle of all, the battle to be the person that he wants to be, irrespective of what his cosmic and public destinies have in store for him. It is this terrible dislocation of the self that gives rise to his anxieties about Sita and his treatment of her. And it is precisely this same dislocation of the self that provides us with the space(s) wherein we can examine the wellsprings of Rama's actions.

As my idea of Rama changes, so, too, must my idea of Sita. She seems less and less a victim and more and more a woman of remarkable strength and fortitude. The larger classical tradition of the Ramayana has glorified Sita for her good-wifeliness, that is, her submission and her chastity, but as contemporary women, we see a host of other much more interesting reasons to celebrate the challenges that Sita presents to the male universe by which she is bound. As her beloved husband battles his internal demons and the external rakshasas to find himself, Sita too, has internal conflicts that she must resolve. Rama and Sita's final separation, after she is asked to prove herself again (this time for the people of Ayodhya) is at Sita's initiative. She disappears into the Earth without even a glance at the man she has loved and it is Rama who is left alone, abandoned to his public life and duties. At the very end of the story, we are left with the man—hero, husband, king, divine reflection—and his emptiness. Glorious Rama, destined for greatness and success from birth, ends up alone and lonely—that should be enough reason for us to read the text anew. For our sake, and not his.

II) WOMEN AND KINGSHIP IN THE RAMAYANA

WOMEN IN THE RAMAYANA

Just as the monkey brothers, Vali and Sugriva, play out an alternate option to the problem of disputed kingship, so, too, does the *rakshasi* Surpanakha, Ravana's sister, provide a distorted mirror image of the chaste and virtuous Sita.

Sita and Surpanakha exemplify two types of women who appear almost universally in folklore and mythology: Sita is good, pure, light, auspicious and subordinate, whereas Surpanakha is evil, impure, dark, inauspicious and insubordinate. Although male characters can also be divided into the good and the bad, the split between women characters is far more pronounced and is always expressed in terms of sexuality.

Surpanakha comes upon Sita, Rama and Lakshmana in the forest. Rama has just fought off the rakshasa Viradha, who had grabbed Sita, a foreshadowing of the more serious abduction that will take place a little later. Surpanakha desires Rama for his good looks and suggests that he give up his ugly human female for her. The brothers proceed to tease and torment Surpanakha, eventually cutting off her nose and ears. Surpanakha's mutilation in the forest echoes the battle the princes had with Taraka in which Rama was reluctant to kill a woman until Vishwamitra assured him that it was all right. The assault on Surpanakha also moves the story into top gear—she complains to her brother Ravana at which point he decides to abduct Sita in order to avenge the insult to his sister.

Both Katherine Erndl and Sally Sutherland demonstrate that the major opposition between Sita and Surpanakha is in terms of sexuality. Sita's is a domesticated, conjugal love while Surpanakha represents untamed, aggressive and, therefore, potentially threatening desire. Sutherland suggests that the encounter between Sita and Surpanakha carries the potential of their becoming co-wives and therefore, they are set up as rivals for the same man's affections. She also interprets the mutilation of the rakshasi as necessary to curb her dangerous sexuality because Rama cannot make the same mistake as his father: he cannot be ensnared by a woman's charms. The Ramayana implicitly argues that it is not wrong for Rama and Lakshmana to assault and disfigure Surpanakha, just as it was not wrong for them to have killed Taraka the *yakshini*, because they are in the forest where different rules apply and because Rama cannot afford to commit the same mistakes as his father.

The same sexual opposition between rival wives is played out between Kaushalya and Kaikeyi, the mothers of Rama and Bharata. While Kaushalya is the respected senior wife of Dasharatha, it is clearly Kaikeyi, the junior wife, who has enthralled the king with her beauty and charm. Kaushalya does everything right, including producing the perfect son, but she has little hold on the king's affections even though she is the ideal wife and mother. Kaikeyi, on the other hand, is wilful and stubborn and gets her way all the time. She conspires to obtain the kingdom for her son and earns the contempt of everyone, including Bharata himself.

Similarly, good and righteous wives recur in the multiple stories of kingship. Vali, the monkey king, has a virtuous and wise wife named Tara, who first urges him not to destroy Sugriva and then cautions him against fighting Rama. Vali does not heed her words and goes out to meet his fate. When Vali dies, Sugriva inherits Tara along with the kingdom. As his senior wife, she remains the voice of righteousness and sanity in his court, whereas Ruma, Sugriva's other wife, becomes the focus of his sexual attentions. The parallels in this case with the Kaushalya–Kaikeyi situation are very clear: Kaushalya and Tara are the wise, older wives who have the king's attention because of their virtues, while Kaikeyi and Ruma are the younger wives whose sexual charms have a hold on the king. Similarly, Ravana's chief queen, Mandodari, tries her best to dissuade him from taking on the might of Rama because she knows that Ravana is acting wrongly, but to no avail. While he holds Mandodari in great respect, Ravana satisfies his sensual and sexual desires with the thousands of other women that fill his palace.

Along with dangerous, demonic women, female ascetics (like Svyamprabha) and the virtuous wives of sages (like Ahalya and Anasuya) also live in the forests. Their rigorous austerities have given them magical powers and a high spiritual status. But once again (as with Sita), because their sexuality has been sublimated, they pose no threat to anyone. In Lanka, the good rakshasis Sarama and Trijata, both of whom help Sita during her imprisonment, mirror the characters of female ascetics of the forest. The female ascetics and the good rakshasis are safe havens in the regions where dangerous, demonic women abound.

These variations on particular themes in the Ramayana are expressed through replication, shadowing and mirror images. Within the text, they explore multiple possibilities in terms of relationships, characters and story lines. The tight normative roles prescribed for Rama, Bharata, Sita and Lakshmana are, in fact, heightened by the more realistic paths taken by the non-human and liminal characters in the text. Apart from presenting a contrast between the prescriptive behaviour of the human characters and the morally ambiguous actions of their non-human shadows, replications also serve to generate the narrative trope of foreshadowing. As in the case when Viradha snatches Sita away, events, emotions and even behaviours are hinted at and suggested in smaller incidents and side tales well before the critical moment actually occurs, thereby foreshadowing acts as a powerful tool in the building and maintenance of a mood for the epic. It also provides a narrative rhythm as it lays out the primary concern of the text.

Kingship in the Ramayana

Since the dominant set of replications in the Ramayana explores the theme of brothers and disputed thrones, one could argue that the central issue which the Ramayana tackles is that of rightful and righteous kingship. Through the multiple variations on the theme of disputed kingship, we see that Rama is clearly both the rightful and the righteous king while Ravana is not. Ravana is the rightful king of Lanka because he is the eldest of the brothers, but he is by no means the righteous king. After Ravana is killed, Vibhishana becomes the righteous and rightful king of Lanka.

It is the relationship between the monkey brothers, Vali and Sugriva, and the throne of Kishkindha that is the most complicated. Vali is the elder brother and from all that we know about him, seems to be a good and righteous king. Sugriva, on the other hand, takes over his brother's throne claiming that he is probably dead. He also takes over his brother's wife, a woman he should have treated as a mother. Sugriva makes Rama kill Vali by saying that he was cruel and unrighteous. Once his older brother is dead, Sugriva becomes the rightful king of Kishkindha. But once again, he takes Tara, Vali's wife, as his own. Ironically, taking another's wife is one of the unrighteous deeds for which Vali is killed. Thus, Sugriva's righteousness would appear to devolve from the fact that he makes an alliance with the righteous Rama and not from any of his own actions.

It is when he acts as the righteous king that Rama commits the two deeds that appear incomprehensible for a man such as him—the killing of Vali and the rejection of Sita. Rama forms an alliance with Sugriva and takes his word that Vali has wronged him and deserves to die. This expediency is compounded by the fact that Rama kills Vali while Vali is fighting Sugriva and Rama himself is hidden behind a tree. As we learn more and more about Vali, it would appear that he was a wise and just ruler, compassionate even towards his brother whom he could have killed on several occasions.

As Vali is dying, he excoriates Rama for his unrighteous act and Rama offers a series of arguments in his own defence. These include the fact that since Vali was a low creature, a mere monkey, Rama could kill him in any way he pleased because the ethics of battle did not apply in this case. At the same time, Rama says that Vali deserves to die because he has violated dharma by taking his brother's wife. The sophistry in this argument is clear: if Vali belongs to a lower order of being and the ethics of battle do not apply to him, why, then, should he be judged by the stringent rules of human dharma in his personal life?

The matter becomes somewhat clearer when Rama states that he is acting on behalf of Bharata and the righteous Ishvaku kings who hold dominion over the earth. There can be no violations of dharma under their jurisdiction. The functions of a king include the meting out of punishments (*danda*), the nurturing of dharma and the righteous organization of society. Rama is attempting to fulfil those functions in this case. He is compelled to act as a righteous king, no matter how specious his arguments may be for doing so.

Rama's unjustified rejection of the chaste and virtuous Sita, not once, but twice, is as problematic as the episode with Vali. Through no fault of her own, Sita is abducted and imprisoned by Ravana. When the war to reclaim her is over, Rama humiliates Sita, first by calling her out in public, and then by saying that he has no use for her any more, that the war was fought to salvage the honour of his clan. Sita walks into the fire but is rescued by the fire god who vouches for her innocence and chastity. At this point, all the gods appear and tell Rama who he really is. Rama takes Sita back because the gods tell him to and also, he says, because he had always believed in her innocence but wanted it to be proved to the common people. Later, after they have lived happily in Ayodhya for many years, Rama hears that the people still doubt Sita. He decides that he must banish her from the kingdom because he cannot allow gossip and scandal to tarnish his reputation.

Once again, in both cases of rejection, Rama plays the part of the righteous king who must always be above reproach. Anything or anyone connected with him must be equally so. Rama has to sacrifice his personal feelings for Sita in order to uphold dharma, as he had to do earlier when his father exiled him to the forest for fourteen years. It is here that the epic trope of the hero's personal destiny being inextricably linked with the plan of the gods is most clearly visible. But Rama as a human hero proves equal to the task. Even though he is not always aware of his divinity, he acts in accordance with a higher law, dharma, which is divinely sanctioned and is his duty, as a king (albeit in waiting), to uphold.

SITA AS GAURI, OR KALI

DEVDUTT PATTANAIK

WHEN A DAUGHTER steps out of her father's house after marriage, the father is supposed to say, 'May you find happiness wherever you go.' But Janaka instead told Sita, 'May you bring happiness wherever you go.' Perhaps because he was a good father who had brought up his daughter to be autonomous and responsible for her life and those around her, or perhaps because he knew his daughter was a goddess—the Earth itself.

The Earth can be wild or domesticated. Wild, she is the forest. Domesticated, she is the field. Wild, she is a woman. Domesticated, she is the wife. In Hindu mythology, wild Earth is visualized as Kali, an unclothed goddess, fearsome, naked, bloodthirsty, one with hair unbound. Domesticated Earth is visualized as Gauri, the goddess of civilization, gentle, demure, beautiful, draped in cloth. Gauri's cloth represents the rules that turn nature into civilization—rules such as marital fidelity, which ensure that even the weakest of men has conjugal security.

Sita is Gauri, the clothed goddess, and this is made explicit in the *Adbhut Ramayana*, where it is said that a demon more frightening than Ravana attacked Ayodhya. All the men tried to destroy this demon but were unable to do so. Finally, it is revealed that only a chaste woman could destroy this demon and save the city. All the women of the city were asked to fight the demon but none were able to defeat him. Finally Sita was called, and she transformed herself into Kali and destroyed the demon as easily as a child breaks a twig. As Kali she was so frightening that Rama begged her to return to her original state—that of Sita, clothed, with tied hair and demure disposition. This tale makes explicit the association of Sita with the goddess—she is Kali but clothed; draped in cloth, she acts out her role as Gauri.

As Gauri she is the wife who follows her husband wherever he goes. When Rama prepares to set out for his exile, she follows him—not because he asks her to do so, but because it is her duty to remain by his side. He tries to stop her but she insists on fulfilling her role as his wife. Rama cannot dissuade her. And so he sets out with her. Sita is thus not the obedient wife but the dutiful wife, one who knows her responsibilities.

When Sita leaves Ayodhya, she prepares to clothe herself as Rama does—in garments of bark and leaves. The women of the palace forbid her from doing so because as a daughter-in-law, she represents the reputation of the royal household. If she is beautifully dressed, it means that the household is beautiful, and if she is shabbily dressed, it means that the household is shabby. Further, her beauty brings luck to the house—if she abandons her finery, bad luck would strike. Thus, Sita's clothes play both a symbolic as well as a talismanic role. If she is well dressed as Gauri, it indicates that Rama upholds dharma and all is well in Ayodhya. That is why Sita follows Rama into the forest in bridal jewellery.

Sita's role as Gauri is further reinforced by Anasuya, the wife of Rishi Atri, who gifts Sita with a sari which never gets soiled. Later, when Sita is abducted by Ravana, she throws pieces of her jewellery into the forest, ostensibly to leave a trail behind her so that Rama can find her. But by abandoning her jewellery, she conveys a subtle symbolic message to Rama. It means that his dharma is being challenged as Ravana, by abducting Rama's wife, has defied the civilized code of marital fidelity. Ravana wants to make Rama's field, his forest; he wants to convert Gauri into Kali. Every piece of jewellery dropped into the forest is a reminder of how close civilization is at risk of being overrun by the forest.

When Ravana is killed and Sita rescued, Rama demands proof that Gauri, the field, which is bound to a single man, did not even momentarily become Kali, the forest, which is bound to no man, and hence available to all men. The only way this can be done is through the trial of fire. Sita goes through the ordeal and the fire does not touch her, proving that neither in thought nor in action did she ever think of any other man.

This story indicates how difficult it is to uphold the social value of fidelity. While it may be easy to uphold fidelity in action, it is not always possible to uphold it in thought. Fidelity in action can be witnessed but fidelity in thought cannot. Therefore, in typical mythological narratives, women who succeed in being faithful to their husbands in both action and thought are elevated to the status of goddesses, unaffected by fire. They get equated with Sati Maharani. Sita is like Sati—chaste in action and thought, able to walk unharmed through flames.

Despite this proof of her chastity given by Sita, the people of Ayodhya ask Rama to reject the queen because of her soiled reputation. The same laws which demanded that Rama should obey the commandments of his father, now demanded that Rama should respect the wishes of his people. And so, Sita is once again sent into the forest. It is strange that Rama, the only Hindu deity known for being faithful to one wife, is also the only Hindu deity to abandon his wife. This is clearly meant to highlight the difference between Rama, the husband, who is faithful to his wife, and Rama, the king, who is sensitive to the wishes of his people. Rama, the king, sends Sita back into the forest but Rama, the husband, never remarries. He places next to him an effigy of Sita made of gold, the metal which symbolizes purity, suggesting that he does not doubt his wife's fidelity but that he respects the laws of Ayodhya and its royal household, however misguided they may have been.

Who is this Sita in the forest? Gauri or Kali? She is Gauri to her children—raising them as powerful warriors, who on their own are able to defeat the mighty army of Rama. But she is also Kali—the one who has shaken off the mantle of civilization. She is no longer bound by its rules. Rejected, she refuses to return to Ayodhya either as a queen or as a wife. She does not feel the need to follow her husband, this time, as his wife. She no longer feels obliged to represent the prosperity of the household that rejected her, or to bring good luck into it. When asked to prove her chastity once more, she returns to the womb of the Earth, whence she came from. Thus, when the people of Ayodhya asked their king to abandon his queen, they inadvertently ended up losing Janaka's daughter, who took away all happiness from Ayodhya with her.

JANAKI: THE FIRE AND THE EARTH

TARUN VIJAY

DURING MY COLLEGE days, we would sound rebellious in declamation contests while trying to bring in Sita's example through various corridors of logic and argument. We had wanted to examine why it was Sita and not Rama who had to go through the trial by fire. Why was Sita exiled to the second *vanavas*—living in a hermitage even after Rama's victorious return to Ayodhya?

My mother never pardoned me for being so 'harsh and rude' to our own glorious past. She would say, 'It was Sita's dharma, her righteousness that gave Rama his essential aura and moral strength, and remember he could never find peace after Sita left Ayodhya, finally taking refuge in the mighty waters of Sarayu.' I remember the lines describing Sita's request to her mother to take her back, which made women cry:

> If unstained in thought and action I have lived from the day of my birth, spare a daughter's shame and anguish and receive her, Mother Earth! If in duty and devotion, I have laboured undefiled, Mother Earth! Who bore this woman, once again receive thy child! If in truth unto my husband I have proved a faithful wife, Mother Earth! Relieve thy Sita from the burden of this life!

We were never satisfied with the innumerable explanations—all justifying Sita's fire test and exemplifying Rama's great love for her. But, and this 'but' always remained a very significant one, Rama was maryada purushottam, the living embodiment of noble virtues, and hence had to listen to his people, even as in this case, to a washerman, to uphold the *rajdharma*—the duties of the king. He had to be harsh with himself and hence Sita had to go to the forest for the rest of her life, until she prayed to Mother Earth to take her back into her affectionate lap. The ultimate refuge of the daughter was again the same earth from which she had been offered to the great sage King Janaka.

We said that Sita rebelled. She never reconciled to the fact that she was made to prove her chastity, her singular love for her husband in full public glare, and was exiled to the forest to prove a point—the righteousness of her husband. And we were certainly never accused of heresy or sacrilegious behaviour. Even the ochre-robed *sanyasin*s who frequented our house, laughed at my logic and said, 'Well, when you come of age, you will understand.'

Now, in more intolerant times, I feel that this could happen only in a broad-minded Hindu family, which has become a rarity today. At that age, perhaps my mother personified the ordeals and rebellious character of Sita, or maybe we liked to see Sita's attributes in her, imparting some sort of divine touch to the daily outbursts of domestic disquiet that we had been witnessing.

We were hardly a happy family. There were always enough reasons for an evening of unrest in our home. My mother remained a symbol of pain and patience. Rising early in the morning, living in utter penury, funding my tuitions, struggling to keep my studies uninterrupted, working late nights, and having the 'Fruities', those twenty-five-paisa candies that gave us immense joy, she moved forward. Her night-time stories and daytime instructions from Tulsidas' *Ramacharitmanas*, the only doses of morality we got, always had references to Sita's ordeals and her patience. These images of Sita were embedded in our lives.

Later, my regard for Sita translated into Janaki's strong, unwavering and extraordinarily patient character that could only be epitomized in a mix of fire and earth—one, a symbol of rebellion, the other signifying unlimited patience. My rebellious characterization of Sita in a revolutionary mould was completely off-track. I learnt that it was not necessary to portray someone in an alien mode to make him or her more acceptable in our own times. They are not stage actors who have to be presented in the way a director would find convenient for a show. Sita represents certain values that have nourished our sensibilities for aeons, and we have to accept them as they are. Sita's patience irritates modernists. In modern times, when everything is available at the press of a button, patience is one word that doesn't find a welcome audience.

Sita's birth from the womb of Mother Earth signifies nature, colour and vivacity. Her father Janaka was an embodiment of austerity, so separated from worldly actions that he was known as 'Videha', one who is above the realm of physical needs and wants. In her previous birth, Sita was the daughter of Rishi Kushadhwaj, who was killed by a demon because Kushadhwaj wanted to marry his daughter Vedvati to Vishnu. In order to fulfil her father's desire, Vedvati began a difficult penance and was sighted by Ravana, who wished to marry her forcibly. Vedvati refused and took her life by jumping into the fire and was reborn as Sita.

Remember Agyeya's monograph, *Jan, Janaka, Janaki*? One of the greatest doyens of our literary world, S.H. Vatsyayan (Agyeya), led a *yatra* of littérateurs to Janakpur Dham, where Janaki was born. The region reverberates with the sacred memories of the daughter who became a *devi* for all. She was everything that a woman aspires to be, pious, devoted, patient, beautiful, affectionate and, above all, uncompromising in her duties as well as her commitments.

She is presented in the Hindu cultural imagination as the epitome of womanhood. That is perhaps why certain modern analysts of women's issues find it so annoying to see M.K. Gandhi's projection of Sita's ideal before the Indian masses as the symbol of anti-colonialism and indigenous cultural values, a powerful icon of the unyielding *swadeshi* spirit. For Gandhi and for many other thinkers rooted in the cultural contours that make us identifiable as Indians, Sita's was a far superior character in the collective psyche than even Rama, who was strictly virtuous. Sita's silent suffering and enduring patience like that of Earth itself made her the touchstone of morality.

Today, there is an attempt to put Sita in the framework of the so-called 'modern' value systems that a Western-oriented contemporary writer would like to see in a woman. Therefore, Sita has to be portrayed as a rebellious, uncompromising, courageous and independent character in the mould of Simone de Beauvoir or Betty Friedan.

Why should this be necessary? Why can't we appreciate and accept what Sita was and has been since time immemorial? Why can't we challenge a colonial mindset that sees Sita's devotion to her husband, her agreeing to pass through agni pareeksha or the fire ordeal, her silent suffering and accepting the forest exile are all signs of a self-effacing woman, who can be pitied but not venerated. All these interpretations are meant to falsify the entire socio-cultural fabric of a land known for its rich civilization.

It is ironic that the values which have sustained our society for thousands of years and have inspired great souls are being 'reformed' and amended by modernists, whose singular passion is to debunk and dispossess whatever India has cherished for ages. It is not at all necessary to denounce the past to glorify the present.

Sita's insistence on following Rama into his exile, and Rama's anguish and lament on seeing her agony while walking towards the forest are vividly narrated in the *Kavitavali* of Tulsidas. Her love for Rama and his deep feelings for her overwhelm any sensitive person even today. Rama's tears rolled down when he saw his beloved trying to walk the rough road covered with pebbles and thorns while following him into the forest. Sita was breaking a convention when she insisted that she would, facing all odds, happily join her husband in his fourteen years of exile. A timid, compromising and traditional wife would not have dared to defy the social principles of her times in such a manner. When Rama tells her about the rigours of life in exile, she says:

> Any term of austerities or forest or even heaven, let it be to me with you only. To me, who follows you, there will be no tiredness. I shall remain in the path without any fatigue, as though remaining in a palace of recreation or as in a state of sleep. While walking with you, blades of *kusha* grass, shrubs of *kaasa*, reeds and rushes and plants with thorns, will touch my feet like a heap of cotton or soft deerskin. The strongest wind that will cover my body will be as sacred sandal dust. Leaves, tubers and fruits either a little or abundant in quantity brought by you will be like nectar to me. Your companionship will be heaven to me. On the contrary, if you do not take me, who is not alarmed of the forest as such, I shall drink poison now. (Valmiki)

Sita's calm, composed yet unyielding behaviour in Ravana's captivity, her dialogue with Hanuman in Ashok vatika, her acceptance later of the changing values of society, her undergoing the fire ordeal, and finally her request to Mother Earth to take her back into her lap, all create a symbolic narrative that has been accepted by people who enjoy a free atmosphere of debate. Sita belongs to the Hindu pantheon for her inner power to reject unacceptable norms with a strength and invincibility of Mother Earth. Rama was never happy without Sita and had to take refuge in the Sarayu river.

Even Lankan authors perceive Sita's character in highly admiring terms and have kept intact Sita's memories with great reverence in the Ashok vatika, where Ravana had held her captive. Sita was chaste even in her thoughts and consistently rejected Ravana's advances, remaining unwavering in her love and devotion to her husband. Rama too grieved for her and mounted a war on Lanka to free his beloved.

When Sita was asked to prove her purity after Rama's victory over Lanka, she was so dejected and even the fire refused to harm her. The gods were pained and protected her. The famous Tamil poet, Kamban, has vividly described Sita's anguish in his celebrated Ramayana, *Ramavataram*, written in the twelfth century AD, saying that the entire universe gets deeply disturbed when she is about to enter the flames. The god of fire is believed to have scolded Rama about his notion of righteousness and declared that the universe stood threatened with destruction because the pious Sita had been questioned. Thyagaraja praises Sita as 'the blessed souls of refugees!' and seeks her protection. She is seen as the powerful destroyer of the 'clouds of demons' like the hundred-headed Ravana. In the popular traditions, without Janaki there is no Rama. Pious devotees remember Sita first in their everyday chanting and Rama comes only after her; it is always 'Sitarama' and never 'Ramasita'. In any case, Sita remains to me the greater icon of patience, dharma and inner strength.

If Sita's character was a weak one, why would people so diverse as Indians and East Asians adore her as the greatest icon of their lives? From Thailand to Laos, Janaki's characterization in literature and in the temples has inspired generations. Her strength and inner integrity have led great poets to admire her and write poems to her glory.

Western scholars have sometimes compared Janaki with Eve, making the point about foundational figures in religious mythology. Comparisons have also been between Sita and other 'earth'-linked women in classical tales, as for instance, Ceres, Persephone and Eurydice. While some aspects are in common if one were to attribute suffering, emotional loss, the motif of journey and abiding love to each of these imagined women, Sita's story offers a living ideal in India in contrast to the others who are locked in the past of Western cultures. Therefore these comparisons seem too far-fetched. The truth remains that Sita, who was also Janaki, Vaidehi, Bhudevi, Maithili and, in fact, the quintessential spirit of our land and minds, was the greatest inspirational icon in our lives in India, and remains so, without there being any necessity to 'modernize' her.

R.K. NARAYAN'S RAMAYANA

RANGA RAO

EARLY IN HIS career Narayan received some sage counsel from his elder uncle, Seshachalam: study a lot more—Shakespeare, of course; but, above all, the Ramayana by Kamban. Then, 'Your writing will gain seriousness and weight.' But Narayan knew from the beginning what was good for him: '. . . I was setting out to be a modern story-writer . . . I listened to his suggestion out of politeness but rejected it mentally.'

In 1938, when Narayan had already had two novels published in England, his idealist uncle renewed his plea from his deathbed. The determined young novelist would not budge: 'I was a realistic fiction-writer in English, and Tamil language or literature was not my concern . . . There was no reason why I should now perform a literary atavism by studying Tamil. So I rejected his advice as being the fancy of a dying man.'

However:

> Strangely enough, three decades later, this advice, having lain dormant, was heeded . . . I felt impelled to write a prose narrative of the Ramayana based on Kamban as a second volume to a work of Indian mythology.

Narayan the Indian novelist was going back to his roots.

The first volume Narayan alludes to in his narrative is *Gods, Demons and Others* published by Viking Press of New York in 1964. Narayan had not anticipated his Ramayana and Mahabharata at this stage. In Gods, Demons and Others, both the epics appear in capsule form, in

'Valmiki' and 'Draupadi' respectively. These sketches were developed later and we have Narayan's Ramayana and Mahabharata.

Narayan retells both the Ramayana and Mahabharata in the spirit of his professional philosophy: the reader and readability matter more than anything else. In these retold epics the common Western reader occupies the centre of Narayan's attention as a storyteller; he sticks to the narrative line to satisfy the needs and expectations of his foreign reader; he chips in occasionally with brief, helpful editorial explanations.

The focus in Narayan's Ramayana is Rama, of course, not Sita. Within the self-imposed limitations Narayan's focus—after Kamban's model—is Rama the man. At the same time he does not overlook 'the splendour of Rama's personality'. He accomplishes the humanization of an epic character—'cosmic personification'.

Love, in its classical form, finds its place in Kamban's classic. Narayan too takes an interest in romantic love; he is at his best, naturally, in describing pangs of love—having experienced them himself. As a young man, the writer had impulsively fallen in love with a young woman drawing water from a street tap. Nothing was right, the sub-caste did not match, the horoscopes did not match. The tenacious young man had his way: his bride Rajam was eleven years younger to him. This young Narayan was so deeply in love with his wife, he could not stand separation from her even for a day. After three years of a deliriously happy life together, Rajam caught typhoid and died. 'Mars kills,' as the family astrologer had warned. (Incidentally, Rajam's death must have confirmed Narayan's faith in astrology. He even had his friend, Graham Greene's horoscope cast and sent to him. Greene's executors should be able to throw light on this, especially whether the British author's life had gone the way predicted for him by a tufted pundit of remote south India.)

Rajam's death shattered Narayan; he contemplated entering the pyre with her body. However, their little daughter helped him recuperate. The memory of his brief wedded bliss led him, a man of great libido, to stubborn sublimation of his sexuality. There was no question of assignations for him, a striking contrast to his friend Graham Greene.

Yet, Narayan remained conspicuously susceptible to feminine charm. In his American travel narrative, *Dateless Diary*, he notices that 'women of tremendous beauty' pass along in the crowds'; or 'I just continued to sit and look away at a pretty girl'. When a secretary commends her own coffee to him because 'I make my own blend and kiss every grain', Narayan responds: 'I think I'll try it even without cream, you seem to have given it the right treatment'. His attention to beauty is evident in his memoir, *My Days*; his second novel, *The Bachelor of Arts*; and another love tale, *The Painter of Signs*, that he wrote three and a half decades later when he was past seventy.

Now, in the hands of a writer of such 'maidenliness', Rama and Sita, the major characters of Ramayana, suffer elaborately, classically. Even Ravana, the demon-king villain of the epic goes through the regulation experience.

Given below is a passage that describes Sita in love:

> They crossed the moat surrounding Janaka's palace, with its golden spires soaring above the other buildings of the city. Now Rama observed on a balcony princess Sita playing with her companions. He stood arrested by her beauty, and she noticed him at the same moment. Their eyes met. They had been together not so long ago in Vaikunta, their original home in heaven, as Vishnu and his spouse Lakshmi, but in their present incarnation, suffering all the limitations of mortals, they looked at each other as strangers. She, decked in ornaments and flowers, in the midst of her attendants, flashed on his eyes like a streak of lightning. She paused to watch Rama slowly pass out of view, along with his sage-master and brother. The moment he vanished, her mind became uncontrollably agitated. The eye had admitted a slender shaft of love, which later expanded and spread into her whole being. She felt ill.
>
> Observing the sudden change in her, and the sudden drooping and withering of her whole being, even the bangles on her wrist slipping down, her attendants took her away and spread a soft bed for her to lie on.
>
> She lay tossing in her bed complaining, 'You girls have forgotten how to make a soft bed. You are all out to tease me.' Her maids in attendance had never seen her in such a mood. They were bewildered and amused at first, but later became genuinely concerned, when they noticed tears streaming down her cheeks. They found her prattling involuntarily, 'Shoulders of emerald, eyes like lotus petals, who is he? He invaded my heart and has deprived me of all shame! A robber who could ensnare my heart and snatch away my peace of mind! Broad-shouldered, but walked off so swiftly. Why could he not have halted his steps, so that I might have gained just one more glimpse and quelled this riotous heart of mine. He was here, he was there next second, and

gone forever. He could not be a god—his eyelids flickered . . . Or was he a sorcerer casting a spell on people?'

The sun set beyond the sea, so says the poet—and when a poet mentions a sea, we have to accept it. No harm in letting a poet describe his vision, no need to question his geography. The cry of birds settling down for the night and the sound of waves on the seashore became clearer as the evening advanced into dusk and night. A cool breeze blew from the sea, but none of it comforted Sita. This hour sharpened the agony of love, and agitated her heart with hopeless longings. A rare bird, known as 'Anril', somewhere called its mate. Normally at this hour, Sita would listen for its melodious warbling, but today its voice sounded harsh and odious. Sita implored, 'Oh, bird, wherever you may be, please be quiet. You are bent upon mischief, annoying me with your cries and lamentations. The sins I committed in a previous birth have assumed your form and come to torture me now!' The full moon rose from the sea, flooding the earth with its soft light. At the sight of it, she covered her eyes with her palms. She felt that all the elements were alien to her mood and combining to aggravate her suffering. Her maids noticed her distress and feared that some deep-rooted ailment had suddenly seized her. They lit cool lamps whose wicks were fed with clarified butter, but found that even such a flame proved intolerable to her, and they extinguished the lamps and in their place kept luminous gems, which emanated soft light. They made her a soft bed on a slab of moonstone with layers of soft petals, but the flowers wilted, Sita writhed and groaned and complained of everything—the night, stars, moonlight, and flowers: a whole universe of unsympathetic elements. The question went on drumming in her mind: 'Who is he? Where is he gone? Flashing into view and gone again—or am I subject to a hallucination? It could not be so—a mere hallucination cannot weaken one so much.'

Within the compulsions of his limited narrative, Narayan focuses on Sita's strength of mind and character: Sita knows her mind:

. . . At the sight of his departure, the women wept. Rama made one last attempt to leave Lakshmana behind but Lakshmana followed him stubbornly. He then went into Sita's chamber and found her already dressed in the rough tree fibre—her finery and jewels discarded and laid aside, although she had decorated and dressed herself as befitting a queen a little while ago. Rama, though he had been of so firm a mind for himself, felt disturbed at the sight of her—the change being so sudden. He said, 'It was never my father's intention to send you along with me. This is not the life for you. I have only come to take your leave, not to take you with me . . .'

'I'm dressed and ready, as you see . . .'

'If it is your wish to discard fine clothes because I wear none, you may do so, though it's not necessary.'

'I'm coming with you, my place is at your side wherever you may be . . .'

Rama saw the determination in her eyes and made one last plea. 'You have your duties to perform here, my father and mother being here. I'll be with you again.'

'After fourteen years! What would be the meaning of my existence? I could as well be dead. It will be living death for me without you. I am alive only when I am with you; forest or a marble palace is all the same to me.'

When he realised that she could not be deflected from her purpose, Rama said, 'If it is your wish, so let it be. May the gods protect you.'

Finally, Sita accepts the ordeal by fire, a disturbing episode for any reader:

A large crowd pressed around Rama. When Sita eagerly arrived, after her months of loneliness and suffering, she was received by her husband in full view of a vast public. She felt awkward but accepted this with resignation. But what she could not understand was why her lord seemed preoccupied and moody and cold. However, she prostrated herself at his feet, and then stood a little away from him, sensing some strange barrier between herself and him.

Rama remained brooding for a while and suddenly said, 'My task is done. I have now freed you. I have fulfilled my mission. All this effort has been not to attain personal satisfaction for you or me. It was to vindicate the honour of the Ikshavahu race and to honour our ancestors' codes and values. After all this, I must tell you that it is not customary to admit back to the normal married fold a woman who has resided all alone in a stranger's home. There can be no question of living together again. I leave you free to go where you please and to choose any place to live in. I do not restrict you in any manner.'

On hearing this, Sita broke down. 'My trials are not ended yet,' she cried. 'I thought with your victory all our troubles were at an end . . . ! So be it.' She beckoned to Lakshmana and ordered, 'Light a fire at once, on this very spot.'

Lakshmana hesitated and looked at his brother, wondering whether he would countermand the order. But Rama seemed passive and

> acquiescent. Lakshmana, ever the most unquestioning deputy, gathered faggots and got ready a roaring pyre within a short time. The entire crowd watched the proceedings, stunned by the turn of events. The flames rose to the height of a tree, still Rama made no comment. He watched. Sita approached the fire, prostrated herself before it, and said, 'O Agni, great god of fire, be my witness.' She jumped into the fire.
>
> From the heart of the flame rose the god of fire, bearing Sita, and presented her to Rama with words of blessing. Rama, now satisfied that he had established his wife's integrity in the presence of the world, welcomed Sita back to his arms.

Narayan was the first to render Kamban's *Ramavataram* into English prose. He may have opted for Kamban as Rajaji had already rendered Valmiki's Sanskrit classic into English or, like any good Tamil, he was proud of his heritage. Narayan did not know the level of Tamil needed to read Kamban. But he went about the job methodically; he engaged Tamil scholars to read the Tamil classic with him. He must have taken notes; if he did they would be informative.

We may briefly compare Narayan's Ramayana with Rajaji's version based on Valmiki. Rajaji—as Valmiki—does not offer, for example, the love episode at all; and Rajaji gives a whole chapter to Sita's resolve to accompany her husband to the forests. Rajaji moralizes purposefully; Narayan does not, never does. As I said elsewhere, Narayan had learned from his precursors in south India that good fiction and moralizing do not go together. Besides, Narayan knew love, knew desire, knew the joy of physical labour, hard work; for him as for Kamban, the Ramayana is divine comedy, spanning *iham* and *param*, the here and the hereafter.

For centuries Sita has been many things to many people. Narayan's Sita must be put alongside some prominent women in his life and fiction. In his first formative period, the novelist was fortunate to have had two strong women in his immediate family, his grandmother Ammani and his own mother: both gave him greater understanding and support in his early struggle than the men in the family. And then he was greatly attached to his own daughter, Hema.

For Narayan, the modern novelist, who did not wear his Hinduism on his sleeve ('Religion is like one's underwear', he said), Sita was a strong-minded woman of great dignity and self-respect; and Narayan followed her up with Draupadi in his Mahabharata, who proves herself more than a match in debates with even Dharmaraja. Thus Narayan's epic women not improbably led to two of his most memorable fictional characters true to our time, Rosie (*The Guide*), a dancer who falls in illicit love to regret it finally, and Daisy (*The Painter of Signs*), a single woman who ends her affair because it comes in the way of her career.

CHITRANGADA NOT SITA: JAWAHARLAL NEHRU'S MODEL FOR GENDER EQUATION

REBA SOM

JAWAHARLAL NEHRU HAD a mind of many layers, a mind which was constantly evolving. As his biographer put it, 'over the years it took in much and rarely sloughed off anything'.[1] One of the deepest layers of his mind was romanticism. His emotions had to be stirred and involved before he could react. Thus it required the massacre of Jallianwalah Bagh to draw Jawaharlal fully into the national movement, and again, it was Kamala's prolonged illness, death and his subsequent role, typecast as the lonely introverted widower, that made him delve into the woman's question. With a rare sensitivity and liberalism which stemmed directly from his wide intellectual exposure, Nehru made a deep analysis of the woman's question in general with all the nuances of a man–woman relationship. As Nehru put it himself, 'I hold rather definite and also strong views on subjects relating to the women of India.'[2]

In following Kamala's development from a shy, sensitive girl to a mature woman of conviction, Jawaharlal had himself learnt much about a woman's inner strength, her own basic compulsions and the need to be herself in the quest for an identity. In the course of time, Kamala became to Jawaharlal a symbol of Indian women, or of woman herself. If Sita was Gandhi's model woman to be emulated, it was Chitrangada, the Manipuri princess immortalized in Rabindranath Tagore's celebrated lyrical drama, that Jawaharlal looked up to. The image of Sita, as handed down through various renditions of the Ramayana, provided a point of reference around which gender constructions were articulated in Indian civilization through the centuries. Mahatma Gandhi, who felt the need to integrate India's past with the enlightened values and notions adopted by the Indian National Congress, tapped this powerful symbol when he called upon the woman of India to join the struggle for liberation. The image of Sita, as handed down by the past and recast by Gandhi, was associated with self-sacrifice, an infinite capacity for suffering, chastity and moral power to inspire men with higher notions. The governing body of gender studies which has sprung up in the past few years has emphasized the limitations of this particular construction of gender relations as far as women's own needs are concerned, particularly as regards their sexuality and material requirements.[3]

That the image of Sita had inherent limitations in terms of women's own needs was realized by a few outstanding thinkers of the Indian Awakening. A remarkable song by Rabindranath Tagore inverted Sita's ordeal through fire to stress on her unspoken rejection of the existing gender regime.

Phire phire amaye micche bhaben swami
Shamay holo biday nebo ami
Apamana jar shajay chita
She je bahir hoye elo agnijita
Raj ashoner kathin asammane

Farewell my lord you call me in vain
She, for whom indignity laid its funeral pyre,
Came out victorious from the fire
The hard dishonour or the throne
Shall never touch her free soul again.[4]

The same Rabindranath recast another mythical image, that of Chitrangada, as a symbol around which a new gender construction could be built that was fairer to women, and which accommodated their needs within the family and the sphere of work. The images, as projected by Tagore, integrated woman's sexuality and her identity as man's comrade in the sphere outside home. The central theme in Chitrangada's philosophy as expounded to the Pandava hero Arjuna, whom she ultimately married, was equality. Chitrangada had warned against being deified and kept on a pedestal as also being neglected and ignored. As the rich and deep personality of Kamala gradually unfolded, Jawaharlal could fathom the passion with which Kamala believed in gender equality. Nehru wrote that ultimately Kamala seemed to come to him as Chitrangada herself, saying, 'I am Chitra. No Goddess to be worshipped, nor yet the object of common pity, to be brushed aside like a moth with indifference. If you deign to keep me by your side in the path of danger and daring, if you allow me to share the great duties of your life, then you will know my true self.'[5] In fact it was this process of sharing in equal measure the common responsibilities arising from a total participation in the national struggle for freedom that created a deep closeness between Kamala and Jawaharlal which long spells of Jawaharalal's incarceration or phases of Kamala's illness could not destroy.

What impressed Nehru most about women's participation in the civil disobedience movement was its equalizing impact. Not only did it bind women from diverse socio-economic backgrounds to a common cause but also made women feel that they were co-sharers with men nationalists in India's destiny. It was women's camaraderie with men evidenced in the civil disobedience years rather than their stoic suffering in the Sita tradition, which was more appealing to Nehru and which he felt had to be publicly appreciated and recognized.

To Gandhi, who had primarily engineered the entry of women in large numbers into national agitational politics, the logic of woman's participation was different. The seasoned strategist in Gandhi quickly realized that women's intrinsic non-violence and ability for silent suffering would lend credence to his non-violent satyagraha. By constantly holding out the example of Sita with her superior moral strength, Gandhi hoped to instill in women a greater tolerance and make them aware of their essential role as peacemaker and balancer. Even when he encouraged women to join the civil disobedience movement, Gandhi was specific about their role. While approving of picketing, he was opposed to women joining the civil protesters lest they become victims of violence. Trapped by middle-class ideological moorings on sexuality, Gandhi prescribed women's participation in politics within certain social parameters. An ardent believer in woman's householder responsibilities, Gandhi discouraged women with familial roles to join his movement. While advocating equal status and legal rights for women Gandhi at the same time felt that the intrinsic difference between man and woman necessitated a demarcation in the vocations of the two. Subscribing to the gender stereotype of the day, Gandhi declared, 'I do not believe in women working for a living or undertaking commercial enterprises.' Using graphic imagery he declared, 'in trying to ride the horse that man rides she brings herself and him down . . .'[6] Gandhi's attempt to channelize women's participation in the movement along a prescribed course was appreciated by most men who saw no threat to their own interests. Many women, however, found it difficult to obey Gandhi's commands. Kasturba Gandhi and Sarojini Naidu broke his strict orders by joining the protest marches and courting arrest. Margaret Cousins, one of the founding members of the All India Women's Conference, wrote to Gandhi: 'Division of sexes in a non-violent campaign seems unnatural and against all the awakened consciousness of the women of today . . . there can be no watertight compartments of service. Women ask that no marches, imprisonments, no demonstrations organized for the benefit of India should prohibit women from a share in them . . .'[7]

This was a sentiment that Jawaharlal Nehru could very well appreciate and empathize with. Indeed, when the ailing Kamala got arrested on 1 January 1931 Jawaharlal shared her sense of fulfillment, and wrote to Indira how she seemed thoroughly happy and contented which was a pleasant New Year gift to him. Nehru was sensitive enough to understand Kamala's compulsions in joining the national movement. He explained that Kamala had wanted to play her own part in the national struggle and not be merely a hanger-on and a shadow of her husband.

While drawing women into the vortex of the national movement, Gandhi had not spelt out any definite programme for women to achieve socio-economic equality, nor did he take up socially divisive issues along caste, religious and sex lines. Instead he devised programmes such as spinning which would bind the various women's social groups together and give them a common agenda and also dwelt on self-effacement and silent suffering, the qualities of Sita which would give women the ideological boost and moral encouragement for sacrifice.

To Nehru, however, the natural corollary to women's participation in the national struggle was the beginning of a greater struggle for finding a proper identity in the Indian social milieu and enjoying equal rights with men. He was perhaps one of the few leaders who sensed this inevitable turn in the women's movement and actually heralded it. He loudly proclaimed that he had the greatest admiration for women and was not afraid to allow them freedom to grow because he was convinced that too much legal constraint would break the social structure.

Nehru's recognition of women's needs to grow and emancipate themselves while working for the larger emancipation of their country from foreign rule was further unique when judged in the context of his times. Recent gender studies have amply demonstrated that the construct of women whether in the social reform era of the nineteenth century or in the subsequent nationalist period was an attempt to 'recast' women on patriarchal assumptions.[8]

The social reformers of the nineteenth century, by projecting the examples of Gargi and Maitreyi, initiated a long tradition of myth about the ancient Hindu women as being free, mobile and intellectual. There was a concerted attempt by reformers to show that women in ancient India enjoyed gender equality particularly in the spiritual domain, which was lamentably lost in the days when sati became an acceptable ritual. Such a construct never took cognizance of the fact that scholars like Max Müller had clearly pointed out that cases like Gargi and Maitreyi were exceptions and not the rule. Also this mythical construct of the enlightened woman of ancient India failed to accommodate the Vedic dasi (woman in servitude).

In the period of nationalism images of Sita–Savitri–Damayanti provided focal points of reference for the qualities of self-sacrifice, chastity and moral power that these heroines possessed. By emphasizing these qualities, nationalists attempted to prove the spiritual superiority that existed within the internal sphere of the home, which compensated for the cultural domination by Western scientific ideas in the material or external sphere which had to be accepted. Feminine virtues of chastity and self-sacrifice, practical skills of literacy, accounting and hygiene and devotion to details of housework were prescribed by nationalist leaders for the education of women, thereby defining a 'new patriarchy'.[9]

Another favourite symbol used by nationalists to project indigenous spiritual superiority was Durga or Shakti epitomized in colonial Bengal by the glorification of motherhood. Bankim Chandra

Chatterjee's *Vande Mataram* became a political battle cry which extremist leaders like Aurobindo and Bipin Pal seized eagerly. The empowering of the symbol of motherhood however created a myth about her strength and power. In real terms, glorification of motherhood meant the glorification of her reproductive powers and her spirit of self-sacrifice. To compensate for the feeling of powerlessness against colonial masters the Bengal nationalist leaders invoked the myth of Shakti as an ideological force which would imply the East's spiritual superiority over the West.

Judged against this background, Nehru's open critique of many of these gender constructs seems remarkable. The repeated references to the pristine purity of the Hindu shastras and the exalted position given to Sita, Savitri, Damayanti and others irked Nehru. While acknowledging that these estimable ladies had no doubt played a very brave part and become traditional heroines, Nehru hastened to point out that they had lived in a particular age and served certain social compulsions which were irrelevant in present times. The silent martyrdom of Sita and the complete internalization of her anguish were certainly not qualities that Nehru sought to inculcate in women. He lashed out strongly against the passive acceptance by women over the years, of man-made laws which were intended to shackle and enslave women and treat them as chattels. In Chitrangada's moral strength and physical prowess Nehru could identify the values of femininity that he admired most, qualities which in the abstract, he could identify and admire in men too.

Clearly Nehru while engaging in the dialogue on feminine qualities was on a different wave length altogether from the colonial discourse of his times which regarded the Orient, as also India, as effeminate, emasculated, weak and powerless, to be resurrected by the manly, strong Occident.[10] To Nehru femininity was not a value-attached term—he used it in the sense of aesthetic, sensitive and morally strong qualities which he admired and recognized in certain men and women.

In a revealing pronouncement Nehru said that he regarded India as a feminine country. As he explained to Frances Günther, India 'has certain feminine virtues and certainly feminine vices. All such generalizations are of course too vague and sweeping but there is a core of truth in them. And that is why I like India and am bound to her and yet feel intensely irritated at so many things. Is that a man's reactions to woman? Our dress and speech and habits generally are inclined to be feminine. Or is it just the climate?'[11]

Between the so-called feminine virtues and vices Nehru drew a sharp line. While addressing a meeting in Madras, he made a subtle difference between being 'womanly' or instinctively feminine and being 'womanish' or indulgent in women's weaknesses.[12] In the same vein he explained to a women's audience in Singapore that he would rather not address them as 'ladies' since the term had a stereotyped value judgment given by men which was 'vulgar'. Instead he preferred to call them 'women'.[13] Nehru was openly appreciative of women. As he put it, 'I can say with considerable confidence that I am proud of the women of India. I am proud of their beauty, grace, charm, shyness, modesty, intelligence and their spirit of sacrifice and I think if anybody can truly represent the spirit of India, the women can do it and not the man.'[14] The woman therefore that Nehru idealized combined strength with aesthetics, which he identified not necessarily only among the women of India but in India herself, transcending gender distinctions and gender stereotypes.

Marie Seton, Nehru's biographer felt that perhaps, more than any other woman, Jawaharlal Nehru saw in Sarojini Naidu the feminine counterpart of man. Nehru acknowledged as much when he declared 'just as the Father of the Nation had infused moral grandeur and greatness to the struggle, Mrs. Sarojini Naidu gave it artistry and poetry and that zest for life and indomitable spirit which not only faced disaster and catastrophe, but faced them with a light heart and with a song on her lips and a smile on her face.'[15] As a politician Nehru valued most Sarojini's role in lifting the Indian national life from the plane of pure politics to a higher artistic sphere.

It was Nehru's strong affinity to feminine sensitivity and admiration for their stoic strength that created strong bonds between him and many women in his times. As Marie Seton pointed out, 'ever and again it would be women who would glimpse the essence of Jawaharlal and bid him from the heart to walk steadfastly along that steep and perilous path that was his destiny.'[16] Jawaharlal thrived on the emotional strength that he derived from his association with women—whether in his family or outside.

As he wrote in his *An Autobiography*, one missed many things in prison but perhaps most of all one missed the sound of women's voices and children's laughter. He felt attuned to the vital energy and strength that he recognized in some of his women associates which inspired him. The active women crusaders of the 40s, of whom Aruna Asaf Ali was one, represented for Nehru new symbols breaking existing stereotypes. They were stern and unbending and with something of iron in their souls. He greatly admired the combination of fiery dynamism and cool restraint in women. Speaking about the vital and dynamic quality of Sarojini Naidu for instance, Nehru said, 'whatever she touched, she infused with something of her fire. She was indeed a pillar of fire. And then again, she was like cooling running water, soothing and bringing down the passion of our politics to the cooler levels of human beings.'[17] In Kamala too he identified this blend of fire and restraint. As he explained to his daughter Indira, it was the character and dignity and quiet restraint of Kamala together with inner fire which had stolen into the hearts of millions. In Edwina Mountbatten, Nehru found the formidable combination of 'beauty, high intelligence, grace and charm' with 'vitality and a dedicated love for humanity'.[18] The indefatigable energy displayed by Edwina during the crisis of human suffering in the aftermath of Partition and the healer's touch that she provided to hundreds of the suffering humanity in the refugee camps earned the deep respect and undying admiration of Nehru. Louis Mountbatten detected the commonality that existed between Jawaharlal and Edwina in their untiring dedication for dearly held causes. Shortly before Nehru's death when he was under severe stress after the China fiasco, Mountbatten wrote to him that like Edwina, he should go ahead with a driving force and not give up.

A committed believer in the principle of gender equality, Nehru strongly condemned men for having exploited women through the centuries. He took upon himself the twin responsibilities of exposing the tyranny of male dominance and, at the same time, encouraging and educating women to strive for equal conditions. As he explained while addressing the All India Women's Conference, 'I would prefer to call you comrades but I have not done so firstly, because I do not know whether you like being called so, and secondly, because I do not know whether you deserve it.'[19] One of the aspects of the Leninist Revolution which had impressed Nehru most had been the equalizing effect it had on women. 'Whatever other failings the Russian women of today may have, she is certainly not a chattel or plaything of man. She is independent, aggressively so, and refuse to play second fiddle to man.'[20] The problem with India, Nehru analysed, was that Indian civilization, customs and laws were all made by man who had taken good care to ensure a superior position and to treat woman as chattel and a plaything to be exploited for his own advantage and amusement. Women therefore had to fight for their own rights since no group, no community, no country had ever got rid of its disabilities by the generosity of the oppressor. Nehru was clear in stating that the association of man and woman should be of perfect freedom and prefect comradeship with no dependence of one on the other.

He was never tired of quoting from the French philosopher Charles Fourrier to point out that the position of women in a country was a sure index of judging its social development. In a deliberate discard of the accepted stereotype for woman, Nehru declared that marriage was not to be regarded as the only goal in life. He exhorted women students to read Ibsen's *Doll's House* and realize how they had been steadily indoctrinated into believing that while man was the bread winner, woman's place was in the home and her ideal should be that of a devoted wife and nothing more. Even in this sole 'profession of marriage' in which woman was trained, he warned that she would not get an equality of status. She would merely be 'the devoted help-mate, the follower and the obedient slave of her husband and others.'[21] Nehru cautioned against entering into matrimony merely as a social requirement. Although marriage was important in life yet it was smaller than life itself. Displaying rare maturity for his twenty-three years, Jawaharlal had written frankly to his mother when she was match-making for him, 'would you like me to marry a girl who I may not like for the rest of my life or who may not like me? Rather than marry in that way, it would be better not to marry at all.'[22]

A truly integrated human being, in Nehru's opinion, was one who had a healthy mind and body. Physical fitness was almost an obsession with Nehru who felt that women should break out of the stereotype of being categorized as delicate and frail and in need of constant male protection. To his daughter Indira, then studying at Santiniketan, Nehru's advice was to go for a run every morning and not be influenced by the 'willowy' Bengali girls who did little physical work.[23] Indeed it was Nehru's dream that in independent India, men and women students were encouraged to do compulsory physical hard work in villages as part of their curriculum. He felt strongly that everybody, man or woman, had to be physically strong and mentally alert to do creative productive work. He felt it was criminal not to look after one's own health. While the average woman in India, Nehru recognized, worked hard in the fields, the problem lay with the urban woman still trapped within the stereotype expectations of society. It was against such women who felt that doing no work was a high status symbol that Nehru lashed out. He declared, 'I do not . . . like the woman who is like the flower in the field and the lily in the valley, which just blooms and does nothing else. I do not like weaklings. I like physically fit men and women who can face mobs if necessary . . .'[24] To Nehru physical fitness was essential for giving women a sense of confidence and an acceptance of the principle of gender equality. Indeed Nehru regarded women's participation in the civil disobedience movement in 1930 as being a social revolution of sorts, particularly because women, hitherto considered quite helpless, were able to demonstrate that they could fearlessly discharge the duties of men and take on physical beating and economic hardships with equanimity. As Nehru put it, 'when their sons, husbands and brothers were sent to prison, they came out of the shelter of their homes and took over the duties of those who had been imprisoned and they discharged those duties excellently and much better than men and because of that India has risen in the estimation of the outside world.'[25]

Another stereotype regarding women forcefully attacked by Nehru was ornamentation as the essential highlighter of feminine beauty. He wrote he could not appreciate the idea of women covering themselves with jewels, like prisoners' chains. While he recognized that women should take some care of themselves and their looks for aesthetic reasons, he protested strongly against the tendency to doll them up, and shackle them with so much jewellery as to restrain their movement and freedom.

Nehru looked for self-reliance and character in women and debunked the non-essential superficialities which many society ladies tended to display. The lady who visited the slums occasionally to relieve her conscience by the performance of good and charitable deeds, he felt, had a patronizing and condescending approach. Nehru felt that a woman's efficiency level could improve considerably if she could adopt a greater simplicity in her lifestyle. His practical advice, for instance, to an Indian women's delegation just before their visit to wartime China was to be mentally prepared for a certain measure of risk and hardship and travel with a very minimum of luggage because of a need for simplicity in a society where people dressed very simply. When his daughter Indira studying at Santiniketan expressed a desire to set up a separate establishment with a cook and staff, keeping apart from the 'common herd', Jawaharlal sternly admonished her. Such preferential treatment generally accorded to royalty, he said, smacked of 'vulgarity and snobbery'. He asked her directly 'do you think any self respecting boy or girl would care to make friends with you under these circumstances?' Any such patronizing, condescending attitude of superiority, Nehru warned, would be insulting.[26]

Often in his impatience to shake women out of their centuries-old complacence Nehru appeared to be brusque. The AICC draft resolution of Fundamental Rights and Economic Policy framed in 1931, for instance, had a clause relating to protection of women workers and especially to adequate provisions for leave during maternity period. Kamaladevi Chattopadhyay objected to the word 'protection' and wished to replace it with 'attention'[27] as she felt that women were not going to tolerate protection from anyone, not even from the state. Nehru reacted to this outburst by saying that though he was personally unconcerned even if the amending word was accepted, he felt Kamladevi Chattopadhyay was overreacting to the word protection. Nehru's Western values and intellectual inclinations made him lash out spontaneously against the social oppressor, whether landlord capitalist or the exploitative male. These outbursts initially caused ripples of uneasiness and apprehension among those under attack. Since the nationalist Congress organization drew support from many of the landed and propertied classes and could not afford their alienation, Gandhi and many of his lieutenants worked hard to tone down Nehru's radicalism. In the course of time Nehru, entrenched in the highest party position, found that his attacks were being discounted as harmless outbursts.

Nevertheless Nehru's forthright social criticism certainly served a purpose. He was able to focus public gaze on specific areas of inequality and injustice thereby encouraging a greater social awareness.

In the early 1920s for instance, when the question of residence of prostitutes in the Allahabad municipal area came up, Nehru's reaction was characteristic. Refusing to address himself to the narrow and immediate question of residence he raised instead the wider issue of the social problem itself. He declared, 'If we could raise the status of women and afford them honorable careers we would do more towards the lessening of the evil than by any number of bylaws.'[28] Further he observed, as 'prostitutes do not carry on their ancient trade by themselves . . . the proper way to deal with the question of prostitution is to make it as dishonorable for a man as for a woman to help in it . . .'[29]

This open denunciation by Nehru can be contrasted with the guarded responses of Gandhi when confronted by prostitutes during the civil disobedience movement. In Barisal in East Bengal, 359 prostitutes wanted to engage in Congress work and contribute from their earnings to the Tilak Fund. The statesman in Gandhi was quick to realize that any association with prostitutes would jeopardize the pattern of women's participation in the movement, and would thereby rob it of its potential success.[30] Elite women appearing in public for the first time were in any case apprehensive of being confused with prostitutes. Apart from this concern was Gandhi's personal belief that sexual restraint was an absolute precondition to social and political reform. Gandhi's suggestion was that they take up spinning instead, since the wheel is a kind of wall for the protection of women. This typical Gandhian platitude which often helped defuse serious political crises seemed anathema to Jawaharlal.

Nehru found his style curbed not only by the restraints of political statesmanship but also by the bonds of Indian tradition which arrested the path of progress. In a candid letter to his American friend Frances Günther, Nehru wrote, 'How I envy you the lack of thousands of years of tradition. It is a terrible and crushing burden. I do not think it is all bad but such a lot of it is just decadent putrid matter. A clean slate to write on—what a joy that would be . . .'[31] The rigidity of society had to be broken and cobwebs of traditional restrictions brushed aside for Indian women to progress. He exhorted women to be 'rebels' and 'soldiers' crusading against 'unjust and tyrannical social customs of the day'.[32]

Jawaharlal was himself, in many ways, a rebel at heart. He was vehemently opposed to any obsessive concern with morality and religion. As he put it, 'I have a feeling that these echoes from the past are raised chiefly to hide our present deficiencies and to prevent us from attacking the root cause of women's degradation today.'[33] It was totally suspect for instance why the examples of Sita, Savitri, Damayanti were constantly flaunted at women, and men never reminded of Ramachandra and Satyavan and urged to behave like them. He wondered whether men were supposed to be perfect, incapable of any further effort or further improvement. Speaking of himself, he frankly explained that unlike Gandhi who was a moralist, he was instead a pagan at heart, and loved the rich pagan culture and outlook on life of the ancients, their joy in beauty of all kinds, in richness of life and a wise understanding of human nature with all its virtues and frailties.

Jawaharlal's attitude to sexual morality differed radically from Gandhi's. He clearly attached no idea of sin to sex and never concealed the fact that he took delight in the company of women with whom he could share an aesthetic and emotional closeness. As he explained to Frances Günther he found her letter to be vivid, vital, impertinent, aggressive and intimate—qualities which sustained him. His relationship with Kamala, dogged as it was with illness, incarceration and her premature death, had a certain element of magic which never wore off. Analysing his own thoughts on man's love for a woman, Nehru wrote, 'love, as I conceived it, and as it came to me, was something different, something electric, something often painful. It was not the conception of duty owed or an obligation to be discharged. I would hate to have someone feel that it was his or her duty to love me. I want no such purchase . . .'[34]

Nehru attached great importance to the sense of equality and mutual respect in a man–woman relationship. Gandhi's belief that sexual attraction even between husband and wife was immoral unless it was for establishing progeny seemed unnatural and shocking to Nehru. Jawaharlal reasoned: 'evidently Gandhiji thinks . . . that if the sexual affinity between man and woman is admitted every man will run after every woman and vice versa. Neither inference is justified . . . for him it is a "soot or whitewash" question, there are no intermediate shades . . .'[35] For Nehru these intermediary shades of grey were vital. As he confessed, 'I presume I am a normal individual and sex has played its part in my life but it has not obsessed me or diverted me from my other activities. It has been a subordinate part.'[36] Nehru made no secret of the fact that his friendship with women friends like Padmaja Naidu or Edwina Mountabatten gave him the vital intellectual and emotional strength that kept him going through periods of grave stress. Physical intimacy, if there was any, would be a mere detail in the totality of this truth. On 14 April 1948, in the tragic aftermath of Partition, Nehru was to write to Edwina, 'I want someone to talk to me sanely and confidently, as you can do so well, for I am in danger of losing faith in myself and the work I do . . .'[37] To Padmaja Naidu or Bebee as he affectionately called her, he reached out in his emotionally vulnerable years during and after Kamala's long illness and death. He confessed to her that after the mad whirl of the day just the thought of writing to her comforted and soothed him. There was no patronizing arrogance in Jawaharlal's relationship with his women friends. Underlying his deep respect and understanding for their growth and development as independent personalities there was an emotional bond of sharing. Edwina recalled that her promise to Jawaharlal before leaving India was that 'nothing we did or felt would ever be allowed to come between you and your work or me and mine.'[38] Jawaharlal treated Edwina intellectually as an equal, sharing with her some of his political ideas and opinions. As Edwina's biographer put it, Nehru thought Edwina's judgement easily as good as her husband's—indeed sometimes better. Edwina felt enriched by this exchange and acknowledged how often she was influenced by Nehru's thinking. Indeed in the highest official circles of London, Edwina enjoyed the reputation of being anti-British, left wing and somewhat pink. There is reason to believe that it was through his deep friendship with women of intelligence and sensitivity that Jawaharlal gained a valuable insight into and understanding of the woman's point of view and could appreciate better the prejudices against which she had to struggle. As Edwina Mountbatten explained to her husband in 1952, 'J has obviously meant a very great deal in my life, in these last years, and I think I in his too. I think I understand him and he me, as well as any human beings can ever understand each other . . .'[39] When Edwina died in her sleep in Borneo in the early hours of 21 February 1960, a pile of Nehru's letters was found on her bedside table—they had been her nightly reading.

With his sensitive understanding and strong convictions Nehru was quick to herald any development which might improve the woman's lot in India. Thus it was Nehru who had been among the first to publicly acknowledge the role of women leaders like Sarojini Naidu in initiating a process which ultimately led to their securing political representation through adult franchise. He felt it must not be forgotten that Indian women had consistently refused special and reserved representation in the legislatures. They had even protested against the partial representation that was given to them. This needed to be appreciated by the nation as a whole. Again, it was at the behest of Jawaharlal Nehru that the Congress decided to enshrine the principle of equal rights for men and women in the Fundamental Rights of the People at the Karachi Congress in 1931. Nehru however warned that this equality won easily through the goodwill of others would be difficult for women to translate into reality, for as soon as they tried to rid themselves of heavy social burdens, they would come up against old customs and man's prejudices and interest.

In the 1937 elections to the provincial legislatures in which Congress decided to participate, Nehru as Congress president made a special plea to involve more women candidates. He felt it was necessary to recognize in practice women's right to an equal share in public and national activity. They had fully earned this right. From the larger viewpoint of national progress it was essential that women should share in the responsibilities as well as the triumphs of the struggle. When the Congress assumed the responsibilities of government in the provinces in 1937, eighty women were included in the legislatures and the assemblies. Under the National Planning Committee which was instituted in 1938, with Nehru as chairman, a special subcommittee was formed with Lakshmibai Rajwade as president and Mridula Sarabhai as secretary to specifically examine the role of women in a planned economy. The report produced by this body included many concepts strikingly bold by contemporary standards, which some of the members of the committee felt were too daring. Begum Hamid Ali, for instance, wrote to Nehru that she would withhold her name from the report. Nehru's reaction to the problem was characteristic. Concerned about the symbolic value and success of the report he was keen to work out an acceptable consensus. To Hamid Ali he pleaded for a reformulation of the report that would be acceptable to all. To Lakshmibai Rajwade he reasoned that the report should carry the approval of a large section of opinion without which it would be condemned as a utopian and airy document with no relation to fact.

So long as the women's movement remained integrally linked to the national movement there seemed to be a general acceptance of its purpose. Gender equality in principle was granted easily enough in 1931 partly because the nature of the envisioned equality remained vague. Although women's associations included in their agenda issues such as equal rights, widow remarriage, polygamy, etc., these were not seriously taken since the general feeling was that nothing could be secured in a colonial state. Imperialism therefore was identified as the major cause of women's subordination and custom. Indeed much of the support to the women's movement for suffrage and greater political opportunities had come from the organizing efforts of men. The political elite gave their support readily because thereby they could show that they were more socially advanced than the British and could counter claims that they were too backward for self-rule. Also, women's suffrage was bound to help the nationalist cause, as any increase in India's political representation would be unfavourable to the British presence.

The deep contradictions in the elite position with regard to the women's movement surfaced dramatically with Independence. In 1948 under Nehru's prime ministership, the Hindu Code Bill was introduced in the Constituent Assembly proposing reform of personal law in marriage, divorce and inheritance. The storm of opposition that this provoked opened up a Pandora's Box of age-old superstitions, complexes, patriarchal feelings and deep-rooted prejudices running along caste, class, religious and regional lines.[40] While the principle of sexual equality and its implementation through woman's suffrage which would help undermine Britain's position of power had been easily supported, the implementation of the same principle of marriage and inheritance which could threaten the privileges of men in the family could not be easily stomached. Jawaharlal Nehru was completely taken aback. He nursed secret misgivings that many of those who had silently voted for the Karachi resolution of equal rights might not have meant what the resolution laid down. But even Nehru was unaware of the extent to which the opposition would go to block legislation on the Hindu Code. To Nehru the call of freedom had always implied a double meaning for women. 'The enthusiasm and energy with which they threw themselves into the struggle had no doubt their springs in the vague and hardly conscious, but nevertheless intense desire to rid themselves of domestic slavery also.'[41] To him, therefore, the passage of personal legislation for Hindus was but the logical culmination of a process to usher in a more equal social order.

The range of opposition against Nehru included conservative hard liners within the Congress Party consisting of veterans like Vallabhbhai Patel, J.B. Kripalani and the president of the Indian republic, Dr Rajendra Prasad; the Hindu Mahasabha and other fundamentalists; the Sikh group who saw the common Hindu Code as a threat to their separate identity; the Muslim group who saw it as a communal measure and many women parliamentarians who felt the measures did not go far enough. In general, the objections were that customary practices hallowed by centuries of tradition could not be suddenly swept aside. Any such move might further boomerang against Congress chances in the forthcoming elections. Specific issues such as compulsory monogamy, divorce, equal property rights were taken to be reckless measures which would destroy the fabric of Hindu society. In his ultimate bid to stall the proposed legislation, Rajendra Prasad even threatened to withhold presidential assent. In utter despair Nehru wrote to Patel that the difference of outlook between himself and his parliament was so complete, that it was driving him far away both in mind and heart. Since the opposition could not simply be wished away, Nehru sought to bide time. As the issue dragged on, the difference of opinion were amply talked out. In course of time many of the controversial points of the original bills were whittled down. With Congress success in the elections were passed the Hindu Marriage Act in 1951, followed by the Hindu Succession Act, the Hindu Minority and Guardianship Act and the Hindu Adoption and Maintenance Act, all of which were passed in 1956 and finally, the Dowry Prohibition Act in 1961.

To Nehru the passage of the Hindu Reform legislation marked a victory. To Aubrey Menen he remarked that they constituted the greatest real advance in his career. The epoch-making legislation pulled out Hindu law from the rut in which it had got stuck, and had given it a new dynamism.

To what extent did this mark a victory of symbol over substance? Even after almost four decades since the epoch-making legislation was made, the condition of women in the country in general remains unequal. Apart from many other factors this predicament can be traced to the fact that major loopholes had remained in the social legislation passed in Nehru's time and that, in the euphoria of having the legislation, a sense of false complacency had crept in and proper measures to enforce the legislation through a functioning infrastructure or attempts to bring in improving legal amendments were not undertaken. For this, both Nehru and his government can be partially faulted.

Unlike customary law which had been simple, inexpensive and geared to local requirements, the separate Act had nuances which were never fully explained or understood at the local level. Moreover, in many cases, those guilty of violating the laws could not be easily brought to book as the offence was very often not cognizable. Or again, as in the case of the Hindu Succession Act, there were several major compromises considered by many to be a sell-out by the Nehru government.

In the ultimate analysis it can be said that Nehru's victory was largely symbolic. He recognized that the legislation as drafted was not perfect. Yet, he was not willing to initiate change which would shake up the social organization too drastically. To him, the Hindu Law Reform Bills were revolutionary in symbol rather than in substance which he claimed to be the outstanding achievement of his time. As he explained, they were not in any way revolutionary. They had broken the barrier of ages and cleared the way somewhat for women to progress. Nehru's symbolical victory did help establish the notion of women's equality as a desirable idea to which the Indian polity was committed. When the Hindu Marriage Bill, the first in the series of the Hindu Code enactments, was ultimately passed, there was a near total approval in the House of Parliament with only one dissident voice. As Nehru's law minister Pataskar said, while successfully piloting the Hindu Succession Act, what was important was that daughters would have a sense of property irrespective of what actual property they would get under the law.

Nehru was deeply conscious of the charges levelled against him that the Hindu social reforms did not amount to much but was satisfied with the spirit that lay behind them. He candidly said that you had to make a beginning somewhere! The gaps in the legislation no doubt could be changed but the struggle to achieve these changes would have to continue. What was important was that 'the essential principles underlying the changes were not given up'. He linked this legal advance in the social domain with the advances in the political and economic areas, for only by way of advance on these three separate lines and their integration into one great whole could the people of India progress. By recognizing and accepting in principle the concept of woman's equality and forcefully advocating it in the face of opposition, Nehru was able to enunciate an emancipated and liberal point of view which was not only unique in the time he lived but also has relevance for posterity.

The shortfalls of this idealistic position are obvious. Nehru comes across as being the visionary who could never match his expectations with his achievements. Although he considered a uniform Civil Code for the whole of India to be essential, he was afraid that any imposition on communities, before they were ready for such changes, would be unwise. Lack of uniformity, he felt, would be preferable to a situation where, because of ill will, laws passed were dead letters in their application. As Ashok Mehta aptly summed up, 'In the case of all leaders of men, there is an angle of refraction between ideas and achievements. In Nehru this angle has grown with unfolding of ideas. That is at once the glory and the tragedy of Jawaharlal Nehru.'[42]

It is important to note, however, that this ambivalence in Nehru between thought and action had also been apparent in the momentous decades of the national movement. Thus, in the 30s, when fired by socialist thinking, he spoke forcefully of doing away with the class structure and taking up the calls of worker and peasant, he was gently made to bow to Gandhian opposition within the Congress. Similarly, on the issue of woman's rights, Nehru who began with the vision of a uniform civil code ended up by accepting a diluted and truncated version. For him, it was not, however, a surrender of principles but merely the pragmatic recognition of reality.

To the credit of Nehru it must be said that he never gave up and without him the legislation would not have been passed at all. Raj Kumari Amrit Kaur said, 'The social reforms, that are now on the Statute Book would . . . have been talked out if it had not been for Jawaharlal's powerful advocacy of and insistence on them.'[43]

It was in the same spirit of scoring a symbolical triumph that Nehru had initiated the entry of women into the Foreign Service. He realized that there would be few entrants just then because of practical problems but he felt in principle there should be no discrimination. 'I do feel,' Nehru wrote in a note dated 26 February 1947, 'that the difficulties that undoubtedly exist are more than counterbalanced by the great advantage of throwing open the doors of the Foreign Service to women . . . Indian women, I think, have something to give which is very valuable and it would be a pity to lose or to close the doors of opportunity to them in this field of activitiy.'[44]

Similarly by spangling his ministries with women of merit such as Lakshmi Menon, Rajkumari Amrit Kaur and Mridula Sarabhai or appointing them to positions of importance such as his sister Vijaya Lakshmi Pandit as Indian envoy and Sarojini Naidu and her daughter Padmaja as governors, Nehru was able to project much acclaimed visible role models. Doubtless this led to a certain degree of complacence regarding the position of women and created a myth about their growing advancement which failed to recognize the extent to which the prejudices and injustices still remained. Judged from his rhetoric Nehru was an untiring crusader for justice, romanticizing the plight of the woman as effectively as he had of the hapless peasant. But in actual performance, Nehru found himself circumscribed by forces which seemed insurmountable. As his biographer rather bluntly put it, 'He combined a lack of reservation in objective with an unqualified adherence to the mildest of methods.' [45] Nehru had hoped that by enshrining gender equality on paper, initiating legislation on personal law and through various high visibility symbolical gestures an important beginning had been made of epoch making proportions. Unfortunately the problem lay in the varying perceptions of the concept of gender equality. Admittedly equality in the face of law was established but the myriads of unobtrusive manifestations of inequality, springing from attitudinal differences and formed over years of discriminatory beliefs, customs and practices, remained operative in a way which was often not even noticed, much less understood. This is why over three decades after Nehru's death, contradictions still abound. While the highest political and civil offices have been opened up to women, the unfavourable literacy and mortality rates of women, their disproportionate ratio in the total work force speak a different story. In a country where goddesses Durga, Saraswati and Lakshmi are worshipped with serious devotion at the same time as young brides are consumed in flames for bringing inadequate dowries, considerable soul searching has to be done.

Real gender equality can only come about when mental blocks and attitudinal prejudices are broken down across regional, class, caste lines. Perhaps the impassioned rhetoric of a committed leader can still serve to keep our minds focused on one of the most important priorities of national life—the position of our women. The old regime which enshrined Sita has gone. The new regime built around Chitrangada is yet to be built. But the Hindu Code Bill, Jawaharlal's single biggest achievement in the recasting of familial relations in independent India does provide a sure signpost in that direction.

SITA: NAMING PURITY AND PROTEST

MALASHRI LAL

IT IS RAMANAVAMI today, the birth date of Lord Rama, heralding the festivities that annually replicate the joyous celebration of Rama's victory over Ravana, the epical triumph of the Good. Theatrical performances of the Ramalila show up in village *chaupals* as well as in sophisticated urban centres. Men and women from all walks of life pay tribute to the enduring mythology of an undated tale.

Where is Sita in all of this? When was she born and to whom? Tulsidas has dwelt on the maternal glances of Kaushalya *ma* when the toddler Rama found his feet. But who was Sita's mother? Who was her biological father? The familiar tale of the baby girl found in the furrow of King Janaka's field is a perplexing riddle to genealogical mapping. Janaka named her 'Sita'—literally meaning 'found in the furrow'. Others call her Janaki, daughter of Janaka, or Mythili, the princess of Mithila. Under patriarchy, women's names—and their roles—are relational, as I understand from my several years of delving into women's studies. Abandoned by a mother (presumably), discovered in a furrow, and finally, at the end of a constantly challenged life, returning to Mother Earth by an act of will, is Sita a self-progenated 'goddess' who can be seen through modern feminism as the unitary woman?

Early texts might even support this view. There appears to be a Sita who existed prior to the Sita of Valmiki's Ramayana. A verse in the *Rig Veda* mentions an earth goddess, Sita, who blesses the crops and brings fecundity and prosperity. But such a Sita is contrary to the Ramayana-related traditions, which prohibit certain forms of agricultural labour for women. According to farming practices in the hill regions of northern India, women are not allowed to touch or use the plough. A poignant folk tale from the upper reaches of Himachal Pradesh recounts how a devoted wife waited anxiously during the planting season, hoping that her man would come back to the village and attend to the fields. The children starved, the earth turned brown, but there was still no man. One day at early dawn, she hitched the oxen to the plough. As the sun panned over the caked earth, the village awoke to the sight of this lonely woman doing an unwomanly job. There was first a sense of shock and the fear of Earth's curse, but finally there was admiration for the woman's courage in breaking meaningless traditions.

In folk tales, the ancient and the modern, the scripted and the oral are often conflated. When I came upon this story, I was fascinated by its emphasis on the earth connections of the Sita myth. Ecology and sustenance are vital in farming communities. The ancient goddess protects the fields but also lays down some laws of labour distribution by gender roles—these have sustained farm practices in traditional communities. Now, a 'money-order economy', as it is called, is prevalent in the hill regions, where the men leave home to get employment in the plains and repatriate their incomes to the village. Who will then operate the plough, a male symbol though it might have been in the past? The ancient Sita who blessed the crops needs to be invoked so that the new exigencies can be met.

This amazing adaptability of myths is seen in many other aspects of Sita's story and its modifications. In the Himachal village, it was a spontaneous retelling of an old tale whereas in sophisticated forums, the Sita story is given deliberate connotations. The name resonates with meaning, its suggestiveness allowing for infinite possibilities of interpreting woman's position in Indian society. It is useful that Sita's genealogy is unknown. She is, in a compelling way, unique, though the Ramayana, traditionally told, binds her to the role identification of the ur-wife within a complex triad of Rama, the 'devoted husband', Ravana, the evil abductor and Hanuman, the supreme follower.

Mahatma Gandhi, for instance, propounded a version wherein the Rama–Sita relationship was one of equal partnership. He famously remarked, 'My ideal of a wife is Sita and my ideal of a husband, Rama. But Sita was no slave to Rama. Or each was a slave to the other. Rama was ever considerate to Sita.' Against the backdrop of nationalism and the freedom movement, the 'wifely role' had to be redefined and there could be no better strategy for change than the evocation of this iconic couple. In his own relationship with his wife Kasturba, Gandhi attempted to demonstrate this 'modernized' companionship, with his autobiography, *My Experiments with Truth*, giving several instances of Kasturba's questioning of Gandhi's choices, their discussions and participation in unconventional modes of wedded life.

Another instance of naming Sita is significantly found in Gandhi's adoption of 'Ramadhun' as it is popularly sung. In the sequential placing of the names, '*Patit paavan Sita-Rama*', he puts Sita first, then Rama. In fact, Rama is deified by the adjectival prefix of Sita's name. Gandhi had adapted a *bhajan* by Vishnu Digambar Paluskar, which was, in turn, based on a *mantra* by the seventeenth-century Marathi saint–poet, Ramdas. Such were the expressions of Gandhi's priorities in which women showed the path that men could follow. It is well known that the Mahatma attributed his methods of non-violence to the influence of women on his political thoughts. The domestic metaphors of a 'fistful of salt' and '*charkha kathna* (weaving)' transformed the patriarchal tools of protest, and women across regions recognized that they could participate in the peace marches on terms that they understood with ease. This in no way belittled the domestic domain; instead, Gandhi's redefinition of the public sphere irreversibly turned global thinking towards an abjuration of violence.

The media too has purposefully played upon the legacy of Sita. Ramanand Sagar's popular TV serial titled *Ramayana*, which was aired from 25 January 1987 to 31 July 1988, marked a critical point in the commercialization of the epic formula. The new-found capabilities of the electronic media were used to their fullest to create flying figures, opulent sets and action-packed scenarios. Few who saw the extravaganza can forget Hanuman cycling though the blue sky, or the fabulous display of martial weapons zigzagging across the firmament. The decorous Rama and the demure Sita did much to freeze a stereotype that lasted many years. Heidi Pauwels points to the interpolations of romantic episodes such as the 'Phulvari' (Rama and Sita meeting in the bower) and the 'wedding night', which were not part of Tulsi's Ramayana or any other dominant text. As the scholar shows, the TV serial upheld a new ideal of partnership in marriage, projecting Sita as the *ardhangini* or *saathi*, a companion of Rama, and not a *dasi* or a slave. This in itself held a contemporary note for the generation that was responding to feminist formulations about self-actualization and identity formation.

The visual appeal of Ramanand Sagar's version was enormous. So was its social impact. At the time, some homes had turned the TV into a shrine for Lord Rama and his consort. Family members took a ritual bath, performed *aarti* in front of the TV and elevated the process of viewing to the seriousness of worship. India saw the emergence of a hybrid form of religious practice, which blurred the distinction between mythology as media entertainment and mythology as a societal model. The transition made by Sagar was symptomatic of many other possibilities. The Ramayana in modern times became once again a text to 'play' with, to innovate and interpret.

Next appeared another mega TV serial produced by Ekta Kapoor's company, Balaji Telefilms, titled *Kyunki Saas Bhi Kabhi Bahu Thi*, airing the elaborate saga of the Virani family. Again audiences stayed glued to their sets at 9.30 p.m. on specific nights. The Ramayana motif in this serial was anything but explicit—the names did not show up, but the plot clearly reflected the perennial triad: hero, heroine, villain, and generations of them. This time Sita, alias Tulsi, was neither submissive nor sacrificial (she never was, but patriarchy had cleverly constructed that legend by reading Valmiki selectively, and yielding graciously to Tulsidas's romanticized version). Tulsi, the *bahu*, the daughter of the poor family priest, elopes with Mihir, the eldest son of the wealthy Virani clan. She is accused of having manipulated the relationship for monetary gain, and her three mothers-in-law (in a joint family, the connection is not only biological) turn abusive and insulting. Through an elaborate process, Tulsi proves her innocence and power over the machinations of her detractors.

The plot commanded an instant contemporary appeal. The serial was about class relations and its shifting signifiers. In the process of modernization of India, class has become an unstable category. While economists project the consequences of the country's bulging middle class, the culture tsars are quick to see the interplay of power politics within family and community. Tulsi Virani, from an economically lower class than her husband, has to prove her worth in other ways, such as a higher morality. Given that the viewing public of the Balaji serials is consistently the middle class, the sympathy lies entirely with Tulsi, the hard-working, right-thinking woman, who suffers silently but cleverly plots her revenge. Although religion is the source of her strength, she is also a practical woman who can bide her time. In a memorable and heart-wrenching episode, Mihir who is trapped into wrong thinking by his family, throws Tulsi out of the house. Her helplessness is acute as she must leave, but Mihir's life also loses its moral anchor. Many episodes later, Mihir regrets his action, but Tulsi may be dead by then. It may be too late to express his repentance. Tulsi, however, is a survivor . . .

The value here resided in capturing the social dynamics emanating from factors such as marriage by choice (not arranged marriages), job opportunities for women, sexual liberation and such-like changes in India. What is in the name? Tulsi—the name is as timeless and self-contained as Sita. A species of the ordinary basil, the *tulsi* plant commands a singular spot in the courtyard and is traditionally worshipped in Hindu homes. The name Tulsi may also evoke Tulsidas's *Ramacharitmanas*, which is the main text for the notions of the submissive Sita. Ekta Kapoor drafted a tale of courage not submission, and therefore uncovered the dynamism of the early Sita legends of strength and fortitude. In Valmiki's Ramayana, there is a telling reference to an avenging figure. Agasthya *muni* relates a story to Rama about Vedavati, a precursor to Sita. Belonging to a vulnerable community, she is molested by the powerful Ravana. In helpless anger Vedavati destroys herself, but swears that she will return to avenge this violation. Ekta Kapoor's Tulsi was the amalgam of many such traditions, and the popular serial showed a modern reincarnation of Sita.

Ekta Kapoor was wise to suggest Sita but not name her. The resonance of the name caused a major controversy in 1998 after Deepa Mehta's film *Fire* was released in theatres in Bombay. The outraged crowds had vandalized buildings claiming that the Hindu religion and the name of Sita had been defiled by its association with a lesbian character. In other words, the name itself was sacred, an utterance which denoted a natural veneration, the context for which had to be suitably pious. Deepa Mehta was compelled to change the name Sita to Nita, at least for the Hindi version of *Fire*, which played to audiences across the country. In several interviews, Mehta tried to sidestep the controversy by attempting to de-link the name from any religious connotations. She went so far as to claim, 'It's a film about choices,' not so much about dysfunctional marriages or about lesbian desire. This was an evasion on the part of the director who surely recognized that the film's primary subject—lesbian activity in a traditional home—was taboo in the public sphere of cinema. Mehta had also embedded visuals from Ramanand Sagar's serial, *Ramayana* to suggest a contrast between the mythic men and women and their real-life counterparts.

A fascinating aspect of *Fire* in relation to the depiction of Sita is that both the women who enact the lesbian partnership are named after mythic deities, but the name change adopted was for Sita, not Radha. One can only surmise on the basis of common cultural practices that the Rama–Sita *jodi* (pair) is one of conjugal love and is accompanied by assumptions of loyalty, trust, devotion, mutuality, progeny and other such connotations. The discomfiture expressed by certain scholars of the Ramayana about the agni pareeksha episode and the second banishment of Sita from Ayodhya are in the context of this conjugal partnership and its expectation of perpetuity. On the other hand, the Krishna–Radha pair is the celebration of *leela* (play)—spontaneous, mischievous, sexual, temporary and joyful—the achievement of a oneness of body and soul in an ecstatic union that is ephemeral by its nature. Hence, the violation of Sita's name is a violation of a construct that has an enduring presence in the family and makes up a society. Radha, on the other hand, remains in the realms outside society. It is by such logic in cultural reasoning that the name of Sita has acquired a resonance that brings sensitivity and reaction.

As compared to the explorations of the Sita prototype in film and TV, its usage in Indian writing in English has been remarkably tame. Anita Desai has a conventional Sita in her novel, *Where Shall We Go This Summer*, in which the protesting woman leaves her home in the state of a fifth pregnancy, but when the husband comes to get her back, she obediently walks five steps behind him.

What remains to be suggested are some things pertaining to the vitality of Sita as a continuing influence in the Indian social polity. The range she indicates is from the minutiae of local practice to the symbols of a globalized India. In her are embedded the aspects of India's burgeoning feminism for which no single image will suffice.

Hence, Sita is multiple in her aspects and deep in her self-sufficiency. Through art and literature, she is reconfigured time and again. Today, the millennium's global agenda negotiates between cultural counters that are difficult to reconcile. Perhaps, it is the right context in which to invoke Sita.

THE JUSTIFICATION OF RAMA

RATNA LAHIRI

ONCE THERE WAS a bird-hunter who shot an arrow at a coupling pair of kraunch birds and the male bird died. That the female bird's lament over her bereavement made a poet out of a sage who was practising austerity on the banks of the river Tamasa, is a well-known story both among the Indian literati and in popular lore. Subsequently, this very sage became the first poet of Sanskrit literature, for he was no other than Valmiki, the author of the legendary Ramayana, the story of which spread all over Middle, East and South-East Asia, sometimes through Buddhist or Jain versions, which modified the tale according to their missionary needs, and at other times, through the word of mouth of travellers who had, in turn, heard it from monks of different orders.

When the sage Valmiki discovered the metre he had created in his first couplet, in which he cursed the insensitive hunter for killing one of a pair of loving birds, he wanted to create an epic in the same metre, and asked Narada who in this whole wide world was worthy enough to be written about. Narada suggested that he should write the biography of King Rama, who was the perfect ruler of the Ikshvaaku dynasty, one who had defeated the demon King Ravana. Apparently, there were many stories prevalent among the folk of those times regarding the handsome exiled king and his victory over the forces of evil.

Scholars often differentiate between what must have been the 'original Valmiki' or *Adi*-Ramayana and the prevailing version, which became popular in three regional adaptations in India—all in the name of Valmiki. Various interpolations took place, especially in the first and last cantos of the Valmiki version, along with sundry additions in some intermediary cantos.

Valmiki's hero Rama was the epitome of male perfection. He had a wide chest and the strong shoulders of an ox, while his arms were long and beautiful, hanging down to his knees. He was the perfect son, the perfect brother, the perfect king. How could he not have been the perfect husband too? How could the sage, who could not bear the separation of two lovebirds, suddenly envisage the separation of such a perfect couple, and in such cruel a manner? Maybe, tragedy was after all the very soul of creativity.

Subsequently, bards sang the story and local poets thought that it was a theme worthy of emulation in poetry, prose, ballad and plays, in various local dialects—for commoners did not appreciate Sanskrit any longer. However, Sanskrit versions of the tale too proliferated for the courtly audiences, and many stories got added to the saga of exile and banishment and subsequent torment. Folk versions continued to flourish. As and when in time a new social phenomenon became popular in the relevant linguistic milieu, it seems to have got absorbed into the local version.

The deification of the hero, Rama became the very soul of the many folk versions, as the notion of a devotionary attitude developed to mark the Indian ethos in early medieval literature. But that is another story altogether. The South-East Asian versions did not subscribe to this deification, but even then they spread and proliferated, with local attitudes inflecting the basic story and characters, while the theme itself remained basically the same. It is interesting to note, however, that most of these changes had their sources somewhere in folk or language versions within India.

The original version of Valmiki became the pride of Sanskrit poetry and soon enough, various additions and embellishments were made to it. It is said that one such instance was the interpolation of the episode of Sita's banishment by Rama, while she was pregnant, in order to appease public sentiment. While many scholarly reasons have been given to prove that large parts of the last canto and especially this part of the banishment story were later interpolations, in the popular version of the Rama story, this episode became so prevalent that it has come to be accepted as a flaw in the character of Rama, and is very much a part of Valmiki's popularized version. The Mahabharata, which contains one of the oldest available versions of the story, does not contain this episode of the banishment of Sita. However, later Sanskrit literary take-offs as well as folk ballads and language versions, all took full advantage of the human tragedy that was epitomized in this great story.

Ever since the legend regarding the banishment of Sita was perpetuated, poets and writers have tried to justify this act as a fait accompli and have claimed that full blame could not be ascribed to Rama. Surely he had his limitations and reasons. It is these justificatory propositions that create very interesting reading.

First of all, it would be engaging to examine the causes attributed to this cruel act, since the 'cause' itself is considered justification enough in some cases. The best-known reason is of course the one mentioned in the last canto of Valmiki wherein Sita, during her pregnancy, asks Rama to let her see the forest areas once again, and Rama promises to send her for a pleasure trip the following day. Subsequently, he is seen as being entertained by his courtiers and everyone is laughing and joking. By sheer chance, Rama asks his friend Bhadra, 'And what do people say about my Sita, etc.?' Then Bhadra tells him about the derogatory rumours being circulated regarding Sita and the fall in the standards of fidelity among women occurring just because of that. People were talking about what they would now have to put up from their wives, since they would be assured of being 'taken back' after having lived elsewhere. The people always follow the standards set by the ruler. '*Yathaa hi kurutey Raajaa prajaastamanauvartati*' (Uttara Kanda, 43: 19). Hearing this, Rama summons Lakshmana and asks him to abandon Sita across the river Ganga. Reluctantly, Lakshmana does this, and leaves her near Valmiki's hermitage.

Kalidasa, in his *Raghuvamsa,* also takes up the same theme, with a slight change wherein the rumour-monger is not a friend, but an official informer, a spy. The *Uttararamacharita* of Bhavabhuti, and other Sanskrit literary works like *Kundamala*, *Dashavatarcharita,* etc., follow the story, wherein the spy is named Durmukh (bad-mouth). In the *Ananda Ramayana* and *Adhyatma Ramayana* of later dates, this person is called Vijaya.

The ninth-century *Chhalitarama* ascribes this disruptive 'gossip' to two disguised spies, sent by the other devious demon King Lawana, who poison the mind of Rama against Sita. The Jain works, using the Rama story for their sectoral purposes, have perpetuated their own take-off on various episodes of the Ramayana, to suit their missionary admonitions. In the *Paumchariya* of Vimalasuri, Rama himself brings a pregnant Sita to show her the various Jain temples when some citizens come to talk to him regarding this problem. They mention how some immoral citizens are indulging in misbehaviour of various kinds. They talk about the blot on Sita's character. Rama discusses the issue with Lakshmana but the latter opposes the abandonment of Sita. However, Rama remains suspicious and asks another commander called Kritantavadana to abandon Sita in the forest across the river Ganga on the pretext of showing her the Jain temples. Fortunately, a Jain king Vajrajangha hears her laments and takes her home where she gives birth to Lava and Kusha.

Ravisena's *Padamacharita* has increased the number of reasons in the list of ills that have resulted due to Rama having accepted Sita. Hemchandra (*Yogashastra*) reports that Rama had gone to look for his wife afterwards but, not finding her there, thinks that she must have been devoured by animals and returns to perform her funeral rites.

Another popular fancy that has prevailed as the reason for Sita's abandonment all over northern India, is the story of the washerman, the *dhobi*, being the generator of such rumours. Father Kamil Bulke has traced the possible origin of this version in the old *Vrihat katha*, which is now unavailable. The *Kathasaritsagar* now records it. The *Bhagavad Purana*, the *Jaiminiya Asvamedh* and the *Padama Purana* repeat the allegation. Later, this reason seems to have been picked up by the Tamil and Gujarati versions, the *Ananda Ramayana* as well as the *Ramacharitmanas* of Tulsidas. Tibetan versions have given similar importance to popular rumour as being the cause of this abandonment.

The Portrait of Ravana

Another frequent reason cited as a trigger for the exile of Sita has been the drawing of Ravana's portrait by Sita, on being asked by a step-sister or mother-in-law about what Ravana looked like. This devious entrapment of the daughter-in-law, commonly accepted in many Indian households as part of the regular harassment of married young women, became very popular in folklore as it touched a natural chord in the hearts of the people. Moreover, it was taken up in great detail in various South-East Asian versions wherein the theme seems to have been extremely popular.

The Bengali version of Chandravati—a Rama story composed by a woman, also gives prominence to this version. Chandravati's Ramayana mentions how her step sister-in-law instigates Sita to draw the portrait of Ravana. But the first ever mention of this episode seems to be traceable to the Jain work of Haribhadra Suri, wherein Sita draws merely the feet of Ravana. Bhadreshwara elaborates upon the theme by describing how the co-wives of Sita become particularly jealous when she becomes pregnant. Needless to say, the Jain versions portray Rama as having many wives, as opposed to the Hindu ideal of fidelity to one woman (ek patni vrata), which is the hallmark of Rama's ideal character as a Hindu husband. The co-wives show the picture to Rama, and he ignores them initially, but they spread the word around and when the rumours get stronger by the day, Rama is forced to take action.

In Hemchandra's Jain Ramayana, there are three co-wives and Sita is forced by them to draw Ravana's portrait. However, she claims never to have actually looked at Ravana, since she used to keep her eyes averted and only saw Ravana's feet, so she could only draw his feet. The *Ananda Ramayana* has her claim that she saw only the big toe of his feet, so she draws just that.

The popular Bengali version by Krittivasa combines all three reasons, including the drawing of Ravana's portrait on the floor. On completing the drawing, Sita is tired, and falls asleep on the floor beside the picture, and is seen thus by Rama. The Kashmiri version also has the sister-in-law causing this misunderstanding and many folk versions have taken up this theme, as it seems to reflect common biases against women. Ramdas Gaudh's magnum opus *Hindutva* mentions a *Suvarchas Ramayana* in which Sita's sister-in-law Shanta commits this misdemeanour. In the *Ramayana Masihi*, again, it is the sister-in-law who cajoles Sita into drawing the picture. The Gujarati *Ramayanasara* shows Rama hearing Sita describe Ravana to a maid while drawing the picture. Similarly, the *Tika Ramayana* of Neelambardas endorses the picture episode as the main cause for Sita's abandonment. Gujarat and Bengal were two main ports of departure for the ships that must have carried the popular versions of the tale to South-East Asia.

In the Malayan *SeriRam*, the instigator is Kikewi Devi, the sister of Bharata and Shatrughna, and Sita is made to draw the picture on a hand fan. While she is sleeping, the fan is kept on her chest and she is shown to Rama in this state as proof of how much she still loves Ravana. Of course, merely drawing the picture may not be reason enough for desertion in South-East Asia, so Rama is told that Sita even kissed the picture before sleeping with it. In the Javanese *Serat Kanda,* it is Kaikeyi herself who draws a likeness of Ravana on a fan and places it on the bed of the sleeping Sita.

In the *Hikayat Maharaja Rawana,* it is a daughter of Ravana who has a picture of her father, which she keeps on the breast of the sleeping Sita. In her dream, Sita kisses the portrait and is seen by Rama as doing so. The punishment in this case is so severe and fatal, as to be totally out of character for Rama.

As for Sita in Sri Lanka, even the gods seem to be in league with forces beyond her control. Uma, the consort of Shiva, herself cajoles Sita into drawing a portrait of Ravana on a banana leaf. Rama enters the room suddenly, and Sita nervously throws the picture under the bed. When Rama sits on the bed, it starts to tremble and thus she is found out. Lakshmana is asked to kill her in the forest.

In the *Ramakerti*, a demoness disguises herself as one of Sita's friends and asks her to draw the portrait, which she then enters by magic so that Sita cannot erase it. The Thai *Ramakien* has the daughter of Surpanakha take this revenge on Sita. She too enters the picture after getting Sita to draw it and causes havoc. In the *Pommachakka* (Brahmachakra), Surpanakha herself comes in disguise to Sita.

Curses That Had to End As They Did—The Inexorable Law of Karma

An indirect cause of Sita's abandonment is mentioned in the last canto of the original Ramayana itself. Durvasa is heard telling Dasharatha that Vishnu had once killed the wife of Bhrigu, so the sage Bhrigu had cursed Vishnu saying that the latter too would have to endure a human birth and a lifetime of separation from his wife. This version is not available in the eastern or north-western versions and must have been an interpolation linked to the Puranic lore that developed later.

Some versions of the Valmiki Ramayana also refer to a curse inflicted upon Sita by Tara, the wife of Vali who had been unjustly killed by Rama. The curse of Tara is mentioned subsequently in many versions like *Ramayana Manjari*, the Assamese Ramayana of Madhav Kandali, the Bengali version of Krittivasa Ojha, the Marathi *Bhavartha* and *Vilanka Ramayana*s.

The *Padama Purana* mentions the entrapment by Sita of a pair of parrots singing the Ramayana. Sita releases the male bird but not the female one who is pregnant. The female bird dies and on hearing this, the male dies too, only to be reborn as the washerman who becomes the cause of the abandonment of Sita in a pregnant state.

The *Paumchariya* describes how Sita had herself indulged in rumour-mongering against one Muni Sudershan in her previous birth, and thus had to face the consequences of the same in this one. In Bengal, we find a legend about Lomash Rishi, who had once come to the palace of Janaka when Sita was a child. He had picked up Sita tenderly and placed her on his lap but Sita's 's soft skin bled on being scraped by the hard hairy skin of the Rishi. This embarrassed the Rishi and he cursed her to endure the hardships of forest life.

The *Tattvasamgraha Ramayana* holds Valmiki responsible for Sita's abandonment. He had performed penance to become the father of Lakshmi and had been granted a boon. Since Lakshmi had promised to come and stay in his hermitage as his daughter, she was born as Rama's wife, Sita.

For the Good of the Gods

A number of Sanskrit sectoral works like the *Adhyatma Ramayana* of an unestablished date (possibly the fifteenth–sixteenth century), have also elaborately engineered a long-drawn-out reason as to why Sita had to undertake a sacrificial role. The gods from the heavens wished Lord Rama to come to them once the 'purpose' of his incarnation in the world had been fulfilled. They requested Sita to come to Vishnuloka first, so that Rama would then soon follow her there. On hearing this, Rama said, 'I know all this, so I will send you away on the pretext of people's gossip about you. You will beget two sons in the hermitage of Valmiki. Afterwards, you will return to take a public oath of fidelity to me and thereafter ascend to Vaikuntha through your descent into the Earth.'

Various sects like the Rasik Sampradaya give no credence to the exile of Sita. According to some of those that delve into the philosophical, it is easy to imply that it were the *rajasic* and *tamasic* parts of Sita that went to exile, as they did when Ravana had taken her by force, because the *sattvic* self of Sita remains with Rama always, anyway.

The sixteenth-century *Ananda Ramayana* depicts a romantic picture of Rama in contrast to the serious maryada purushottam character that other medieval devotees have chosen to portray. Apart from all the other reasons, a new innovation is a carnal reason indicating the intense desire of Rama to cohabit with Sita. Rama believes that it would not be good for Sita if he were to indulge his desire during her pregnancy, so he confides in his in-laws that he is about to send her away to Valmiki's *ashram* and that they too should go and live there. Were she to go just to Mithila, the kingdom of Janaka, Rama would have surely rushed to visit her there. Being an epitome of perfection, he would have to mind his behaviour in a hermitage. Later on, Rama tells Sita one day that she would be going to stay at Valmiki's hermitage for five years or so, would give birth to two sons, and return to publicly promise her purity. The Earth goddess would vouch for her innocence. Sita then makes a shadow out of her rajasic and tamasic parts while her real sattvic self merges to dwell on the left side of Rama (as the wife is the left half of the husband—*vaamaa*—in Hindu philosophy). It is only after all this divine planning that, almost on cue, the washerman's allegation on Sita's character occurs and a friend named Vijaya duly reports this to Rama.

However, the one purported reason for Rama's action, which surpasses all others, is perhaps the incredible imagination of Tulsidas, an ardent devotee of Rama. Tulsidas, in his magnum opus *Ramacharitmanas*, which is read in almost every north Indian household, does not even refer to the episode of Sita's abandonment in his last chapter. The story ends with the glorious reign of Rama, with his three other brothers and Sita at his side. However, he could not altogether ignore this episode in the life of his deified Lord Rama, so in *Geetavali* he brings up a very interesting set of causalities. Dasharatha had died before his time and so the gods had given that 'unlived' time to Rama, his son. In the last hundred years of his reign, therefore, Rama was, in fact, living the life of Dasharatha, the father-in-law of

Sita. How could he then indulge in any cohabitation with Sita during his 'Dasharatha years'? So he finds an excuse to send her away to Valmiki's hermitage. This seems to be the most convoluted 'reason' of all, but Tulsidas had to try to find a better excuse for Rama's behaviour than merely the latter's acquiescence to popular sentiment.

Thus, in the Indian Ramayana versions, the ideal of Rama's character does not get diluted as it does in some South-East Asian versions. Even in the exposure of a tragic flaw, we find the ideal of Rama's perfection maintained, as always, for he is seen sacrificing for the greater good of his subjects, proving himself to be a perfect idealistic man, a maryada purushottam, by remaining single and devastated due to the very act of banishing his most beloved wife, and yet upholding his greater duty to his people before whom he has set out to establish the ideals of kingship, as also those of fidelity in marriage.

Rama could have married again, as not only did kings normally have many wives, but they were allowed to perform *yajna*s with only their chief wives by their side. Rama, however, did not acquiesce to public sentiment or prescribed law in this matter and performed the Asvamedha sacrifice with an image of Sita carved in gold placed by his side.

It is sad that critics seldom highlight this aspect of Rama's character or that none of the South-East Asian versions find it to be a uniquely appealing characteristic, though they mostly accept the fidelity of Sita and the fact that fire or some natural phenomenon would always protect Sita's 'purity'. Before Rama, it was considered natural for royalty to have a large harem of wives and mistresses, and Rama's dearly revered father himself had a large harem, with three major queens. The strictness of Rama in adhering to monogamy is, therefore, all the more exemplary, and it did become the ideal in subsequent Indian thought, so that the idea of polygamy became a matter of discomfiture for all time to come, and monogamy became the model forever. Perhaps that is the reason why even the elitist practice of having two wives was easily dispensed with within a generation or two when the British enforced monogamous laws as being mandatory for anyone wishing to join government service. Rama, to that extent, still provides an ideal for others to follow.

MATRILINEAL AND PATRILINEAL

RASHNA IMHASLY-GANDHY

BEHAVIOURAL PATTERNS ARE linked to thought patterns within the mind. Deeply entrenched ways of behaviour, even in modern-day society, have their supportive myths and legends that pass on the collective thought forms. If we look back at our history, we could claim that Dravidians were the founders of the earliest Indian civilization that was matrilineal and shared an attachment with the great Mother goddess. The traditional confrontation between the sexes in contemporary India has traces and mindsets that were established during the initial subjugation of the patrifocal Aryan system over the matrifocal non-Aryan one. Patriarchy was established via Brahmanization/Sanskritization, wherein most of the spiritual disciplines were ascetic and life-denying. It relegated the female to the position of a devotee. It used mythological weaponry and religious licence to transform culture and induce a societal and sexual shift away from the strong position that women had originally occupied. The epic struggle for moral supremacy can be observed through the centrality that the Ramayana has occupied and which lasts up to the present day. The Ramayana is the exponent of rigid Brahmanical standards of male–female relationships. Although it draws inspiration from a broad canvas, that is, the confrontation between non-Aryan and Aryan cultures, it can be interpreted as an encounter between the patrifocal social systems and the matrifocal ones, with the former subjugating the latter. The sexual initiatives of both Ravana, the rakshasa (the darker-skinned Dravidian) king and his sister Surpanakha have to be curbed or, better still, destroyed.

Looking at the matrilineal Dravidian social system in ancient India, and drawing from a layered fabric of our multicultural strands, one can identify traces of heavy resistance in the Aryan tribes towards the mother-right features that were strongly implanted in the existing society and religions. 'The threat lay partly in the diametrically opposing sexual patterns of the natives, specifically their recognition of woman as central in familial and social orders.'[1] Classical Hindu tradition abounds in intriguing examples of the confrontation between patrifocal and matrifocal societies. 'If one earnestly approached this study in India, one could probably discover an epic struggle of mother-right and father-right traditions based entirely on an intellectual reconstruction of the history of the Indian people in the form of their myths and legends.'[2]

The Ramayana therefore symbolizes a cultural, historical as well as a socio-anthropological material which deals with normative and prescriptive behaviour. On the other hand, while scanning the Mahabharata, one can see that many of the important characters are 'illegitimate', that is, they are born out of wedlock or outside conventional morality. The most prominent system is the polyandrous union of Draupadi with the five Pandava brothers, with all of them being married to one woman, each having a child with her, but never remaining faithful to her. Throughout the epic, one also finds Aryan noblemen marrying non-Aryan women because they are seduced by the latter's beauty, boldness and a certain sense of loyalty that these women embody.

With the spread of the Brahmanical norms, intellectual indoctrinations and interpolations sterilized sections of even the older compositions of the Mahabharata. A lot of the folk traditions and cultural diversity was lost in the north Indian version of Valmiki and Tulsidas. The dominant versions of the Ramayana influenced the collective consciousness of a majority of the people.

What we will be focusing on is the material surrounding the man–woman relationship within the myth. We will be examining the story that acts as an organizing agent, explaining the way natural instincts get expressed in a cultural context, and the resulting experience which brings out the depths of emotions and experiences that are archetypal. Reality can only be understood experientially, and the best way to convey it to the masses in a culture is through a myth or a tale.

We see how the union of Rama and Sita becomes the ideal monogamous model for the Hindu marriage. The woman must henceforth regard her husband as a near god. The ideal of womanhood is projected onto Sita, who becomes the perfect role model as partner and mother. She, like her Western counterpart, the Virgin, is sanitized and made out to be an asexual person, belonging to a higher and purer self, but one who is constantly separated from her husband. Sita's questioned fidelity when she is in Ravana's power is a major theme that constitutes a reference for women even today. There is a kind of collective cultural conditioning by which male folk wisdom portrays the female sex as lacking both sexual morality and intelligence. Sudhir Kakar cites a number of ancient texts which are exponents of this belief, and which stem from various regions of India.[3] 'Is it any wonder then that with such a collective fantasy . . . the fate of sexuality within marriage is likely to come under an evil constellation of stars? Physical love will tend to become a shame-ridden affair, a sharp stabbing of lust with little love and even less passion.'[4]

What are the covert messages that such a traditional mythological epic conveys to a woman? Men have complete dominance in every domestic and public relationship. Sexual activity is restricted to marital relations, and it is deemed correct for the purpose of procreation alone. It controls women from undertaking any independent activity and gaining self-confidence. Women are denied participation in important religious rituals and are exiled from the political arena; they do not inherit the properties of their fathers and widows are not allowed to remarry.

Even now, many Indian women, like Sita, are subdued in their marital homes, and their spirits are broken. They have learnt to subordinate themselves to the male ego; they must love and worship the husband and must believe that they are dependent on him. A wife is to support her husband's decision even if he deems it right to abandon the woman along with her children as the Ramayana myth portrays. Why? we may ask. Is it because both the fate of the woman and her children depend upon him?

When the energy of the Great Mother in a culture is suppressed in such a way, the power of the Great Mother rises in a different form—the Feminine. Swami Vivekananda, told an audience during his famous speech at the World Conference of Religions at the turn of the nineteenth century: 'In the West woman is wife. The idea of womanhood is concentrated there—as the wife. To the ordinary man in India the whole force of womanhood is concentrated on motherhood. In the Western home the wife rules. In an Indian home the mother rules.' Modern anthropologists testify to the exalted position that the human mother, especially the mothers of sons, and not the Mother goddess, occupies among Hindus. She, in turn, strengthens the umbilical cord during childhood, knowing that it is her only means of gaining a status in her new family and society.

Psychological studies show that this makes the Hindu male a narcissistic personality. It is a well-known fact that Indian male narcissism is a trait which is fuelled by his mother, and which develops into a classical mother fixation. Indian mothers have made the most of the attachment and veneration that their sons feel towards them, and it is often alleged that the mothers make no effort to rear independent and self-sufficient boys and men.

A strand of the same belief system, however, gives rise to a different theory which derives from the Vaishnava tradition of the *Bhagavad Purana*, based around the Krishna cult. God is depicted frolicking with the love-stricken *gopi*s, a metaphoric symbolism of the joint dance of the gods and the mortals. India is also the land where one finds erotic sculptures depicting loving couples on the temple walls of Khajuraho and Konarak, suggesting the union of the temporal physical and the spiritual. It is also the land that produced the *Kamasutra*, a text that investigates the full range of human sexual impulses. The Shiva–Shakti cult is yet another form that is present in the collective consciousness of India. One may further list the *Tantra Shastras* based on matri-centred values, as affirming life processes, based on the equality of the male–female balance, the Shakti and Shakta.

However, despite the various and diverse images that enter the collective Indian psyche, the Ramayana still stands out as the predominant myth. It acts like a religious template that affects and influences the collective consciousness of a majority of the people. Sita being banished means Shakti being banished from her role as wife and partner, from her rightful position in society. It appears that the male is unable to relate to the feminine principle. The psyches of individuals have been confused with the tensions of religious conditioning. While Sita is banished in the story, she returns as Shakti—the potent feminine force in everyday life. The strong mother–son dyad of the Ramayana is lived out. Lava and Kusha become symbolic of every new generation of males that grow up in a fatherless family, brought up as they are, by a single mother. Often, the father may not leave the home, but he is absent as a parent, psychically. When there is a lack of a positive father figure as a role model, how can we expect the future generations to mature in a healthy way? But are not mothers also responsible for creating the next generation of narcissistic males by ensuring the attachment of their sons and not allowing them to become independent, self-sufficient men? And does this not perpetuate a karmic cycle of mother-love?

We must be able to dispassionately and creatively examine the doctrines of our culture in order to confront its anxiety-laden polarities. Only when we question our impulses and realign our attitudes towards the sexes, will we be able to bring a gender balance in our present-day culture. The greater the equality the more will it strengthen both the sexes. Only then will Shakti, the feminine force within each one of us, no longer be destructive but become a co-creator with Shiva in the metaphoric union of partnership.

DRAUPADI'S MOMENT IN SITA'S SYNTAX

KAREN GABRIEL

THE STORY: The film *Hey! Ram* begins on 6 December 1999 in the sickroom of eighty-nine-year-old Saket Ram (played by Kamal Haasan). From there it moves in a flashback to August 1946. The young Saket Ram is an urbane south Indian Vaishnavite Brahmin archaeologist who works at the Mohanjedaro excavations in Lakhana, now in Pakistan, with his Muslim colleague and good friend Amjad (Shahrukh Khan). Saket Ram is married to Aparna (Rani Mukherjee) and because his family disapproves they live as a nuclear unit in Calcutta. When Saket Ram returns to Calcutta from Karachi on 16 August 1946 (Direct Action Day), the riots have begun in Calcutta. That night, Aparna is raped and killed by her tailor Altaf and a gang of Muslims. During this incident, Saket Ram is himself almost sodomized by her rapists. While wandering the streets later that night, he meets a Hindu extremist Shriram Abhayankar (Atul Kulkarni). Later Saket Ram giving into family pressure marries again, but he cannot consummate his marriage with Mythili (Vasundhara Das), haunted as he is by his love for Aparna and by her death. Subsequently, through Abhayankar, he meets a Rajput maharaja (Vikram Gokhale) who supports and funds what appears to be an RSS shakha. During the Dussehra celebrations at the palace, the Sangh lays its plan to restore the glory of the Hindu people through the assassination of Gandhi and the task eventually falls to Saket Ram. His austere training begins, at the end of which, while waiting to fulfill his mission, he accidentally meets Amjad, now ghettoized and hiding in fear. Amjad gets killed trying to organize Saket Ram's escape from his home. Saket Ram's confusion slowly becomes a change in heart after his meetings with Gandhi who is, in any case, assassinated. The film closes with the death of Saket Ram and ends with a conversation between the two grandsons [Saket Ram's (Gautham Kanthadai) and Gandhi's (Tushar Gandhi)].

Hey! Ram (2000) engages in some very important, intelligent and sophisticated ways with the distinctions and continuities between cultures and communities and in the manner in which communities render their history. In a suggestive pan-Indianism the director distributes the action of the film in all four corners of the country (Calcutta in the east, Karachi and Delhi in the north, Maharashtra in the west and Tamil Nadu in the south), locates the key actors across the territory of the nation and chooses a south Indian protagonist. Through this, he doesn't merely bring what have frequently been understood to be concerns of the North (Partition and communal hostility) to the South, but claims that history is equally an Indian history that the South has negotiated as well. The film straddles the period 16 August 1946 to the 1999 anniversary of 6 December 1992, dates that suggest an important historical and political continuity. On 16 August, Jinnah called for 'Direct Action' by the Muslims to demonstrate their will for sovereignty, and in December the Babri Masjid was demolished by Hindu extremists in response to a long-drawn call by the Hindu right to 'Hindus' to assert their sovereignty. However, the historical sweep of the narrative includes Harappa and Mohanjedaro and is further expanded as the film undertakes an examination of the revived mythologies of the nation-state. Both the historical moments, and the figures chosen, their reconstruction, and the suggested correspondences are remarkable.

Draupadi's Moment in Sita's Syntax

Teresa de Lauretis (1986) argues for the inseparability of representations of violence from the notations of gender, both of which are contingent on the reciprocal discursive relation of power to the deployment of sexuality. This partially explains how self-violative femininities in Hindi cinema are legitimized through invocations of personal or situational mythic 'equivalents'. A classic instance of this is the mythic motif of the lakshmana rekha[1] in the Ramayana which is frequently used in the Hindi cinema to signal both social and sexual transgression. While there is no such clumsy use of it in *Hey! Ram*, the erotic and even female desire enter the narrative somewhat typically, as a prelude to crisis. We see that the early love sequence between Aparna and Saket on the balcony is followed by her rape via the balcony which, we realize, signifies both a frontier and a liminal zone. Saket Ram playfully refers to their passionate lovemaking on the balcony as sexual assault ('But you were just sexually assaulted' in response to Aparna's resolute declaration, 'I do not want to be sexually assaulted') implying a possible confusion between consensual sex and rape, and a continuum between sex and violence. The apparent confusion of categories here, the liminal nature of both the erotic and the violent are explored quite literally through the subsequent rape which drives the rest of the narrative. Sexual desire again provides momentum for a critical development as the love-making between Mythili and Saket is followed by Saket's induction into a deadly machismo. Again, the bloody exchange at the ghetto and the death of Qureshi precede the birth of his child, corroborating the link between sexuality and death. But to return to the relation between expressions of female sexuality and male subjectivity, and how this is symbolized by the lakshmana rekha . . .

The mythic metaphor of the lakshmana rekha (rather than a *rama rekha*) functions as a general principle of control and boundaries which indicates the significance of Ravana's infringement and initiates the beginning of a territorial and dharmic contest. The territory, includes both the material female body and the vast range of its significations. Importantly, the lakshmana rekha records Sita's accountability to patriarchy, i.e., her accountability not as individual to individual but as woman to the laws of man. Equally it is a principle that organizes the spaces of her gender, the transgression of which condemns her to incarceration, self-exile and/or death. The neat but discomfiting fit between this epic narrative situation and the crisis that generates the dharmic dilemma within *Hey! Ram* is not accidental. Suitably, within the terms of the larger narrative in popular versions of the epic text, the appropriation of the violator's geographical, ethical and bodily spaces (Ravana in the mythic text and the rapacious assaulter in the cinematic one) constitute his punishment and the basis for the subject-formation of the hero-rescuer (say, Ram). The film retains some of the complex moral and situational ambiguities of the original in its deployment of this motif, and focuses on examining the control implied by the lakshmana rekha as a prime univocal patriarchal law. In the case of Draupadi, the chief female protagonist of the other epic, the Mahabharata, patriarchal injunctions towards controlling her sexuality, while containing her, cannot sustain her repeated interrogations of them.[2] In fact Draupadi embarrasses both the law and its keepers, including, and especially, her husbands. Of the two central female protagonists in the epics, Sita is celebrated not because she suffers less visible violation from the 'villain' but because she suffers great humiliation from the hero, her husband–judge Ram. It is important to cognize the implications of what has come to be honoured as Sita's mode of expression and syntax, based as they are on appeal, apology and self-violation, over Draupadi's, exhortative and interrogative dialogue with patriarchy.

This has gradually expunged from active memory Draupadi's assertive subjectivity though not her critical moment of public humiliation which evidently retains its appeal: It is a situation in much mainstream Bombay cinema. This rather licentious mode of remembrance is the eviction of Draupadi as subject and the violative conversion of her into a mode of femininity in which she may be simultaneously dematerialized and (paradoxically) reified. Thus, it becomes not just possible, but necessary, to have Draupadi's moment of violation rendered in Sita's syntax of apology. The female body is ceaselessly and simultaneously split and dichotomized into the affective dematerialized space of positive values (purity, maternality, sacrifice, selflessness, etc.), and an erotic space of negative values (vulnerability, seductiveness, provocation of invasion or treachery, etc.). Within the context of the film, this is effected through the replacement of one kind of femininity with another, while retaining the situation of violation. The argument that Draupadi was punished because she was polyandrous (perverse within a patriarchal sexual economy) or haughty, assertive, mocking (possessing of an 'improper' subjectivity) and therefore blameworthy misreads the nature of patriarchy in which the causes for punishment may be so contradictory and arbitrary that cause may not be required at all: being woman may be sufficient cause for punishment.[3] Nevertheless penalizing errant and 'difficult' modes of femininity is a necessary part of reifying and idealizing femininity. It is for this reason that Aparna must both be raped and die. She must make way for the adaptable and often silenced version of Sita, Mythili, if at all the narrative can progress in accordance with the agenda of the film: to examine the logic of the Hindu right. In short it is necessary to replace Aparna with Mythili, but after her rape and before she speaks it. Inscribed thus, the female body is 'always already' metaphorical: always in transit between two interpretations. Because it can never be either one or the other only, its identity must be harnessed to a stable masculine presence: father, son or (in the context of the nation) the ghost of death. Her body may thus feature (literally in cinema) as a spectacular metaphor, it will meet the paradoxical criteria of being spectacularly visible and yet invisible, i.e., as necessarily duplicitous and mythified . . .

The dichotomization of this figure—Sita and Draupadi—is interrupted by its maternality. The Sita–Draupadi dichotomy drawing on specific legends and modes of feminine subjectivity, is often subsumed by the larger figure of the Mother goddess. The masculine subject is thus also drawn into a filial relation to these figures because of traditions of mother-worship. In fact the maternal, now a principle, within a patriarchal interpretation of it, threatens to turn authoritative in its own right in versions of the potent mother or in versions of the castrating mother.[4] The Sita–Draupadi dichotomy and its vacillation between abjection and authority may be seen as the attempt to neutralize this tendency, to make manageable the power of the mother. The mother figure is disarmed in the dichotomy, even as she becomes the reason, the cause for, say, nationalistic masculinities to be armed, both in defense and in judgment of its mother. We now begin to understand how these dynamics interrupt the social construction of desire, gender subjectivity and narrative.

IN DIALOGUE

SITA'S VOICE

MALASHRI LAL AND NAMITA GOKHALE IN CONVERSATION

Dr Malashri Lal and Namita Gokhale have collaborated on a number of projects, most recently *In Search of Sita.*

Malashri Lal is a professor in the department of English, and the current joint director of the University of Delhi, South Campus. She has written and lectured extensively on women's socio-cultural positioning and women's writing. Her publications include *The Law of the Threshold: Women Writers in Indian English* and the co-edited volumes, *Interpreting Home in South Asian Literature* and *Speaking for Myself: An Anthology of Asian Women's Writing*. Malashri Lal is presently exploring women's viewpoints in folk narratives of Rajasthan and Himachal Pradesh.

Namita Gokhale is a writer. She published the film magazine *Super* from Bombay in the late 1970s. Her first novel was the critically acclaimed *Paro: Dreams of Passion* (1984), followed by *A Himalayan Love Story* and *Gods, Graves and Grandmother*. Her other works include *The Book of Shadows, The Book of Shiva* and *Shakuntala: The Play of Memory*. Most recently, she retold the epic *The Mahabharata* for young readers. Namita Gokhale is a director of Yatra Books and one of the founder directors of the Jaipur Literature Festival.

Malashri Lal (ML): *In a globalized India, the Ramayana has taken on a new relevance. While young people such as students and highly qualified professionals are connecting up with transnational impulses, travelling widely, seeking job opportunities far from 'home', they are also finding in the Ramayana core issues on value and tradition. But it is not a fixed paradigm. The Ramayana speaks of feminism, environment protection, rights and duties, the problem of choice, of power. In other words, most modern dilemmas are reflected in the mythic lore, to be interpreted in contemporary terms. My involvement with the project seeks to understand the stability of an ancient narrative in relation to its new orientations. For me, Sita is the key to this understanding for it is in the rethinking about patriarchy that the greatest social changes have evolved.*

Namita Gokhale (NG): Ever since my curiosity about Sita was aroused during a trip to Sri Lanka, I resolved to work on this book, making what is called a *sankalp*, a private determination. Our project, like the story of the *Ramayana*, is situated in a cultural and mythic space which is specific to South Asia and also permeates the world view of the Indian diaspora. After we began working together, my responses were an initial sense of indignation at the unfair lineaments of the story. Sita's abandonment is a prickly subject, one that many Indian women are uncomfortable with. There is an inherent inequity in the idea of a pregnant woman's loyalty and fortitude being repaid with harsh banishment. Surely she too was entitled to the compassion of Ramrajya? And then, the integrity of the Sita–Rama concept continues to be further devalued in our culture—as in the combined invocation of 'Jai Siya Rama' morphing into the exclusively masculine 'Jai Shri Rama'. But slowly, the ambiguities of Rama's difficult decision and of Sita's return to the lap of her mother, the Earth, began asserting themselves in my perspective. This graduated to an appreciation of the range of scholarship, historical and contemporary, on the subject, and a realization of the deeper strengths of Sita, and of Indian women, or perhaps women everywhere.

ML: *In the depictions of Sita's birth, we see the beginnings of the mythologizing process and note the timelessness and the reliance on the* *fantastical. Sita, daughter of the Earth, was found in a furrow while her adoptive father Janak was ritually ploughing the ground. How Sita came to be in the furrow is told differently in many regions. But what is evident is the dominance of the earth myth emphasizing Sita's link with nature. As in many other mythologies in world civilizations, the woman is associated with nature: in Japan is the figure of Amateresu, in Greece, we have Gaia. Women have the strength of the Earth, they are nurturers and life-givers. But their strength is foolishly disregarded and civilizations have to go through a cycle of trials before the acknowledgement is made once again. In our own times, eco-feminism has established the connection between woman and nature, man and technology—a questionable equation no doubt but it will set us thinking about the origin of such ideas. In India, the feminization of agriculture is being spoken about and Sita becomes a convenient point of reference.*

NG: Sita is the unusual girl child too, endowed with divine power. When Sita was a child, she was swabbing the floor of the rustic temple which housed the Bow of Shiva. Janaka, who happened to walk by, was astounded to see her lift the bow with her left hand (the left hand being the source of intuitive, instinctive strength) and resolved that only the man who could string and break Shiva's bow was fit to marry his daughter. Rama's winning Sita in a *swayamvara* by breaking the bow was an acknowledgement of that power. The unuttered strength of women, which is mute, not valorized, is given heroic dimension.

ML: *Sita has a quiet determination and a resolute mind even as a young wife in the hierarchical family headed by Raja Dasharatha. Note that when Rama wishes to proceed on exile alone, Sita asserts herself by insisting on accompanying him. She wishes to give away her fine jewels and clothing, and she would like to assume the appearance of an ascetic, in keeping with the new status of Rama. The two brothers leave for the forest, accompanied by the determined Sita.*

This is a pattern in many mythologies. The fourteen years of vanavas or forest exile are paralleled in the wanderings of the hero in tales around the world. The contrasting theme of a corrupt state and the innocence of nature is foregrounded. But of course, the pastoral idyll is rudely interrupted, setting the premise for the war between the forces of evil and good.

NG: Represented as a mighty figure with ten heads, Ravana is both saint and sinner. The heads represent his extraordinary capabilities and culpability. Indian myth is morally ambiguous, and Ravana is still acknowledged as a great if misled saint–scholar. He did not assault Sita, but kept her hostage and tried to terrorize her into sexual consent. Sita again displayed her moral and emotional strength, but her honour was not in her individual custody: women were trophies of the male honour system.

ML: *A series of evocative pictures, created by Raja Ravi Varma, show King Ravana abducting the young Sita. Trying to save Sita is Jatayu, the king of eagles. One notes that Varma does not depict Ravana with ten heads but concentrates on the brute force of a man exerting power over a woman. The painting is deeply emotional and captures the sense of movement, of brutality and violence. Sita turns away her face as much from Ravana as the sight of Jatayu's dismemberment.*

Mythology and realism are interwoven in such a rendering. Depictions such as these relate mythology to current discussions of sexual violence and rape. Ravana was motivated as much by revenge as lust. Rama's brother Lakshmana had spurned Ravana's sister and mockingly cut off her nose. To avenge such an insult to his family, Ravana produced the illusion of a golden deer to entice the attention of Sita. This directly leads Sita to step over the line drawn by Lakshmana and be taken captive by a powerful male. To this day, the lakshmana rekha denotes the common idiom for women transgressing a prescribed boundary.

There are several themes at play here, but chiefly the linking of family and national honour and female chastity. There is a perennial relevance of such myth. In war, as we know, women's bodies are the pawns of power. Stories of violence against women, committed during the Partition of India in 1947, were brought to public scrutiny by feminist scholars in 1997 when India marked fifty years of Independence. Many abducted women compared themselves to Sita.

NG: After the epic war is won, and Rama's familial and male honour restored, the common motif of sexual doubt and reproach creeps in. Even if she had not been violated, Sita had lived under the protection of another man. The onus of proving her purity fell on her, and she underwent the humiliation of a public test of her virtue. Invoking the elements, she emerged unscathed from the test of fire, with Agni, the fire god, standing witness to her purity and virtue. Later, after Sita was crowned queen of Ayodhya, a citizen's comment led Rama to decide that his public role as king would override his private desires, and an unsuspecting, pregnant Sita was cruelly abandoned in the forest.

Popular calendar art often details Sita's second exile. She is a single mother, a survivor. Her twin sons, Lava and Kusha, are warriors, holding the bow and arrow as proudly as did their father and royal ancestors. This is the pastoral idyll repeated, but in a darker, bleaker vein, with few illusions of a happy ending.

In the course of time, Rama rediscovers his sons, and reappropriates them. He has been faithful to Sita in his way; he has not married again, and kept a golden image of his estranged wife beside him for public ritual. In most versions, he now seeks Sita's return to his kingdom of Ayodhya, conditional to a second test, a new ordeal to establish her innocence.

It is now that the silent, nourishing, enduring strength of Sita finds voice. She finally exercises her choice. Calling upon the Earth as witness, Sita rejects the patriarchal power system that has so devalued her.

Here, in the myth, we see the internal growth and individuation of a woman who has been rejected by state, monarch, husband, family, and yet has not abandoned the constituents of her *dharma* and individual duties. There is a deep resonance in all the versions and surrogate stories, of inner resolve in the face of societal marginalization. In the Indian psyche, the enduring appeal and relevance of the Sita myth resides in its embodiment as a journey into examining our collective and individual woundings, betrayals, losses, yearnings and initiations.

ML: *We have attempted, in and through our project, to look in a nuanced manner at the contemporary presence of Sita. The diversity of India encourages the depiction of many Sitas—protean, culturally authentic and specially inspiring for a gendered approach to mythopoeic understanding. She speaks not just for women but also for the marginal people, the ones who are compelled to receive the dictates of power. We* *wish to foreground Sita's voice and her subversive authority. Daughter of the Earth, touched by the anguish of mortality, she is both a conformist and a rebel, mystic yet real.*

SITA'S LUMINOUS STRENGTH

SONAL MANSINGH AND RINA TRIPATHI IN CONVERSATION

SONAL MANSINGH IS an eminent Indian classical dancer and a leading exponent of Bharatnatyam, Kuchipudi, and Chhau. Besides being a dancer, Sonal Mansingh is a well-known choreographer, teacher, orator and a social activist. Reworking mythological tales in some of her performances, Sonal brings a new value to traditions. For her contributions in the field of classical dancing she has received accolades from many national and international organizations. She was the youngest recipient of Padma Bhushan, in 1992. In 2003, Sonal became the first Indian woman dancer to be awarded with Padma Vibhushan.

~

Rina Tripathi (RT): *Would you consider our epics to be women-centric? What would be your observations on how 'moral issues' are presented in the two great epics, the Ramayana and the Mahabharata?*

Sonal Mansingh (SM): Both the epics revolve around women's honour and dishonour. In the Ramayana, Surpanakha, who is the governor of Dandak *van*, seeks revenge when she is humiliated by Rama and Lakshmana and they, in turn, wage a war when Sita is abducted. In the Mahabharata, Draupadi's dishonour results in the great war between the Pandavas and the Kauravas. The two epics, however, show marked differences in moral values. The Ramayana is fairly rigid and reticent about domestic matters, and accords no special importance to the conjugal relationships of its characters, while the Mahabharata speaks of nuanced, romantic attachments and various children are born out of wedlock. The extreme morality of the

Ramayana may be the result of the social conditions in which it was written. There is a possibility of extreme chaos, anarchy and atrocities associated with those times. The collapse of the social order leads to rape, loot and violence, and in order to curb this breakdown of civil society, strict moral codes are enforced. The disturbed social conditions probably led to the creation of an epic such as the Ramayana. The magnificent story carries a cautionary message for the coming generations—'Let not this happen to you!'

RT: *How would you compare the female icons—Draupadi of the Mahabharata and Sita of the Ramayana? Do you find any similarities? How are they different?*

SM: Both Sita and Draupadi are extremely powerful women who not only have a firm grip over their own lives, but also greatly influence events and personalities with their strong convictions and ideas. However, there are some striking dissimilarities—unlike Draupadi, Sita has no friend or confidante. There is a kind of brother–sister relationship between some male and female characters in the Mahabharata, such as that of Draupadi and Krishna. Sita has no such friend, so the *sakha* element is lacking in the Ramayana. Sita is often depicted as Sati—the sacrificing wife. Also, while Draupadi's identity is not dependent on any male character, Sita's personality is centred on Rama's elevated status.

RT: *We are often made aware of the power of the visual medium in shaping our world view. In relation to the electronic media in India, where would you place dance and performance on stage in terms of their impact upon the audience?*

SM: In theatre, the characters of Sita, Mira, Radha, Parvati are reworked for contemporaray audiences. These are popularized by the electronic media too. Earlier, theatre was very different—the *nautanki*s, *yatras*, *bhavai,* all were based on regional culture. The entertainment was rooted in a local milieu. However, television has reached out to the masses across regional barriers. It has homogenized entertainment by targeting the lowest common denominator. In the fine arts such as dance, drama and theatre, there is a vital interaction between the performer and the audience. The people involved in creating dance and drama question mythology. However, television is a relatively passive medium, and it often dilutes the content and message in its quest to relate to the masses and thus achieve high Tele Rating Points (TRPs). The subtleties and nuances thus do not percolate down to the masses. The electronic media is simply reinforcing patriarchal values while social development is moving in another direction. There is a need to finance new channels and projects which can fill this widening gap. Innovative and creative artistes should be able to get a foothold in the popular media and say we would like to do it *this* way.

RT: *In your research on Indian mythology and Odissi dance forms, have you come across any startling or unusual depictions of Sita? Could you please share those with us and also comment on these aspects of Sita?*

SM: Yes, there have been many such instances. To recall a few—an interesting episode that is different from the usual version is found in the Jain Ramayana wherein Sita tells Rama about the weak joint in Shiva's bow from where he should attempt to bend it. She conveys this secret to Rama and he is successful in breaking the bow. Also, in the Champu Ramayana of Kerala, Tara, the wife of Vali, is shown taunting Rama, daring him to kill her. She challenges him to try his skill on her, calling herself a *vajra hridaya*, meaning one with a heart of stone. She further mockingly says that if Rama is a great *dhanurdhar*, why did he kill Vali while hiding behind a tree and not from the front as a true warrior would? I can recall another interesting episode from a text in which the wedding night of Rama and Sita is described. Here Rama is shown as an expert lover, highly adept in the art of love-making. Such a description is normally unavailable elsewhere. Hanuman is present in this scene but is invisible, as he is the *ansh* of Lord Shiva as *ekadash Rudra*. In the commonly sanitized text of the Ramayana, the conjugal aspect of Sita and Rama's marriage is almost missing, so it is only in songs sung at Indian marriages and ceremonies that a little of this aspect can be discovered. In most of the other relationships in the Ramayana, conjugal sexuality is mentioned only indirectly.

RT: *What fascinates you about the women in Indian history, legend and mythology that you have woven so many powerful dance performances around them?*

SM: The epics revolve around the strong characters and bold decisions taken by women. In the Mahabharata, Matsyagandha, a fisherman's daughter, is beautiful, sultry and enchanting. Sage Parashar falls in love with her and Ved Vyas is born out of this union. The child is born on an island in the Ganga and is therefore named Krishna Dvyeepanya Vyas. When the sage leaves her, he gives her a boon that the smell of fish would leave Matsyagandha's body and that she would become a virgin again. (Similarly, Draupadi who cohabits with her five husbands becomes *kumari* or virginal repeatedly). Later, the king of Hastinapur, Shantanu, is attracted to Matsyagandha and proposes to her. She lays down the condition that he will not question her doings and seeks a commitment from Shantanu that her children will ascend the throne. This leads Bhishma, the son of Ganga by Shantanu, to take a vow to never covet the crown, and he takes upon himself the responsibility of mentoring the royal clan.

RT: *Do you see Sita as a woman of exceptional strength though she sacrifices none of her 'feminine' attributes? How does she relate to other women in the Ramayana?*

SM: In the Ramayana too, one comes across very strong women—Sita's own luminous strength determines her identity and self-respect. She has an aura about her, which does not admit contrary intrusions. The woman, Trijata, who is given the charge of protecting Sita when she is kept a prisoner in Ashok vatika, is also very sympathetic towards her and does not allow any person to misbehave with Sita. Although Trijata is of lower status than Sita, she shows a sympathy arising out of feminine bonding with Sita and ensures that Sita is safe and kept respectfully by Ravana during her captivity. Mandodari is another strong woman portrayed in the Ramayana. She warns her husband Ravana that Sita would be the cause of his downfall and destruction. Even when Ravana is on his deathbed, Mandodari questions him about his actions. She asks him poignantly why he lusted after Sita and what Sita had that she, the rightful wife of King Ravana, lacked. She asks Ravana in what manner—*roop* (beauty), *kula* (lineage) or *guna* (qualities)—Sita was superior to her.

RT: *You have become an inspiration for many young women who hope to carve out a space in the realm of dance in India. Do you believe in mentorship? Are there models of mentorship available in our epics and legends such as the Ramayana and the Mahabharata?*

SM: The powerful women in the epics are akin to the leader of an elephant herd, who is a female and who guides and protects the whole community. Draupadi is one such woman mentor who looks after her five husbands, their children and their other wives as well. In the twelve years that she spends wandering about in the forests with them, she faces all kinds of challenges. Once, sage Durvasa is sent to the Pandava camp by Duryodhana who, after entertaining the ill-tempered sage, wants to see the Pandavas ridiculed and cursed. He knows that in the wilderness the Pandavas would not be able to feed the sage properly and would thus invite his terrible wrath. Draupadi had a great friend in Krishna and on this particular day when the sage arrived, she had finished feeding all her family and dependents, and had washed the *akshaya patra*, which had been gifted to her by the Sun God. The magical akshaya patra could feed any number of people as long as there was some food left in it. Draupadi was told by Durvasa to prepare a meal while he and his compatriots bathed in the river. As a homemaker obligated to serve visitors, Draupadi was unnerved as there was no food left. In desperation she called on Krishna who then asked her to look closely inside the pot. At this point, she discovered one grain of rice stuck inside the akshaya patra, which she proceeded to offer to Sri Krishna on a tulsi leaf. When the sage and his thousand disciples came back from the river, they felt as though they were well fed and satisfied. In this episode, we witness a rare kind of sakha relationship for a woman in epic literature. It is about mentorship and friendship between a man and a woman.

RT: *At the end of the Ramayana, we see the strong Sita who makes her own decision. Is the Ramayana the journey of a woman's self-discovery and her potential as a decision-maker?*

SM: There are certain instances in the Ramayana where the forcefulness of Sita's character gets highlighted. When Rama prepares to go into vanavas, Sita insists that she will accompany him even though Rama is reluctant to take her along. In a critical episode, Sita again expresses stubbornness and cajoles Rama into getting her the golden deer, though Rama keeps telling her that there appears to be some trickery involved in it. She also forces Lakshmana to go to the aid of Rama in the forest. When Lakshmana shows reluctance, she speaks in a harsh manner, alleging that he harbours a desire for her and therefore does not want to go to the rescue of Rama, who is calling out for help. This she says knowing fully well that Lakshmana had imposed strict injunctions upon himself and that he had never even seen Sita's face. In fact, there is an incident where Rama asks Lakshmana to identify Sita's ornaments brought in by the monkey soldiers and Lakshmana says that he cannot recognize the ornaments as he has only seen Sita's feet. Further, after the defeat of Ravana, Rama humiliates Sita in front of everyone and does not accept her. This enrages Sita and she goes through an agni pareeksha to prove her chastity. Finally, when she is abandoned in the forest in the final sections of the Ramayana, Sita, to avenge her insult, does not tell her children the name of their father. Asked to prove her purity for the second time, she despairs at the limits of masculine strictures on women, and prefers to return to her mother Earth. Sita asserts her choices but in the context of social interactions.

RT: *What are your views on the character of Ravana?*

SM: Ravana was a very learned man and a great scholar, yogi and a *sangitacharya*. He composed the '*Shiva tandava stotra*', which spoke volumes about his capability as a scholar and devotee of Shiva. Further, though he abducted Sita, he never made lustful advances towards her. He was also a mighty warrior and even though he knew that he was destined to be killed by an avatar of Vishnu, he still took on the might of Rama and battled valiantly. By virtue of his dignity, valour and erudition, he was a worthy opponent of Rama. However, it is the identity and forcefulness of Sita that determines the narrative of a great epic that continues to fascinate our imagination and gathers relevance for every generation.

RAMAYANA: THE HUMAN STORY

INDIRA GOSWAMI AND MANJEET BARUAH IN CONVERSATION

JNANPITH AWARDEE INDIRA Goswami is widely known for her literary writings and her research on the Ramayanas. Her research in comparative Ramayana was one of the early works in the field in the 1960s. Some of her famous novels include *Datal Hantir Une Khowa Howda* (*The Moth Eaten Howdah*), *Mamore Dhara Taruwal* (*The Rusted Sword*, which won her the Sahitya Akademi award, 1982) and *Chinnamastar Mahuhtu* (*The Man from Chinnamasta*), besides others. Presently, she is completing her new novel *Thengfakhri*, based on the life of a woman revenue collector of the Bodo community of Assam.

Manjeet Baruah (MB): *Greetings, Baideo. You have been speaking at several conferences on the Ramayana. I would like to focus on Assamese literature and the topic of Sita in Assamese Ramayanas. But firstly, what inspired you to take up the Ramayana as your research subject?*

Indira Goswami (IG): It was in the late 1960s, after the death of my husband in Kashmir, that I was planning to pursue my Ph.D. I had almost decided on *tantra* as my subject. We know that there is a highly developed body of tantra literature and practice in Assam. But two factors made me change my decision in favour of the Ramayana. One was my guru, Professor Lekharu. In one of my conversations with him, I learnt about the greatness of the Ramayana story—as a story of human beings and not gods. I saw Ramayana, especially Madhav Kandali's *Sat Kanda Ramayana* (fourteenth century), in a whole new light. The other factor was the poetry of the Sufi poet Mullah Masiha.

He flourished during the time of Jahangir. His *shers* on Sita deeply touched me. I recall the lines in my own way:

> One can never see Sita disrobed, but always covered in clothes
> Just the way one can never see the soul, but always covered in the body.

His poetry was profound. I began reading more and more of him and the other Persian and Urdu poets. Each time I read them, I could feel a motivation growing within me to undertake research on the Ramayana. It was a unique beauty to experience Hindu spirituality through Sufi idioms.

MB: *Thus, from tantra you moved to the Ramayana.*

IG: Yes, and look at the contrast. I was planning to pursue my studies in the US. I landed up for my research in Vrindavan, at the Institute of Oriental Philosophy. I think there is a wrong opinion among people that my research topic and the place where it was carried out had to do with my personal tragedy. In reality, it was just a coincidence, like so many others in life.

MB: *I suppose your research was one of the earliest in comparative Ramayana studies?*

IG: I guess so. It was a comparative study of Kandali's Ramayana and Tulsi's *Ramacharitmanas*. That study was a heuristic experience for me. The same story could become different in different regions. Its message could change. I think it would be more appropriate to say that the same story took on a different meaning for different people.

MB: *For example?*

IG: Since we are to discuss Sita, let's take Sita and women in general as an example. A most notable thing about Kandali's Ramayana is that in it, the women do not appear subdued as they do in Tulsi's. When Rama goes into exile, the common women of Ayodhya force their husbands to go, plead with and bring Rama back to Ayodhya. But the husbands return empty-handed. At this, the women do not hesitate to beat them up on the roads out of sheer anger and sorrow. Sita in Kandali's Ramayana is a powerful character. In the palace, when people ask the newly wed Sita to pay her respects to Kaushalya, her mother-in-law, and learn from her, Sita is brave enough to say that she does not need to *learn* anything from her mother-in-law.

Another funny but interesting episode is when Hanuman goes to Lanka in search of Sita. He does not know how she looks. When he reaches Ravana's *madhushala*, he sees Ravana and his several beautiful concubines in deep sleep together, 'like creepers tied to the body of a massive tree'. Hanuman becomes a honeybee and smells the mouths of all the sleeping women. He thinks that Sita at least would not drink wine! Such incidents are impossible in *Ramacharitmanas*. In the Ashok vatika of Lanka, where she is a prisoner of Ravana, we do not see a cowed, tamed Sita. Her open defiance of Ravana is as much responsible for her survival as her great love for Rama. Similarly, Kandali does not shy away from the physical description of Sita. He describes her body to be like the beautiful Brahmaputra and her breasts like the waves of the river.

I think we can see this in the larger context of the characterization of women by Kandali. For example, Manthara is portrayed as a shrewd politician, who devises plans to become Bharata's chief concubine (she was old enough to be his grandmother) and thereby indirectly rule Ayodhya. Thus, the good or the bad aspects of Manthara's character are depicted more in terms of her as a politician than a human being. This is not found in the other Ramayanas.

MB: *What, according to you, could be the reason for this difference between the two Ramayanas?*

IG: It's the context and the respective predilections of the poets. Patriarchy was strong in north India; the caste system was more deeply entrenched. Since Tulsi wrote a sacred text in Hindi, the people's language, he had to run from place to place for fear of being persecuted. Moreover, Tulsi wrote *Ramacharitmanas* out of sheer devotion to his god Rama. All these factors together give *Ramacharitmanas* its character.

Kandali's case was very different. He received support and protection from the Kachari king of Jayantapur, Mahamanikya himself, to write his Ramayana. Secondly, Kandali wrote it for the common people. Therefore, their society, norms and economy are overwhelmingly present in the text. Kandali's characters are not gods. They are human beings, driven by common feelings of love, passion, hatred, jealousy or goodness. His Ramayana carries the message of victory of good over evil. But unlike Tulsi, the contention that the good is divine and the evil is demonical is absent in his text. Kandali's Ramayana differs from Tulsi's in both conception and execution.

MB: *The title of your book, therefore, appears very suggestive—Ramayana from Ganga to Brahmaputra.*

IG: (smiles)

MB: *More than one Ramayana has been written in Assamese. Do you see any changes in the portrayal of Sita?*

IG: Madhav Kandali's Ramayana has always been the standard and the most popular in Assam. Ananta Kandali, a poet and a Sanskrit scholar, asked Sankaradeva, the great Vaishnava reformer, if he should rewrite the Ramayana. He was upset that Madhav Kandali's Ramayana was not about the divine Rama and Sita. Sankaradeva disapproved of the idea of recasting the Ramayana. He believed that Madhav Kandali's Ramayana had been supremely successful in spreading the story of Rama among the common people.

By the time of Sankaradeva (sixteenth century), the Adi Kanda and the Uttara Kanda of Kandali's Ramayana were believed to be lost. Madhavdeva (Sankaradeva's disciple) and Sankaradeva added the two parts. But the character of Sita continues to be powerful in their depictions too. In the Uttara Kanda, when Sita returns to Ayodhya with Lava and Kusha before disappearing into Mother Earth, she stands defiantly in the open court and lambasts Rama in front of everyone for his mistreatment of a woman and a queen that Sita was. She is candid and fearless. When Sita decides to retreat into Mother Earth, it is a decision based on her outright refusal to be a part of an order where she never received her share of respect. She is quite vocal about the reason behind her decision. I think that is very important.

MB: *Isn't this a very unique feature of art in Assam, especially between the thirteenth and nineteenth centuries—that the language of the court and that of the common people was the same, Assamese? Therefore, the classical and popular in art were uniquely connected. We generally don't find this in other parts of South Asia during the period. It seems to have influenced the nature of the Assamese Ramayanas too.*

IG: That's a very important point. Whether in literature, music, dance or miniature painting, by the time of Sankaradeva, the classical expressions in the arts had acquired form and sophistication. What was distinctive is that the same art could cater to both the court and the common people. It's a very unique moment in art indeed. And certainly, I think, the fact that the language or the medium of the art was Assamese in either case helped to disseminate a shared culture. The art that the monarchies institutionalized were people's arts and people continued to participate in their evolution. The Ramayanas as both literature and performing arts are an example of this fact.

MB: *I think what was unique in the method in art was that the classical and the popular could combine together without a clash of values. It shows that the Sanskritization process, in its theoretical sense, did not operate in Assam too well, except to some extent with the Ahom monarchy in the eighteenth century. But quite possibly, this very attempt by the Ahom monarchy led to the popular Moamoria uprising, which marked the beginning of the downfall of 600 years of Ahom rule. Perhaps the fact that Assam was located at the intersection of South Asia and East/South-East Asia and imbibed the cultures of these regions explains the amalgam. But coming to contemporary times, has the Ramayana influenced your creative writing?*

IG: Certainly. I have travelled throughout the world while participating in the Ramayani conferences. Based on my experiences in Nepal and Mauritius, I wrote one of my novels, *Daxorathir Khuz*. But many of my other novels have characters inspired by the philosophy in the Ramayana. Sita, with her defiant and yet tragic life, Ravana, who was a great villain and hero rolled into one, and Rama himself, with his qualities of love and forgiveness, have influenced several characters in my novels. Valmiki's Rama has many great qualities. I discovered these qualities once I could tear away the interpolations from the original. Father Bulke, the meticulous scholar, was instrumental in making me see the greatness in the character of Rama. I think my novels never have villains. The problem lies in the situational context. Human beings are not born good or bad. This probably is the essence of Kandali's Ramayana too.

As you know, the place where I did my research, Vrindavan, has also been a part of my writing. My entire experience in Vrindavan came out in my novel *Nilkanthi Braj* (*Under the Shadow of the Blue God*). I cannot deny that it too was a part of my Ramayana studies.

MB: *One last question. Tell us something about your forthcoming books.*

IG: One book is on Ravana—*The Journey of Ravana*, perhaps the greatest 'villain' in world literature. You too are a part of the project. I think greatness may not always have much to do with goodness. Had it been so, Vibhishana would have been a higher character than Ravana. However, Ravana, as a character, is complete in himself, as complete as Rama and Sita, and I wish to explore his complex psychology. The other book that I am working on is the novel *Thengfakhri,* named after a Bodo woman who was appointed as a tax collector by the British. Later she died tragically at their hands. I came across her story through oral narratives when I organized workshops to know more about her. The Bodos of the area themselves seem to have forgotten the details but now they are raising a memorial in her name. Thengfakhri was a woman who had the tenacity and self-confidence of a classical Sita.

MB: *Thank you, Baideo, for your time. Wish you the best for your forthcoming novels.*

IG: Thank you too, Manjeet.

TRIAL BY FIRE

MADHU KISHWAR AND RINA TRIPATHI IN CONVERSATION

MADHU PURNIMA KISHWAR is Senior Fellow at the Centre for the Study of Developing Societies (CSDS). She is the founder editor of *Manushi*, a journal about women and society being published since 1979. The journal, run by a non-profit organization, tries to bring together the diverse fields of academia and activism. She is also the founder president of Manushi Sangathan, an organization committed to strengthening women's rights through activist interventions. She has authored or edited several books, such as *Deepening Democracy: Challenges of Governance and Globalization in India*; *Gandhi and Women* and *Religion at the Service of Nationalism and Other Essays.*

Rina Tripathi (RT): *Do you think Sita accepted Rama's demand and went through the agni pareeksha to prove her chastity? Do you think it has been influential in defining a low status for women and patriarchal control over women's sexuality?*

Madhu Kishwar (MK): While Rama's demand for an agni pareeksha is indeed offensive, Sita's act of undertaking the fire ordeal is presented by the various writers of the Ramayana more as an act of defiance, rather than as submission to Rama's tyranny. I find it very strange that most feminists see the agni pareeksha as proof of our culture's endorsement of women's quiet suffering and submission to the tyranny of their husbands.

For them, a 'Sita-like' woman is synonymous with a slavishly dutiful wife. It is as though the main purpose of the authors of the epic was to brainwash Indian women into accepting a servile status for themselves. They tend to forget that the Ramayana is not a commandment-giving religious text in the way that the Bible or the Koran is. Valmiki's Ramayana is first and foremost a literary text like Homer's Iliad. And yet feminist critiques tend to treat the Ramayana as a 'religious' text.

Even a casual reading of the text shows that like any astute literary writer, Valmiki develops the two agni pareeksha sequences as great dramatic moments to evoke a sense of utter shock and disbelief in the reader as well as all those characters who witness Rama demanding them of Sita.

It is similar to the dramatic horror evoked by Othello's murder of Desdemona. No one would be naïve enough to suggest that Shakespeare wrote the play *Othello* in order to valorize jealous husbands who murder their wives and that the aim of the play is to exhort women to gracefully accept insults and even death at the hands of their suspicious husbands. This is despite the fact that Shakespeare treats Othello's fits of jealous rage with a lot of sympathy. In contrast, Valmiki does not build any defence whatsoever for Rama's behaviour. In most versions of the Ramayana, Rama is projected as being highly flawed in his moral judgement, in his treatment of Sita. Everyone who witnesses the agni pareeksha episode is on Sita's side and openly disapproves of Rama. That includes his own brother Lakshmana, his mother Kaushalya and all other relatives, associates and even a devotee like Hanuman.

This unease has led to numerous versions of Rama's conduct in diverse Ramayanas. In many latter-day Ramayanas, Rama is seen either as behaving more responsibly towards Sita or being soundly condemned by those around him. A Rama devotee like Tulsidas in his *Ramacharitmanas* just glosses over the first agni pareeksha altogether. This indicates the unease that Tulsidas felt at Sita's ordeal by fire.

Ramanand Sagar's TV serial *Ramayana* presents the agni pareeksha as part of a pre-planned pact between Rama and Sita whereby Rama leaves the 'real' Sita in the safe custody of Agni Deva to save her from the travails of his exile. Agni Deva endorses the truth of this pact by appearing in person to return the real Sita and explains that the Sita who was abducted by Ravana was a 'shadow' Sita. As per this version (which is influenced by some of the regional Ramayanas), when Rama asks Sita to walk through the *agnidwar*, he is not asking her to prove her chastity but asking her to take leave of Agni Deva's protection and walk back into the world of ordinary mortals. It is noteworthy that several months before the agni pareeksha episode, Ramanand Sagar was flooded with letters from viewers advising him not to allow Rama to subject Sita to the humiliation of an agni pareeksha. He explained that this had influenced his choice of interpretation of the episode.

RT: *Do you think the practice of bride-burning in India has been influenced by Sita's fire ordeal?*

MK: In my view, attributing the incidence of bride-burning in India to the negative influence of Sita's agni pareeksha is a very naïve response. We have to distinguish between two kinds of bride-burning: when a woman is burnt to death by her husband and/or in-laws; when a woman burns herself to death. In the first instance, it is a pure and simple case of murder, a crime no different from a man shooting, battering or strangling his wife to death. In most such cases, the woman is first battered and strangled and then burnt to death. Burning a woman by dousing her with kerosene and then setting her on fire is resorted to more often in India mainly because people have discovered that it is easy to destroy evidence of battering and pass it off as a case of suicide by the woman or a case of an accident in the kitchen, especially since police investigation can be tardy.

In the second instance of a woman burning herself to death, one can see a definite unconscious influence of Sita's agni pareeksha, even though the woman who chooses to do so knows very well that unlike Ramayana's Sita, she is not going to come out unscathed and Agni Deva is certainly not going to step forward and offer her a good character certificate.

A woman who chooses the most painful way of killing herself is, in effect, saying, 'I consider living in my marital home more hurtful than burning myself to death. I reject this relationship and this marriage because there is no sanctity left in it. The oaths taken by my husband with Agni Deva as witness have been trampled upon. Therefore, I surrender myself to *agni*.'

I read this as a strong statement of protest and rejection, similar to Sita's plea to Mother Earth to swallow her because she finds the demand for a second agni pareeksha so utterly humiliating that she would rather be dead than live as Rama's queen.

A woman who chooses this form of death leaves a permanent blot on the marital family, just as Ramayana's Sita leaves Rama permanently stigmatized. When a charred body is found in a house, the sight itself is so horrific that it leaves no one in doubt that the woman suffered endless cruelties and indignities. In such cases, no matter what the verdict of the court is, the social verdict goes against the husband and in-laws. It is a very deadly and unforgettable way to register protest and damn your torturers, especially in a country where people can't depend on the police or the law courts to provide them redressal and justice.

This perhaps explains Indian women's fascination with and psychological connection to Sita. Through the ages, Rama's conduct with regard to Sita has earned the disapproval of even his devotees, who have not been able to either justify or forgive him for such a grievous insult and injustice. Rama shrinks in stature due to his cruel and flawed judgement, while Sita rises in our estimation by defiantly rejecting his demand and his moral code and instead preferring to be swallowed by Mother Earth.

RT: *Were you influenced by Sita's character in your growing years?*

MK: Far from it. She was never a role model for me. I was more influenced by the likes of Rani of Jhansi and Joan of Arc rather than the Sitas or Savitris of India. However, I was also deeply influenced by Mirabai's life and her rejection of matrimonial ties and queenly comforts in order to pursue her chosen goal and a life amidst ordinary people, challenging all possible social hierarchies such as those imposed by caste, class and gender. Mirabai for me was a symbol of feminine freedom and autonomy. Even today, I don't have the *grahasthya ashram* mindset simply because I was never inclined towards matrimony and did not want to channelize my energies towards seeking a spouse and bringing up my own children. I love other people's children. I would rather work for all those children who are deprived of a dignified life rather than focus on bringing up one or more of my own.

I got interested in Sita only because I witnessed the widespread obsession with and admiration for Sita among Indian women and men alike, cutting across caste, class, regional, religious and educational divides. I found it very puzzling that while most feminists hold her in contempt and treat her as a negative role model, the vast majority of women across the country admire Sita as a symbol of perfect womanhood. The feminist mission or counter obsession is to 'cure' Indian women of their tendency to idolize Sita and instead urge them to adopt Western notions of women's equality and freedom, or else adopt Durga and Kali as their role models. However, they tend to overlook the fact that Durga is not just a warrior goddess, a slayer of evil demons but also a compassionate mother who is nurturing and forgiving. People respect her wrath because it is focused on combating evil but this is not her permanent stance. People reach out to seek her love and protection. No one would go near a woman who is permanently wrathful, who has no compassion or love to counterbalance it.

A lot of my writing, including the essay 'Yes to Sita, No to Rama!' as well as the special issue 'Women Bhakta Poets', has been motivated by the desire to counter the simplistic negative stereotypes held by many feminists regarding our cultural heritage and traditions. Very often, such critics pick up two couplets from Tulsi's Ramayana, four lines from *Manusmriti*, a para from here and a para from there—all out of context—and present the case that our entire civilizational history is about oppression, subjugation and brutalization of women. They forget that for every loyal spouse like Savitri or Damayanti, our mythology provides us hundreds of thousands of Durga–Chandi type goddesses, who are revered through the length and breadth of the country. No doubt, contemporary Indian society practises unacceptable forms of discrimination against women. But the continuing hold of the tradition of goddess worship in India and the belief that the feminine represents the *shakti* that energizes the entire universe makes for a strong counterbalance to the woman-hating aspects of our culture.

Our goddesses believe in peaceful co-existence, in graceful acceptance of each other's worth rather than claiming or establishing superiority over one another. For example, a martial goddess like Durga does not consider herself superior to a patient sufferer like Sita. Nor is Radha treated with disdain for being lost in Krishna's love despite his polygamous dalliances. It is accepted that they represent diverse aspects of the feminine shakti, and diverse responses to similar and varied situations. Therefore, devotees of one are not expected to disparage other manifestations of shakti.

The range of moral exemplars available to Indian women is indeed spectacular. Apart from goddesses who work hard to win respect as wives, at the other end of the spectrum are those who consider it an affront that any male should dare consider them sexually accessible or that they should condescend to be mere consorts. Radha's complete abandon to her extramarital love with Krishna is no less deified than Sita's steadfast devotion to her husband.

My experience tells me that women who display strength and courage come to be revered with much greater ease by traditional sections of society in India, than in many other parts of the world. A woman who acts like a mother figure, and can order men around while exercising her authority, but who is also compassionate and nurturing at the same time, is put on a special pedestal and treated like a virtual goddess. In contrast to men rooted in traditional Indic values, Western-educated men in India, who are liberal in mouthing the rhetoric of women's equality, are much less able to accept women in positions of authority because Western culture is traditionally more macho and male-centric.

RT: *Why did you write 'Yes to Sita, No to Ram!'?*

MK: This happened by chance. I was invited to a conference organized by Julia Leslie in SOAS on the woman's status in Indian culture. I had read her book *The Perfect Wife*, which deals with some aspects of the Sitas and Savitris as models of servile and masochistic behaviour. By then, I had conducted numerous formal and informal interviews with both men and women on their idea of traditional role models of perfect conjugality. I was pleasantly surprised to find that while most men and women held up Sita as an awe-inspiring role model of a perfect wife, hardly anyone ever mentioned the otherwise revered maryada purushottam Rama as a good husband, leave alone a perfect one. The top slot for a well-matched relationship went to Shiva and Parvati. Therefore, I decided to write a paper based on my perception of popular notions regarding Rama and Sita. That essay attracted a good deal of attention, especially after it was published in *Manushi* as well as in an anthology edited by Paula Richman entitled *Questioning Ramayanas.* Not long after the SOAS conference, I was invited to deliver the keynote address at a conference in the USA. That gave me time to study several versions of the Ramayana, including the immensely popular television serial of the same name by Ramanand Sagar.

That study further confirmed my initial findings that the standard 'feminist' response to Sita was at war with the people's version of Sita. This variance and conflict provides a key to understanding the limited appeal of Westernized feminist politics and ideology in India. If you treat women's own ideals and aspirations with disdain, and assume that only those who draw their inspiration from Western feminism have the right to decide what role models women should choose for themselves and what should be their idea of a good life, you are likely to be ignored and avoided rather than accepted and embraced.

This is not to say that I negate the achievements and role models of Western feminism altogether. The history of women's rights movements in the West is very impressive and the lives of many of the women who played a leading role in them are very inspirational. However, copycat feminism is a sign of intellectual slavery. We have very different histories and cultures. Therefore, our problems, our solutions and our aspirations cannot be identical. We must learn to take our civilizational specificities into account if we are to play a creative role in our society. That is why I take Sita seriously, even if she may not be my personal role model.

RT: *Any memorable responses to your work on Sita?*

MK: I must say that the most rewarding experience for me was my own mother's response to my writing on Sita. She was a great supporter of *Manushi* and used to read it regularly. But the 'Yes to Sita . . .' article moved her far more deeply than anything else I wrote. When this essay was published, my mother was in poor health and her eyesight was deteriorating, thus making it difficult for her to read anything at length. I was deeply moved when she phoned to say, '*Meri* Rano (that was her affectionate term for me), in this article you have articulated my own deepest sentiments. I had no idea you could read your mother's heart so well. I was so moved by the article that I read it at one go, even though my eyes were terribly strained. I could not put it down after I started reading it.'

My mother was indeed as resilient and dignified as Sita but she was by no means a servile woman. Like Sita, she too never indulged in tit-for-tat. All the rest of us—my father, my two brothers and I are tempestuous creatures. We gave her plenty of trouble. But she never retaliated, no matter how unreasonable the behaviour of others was and no matter how much their actions hurt her. I don't remember her saying harsh words to any of us, ever. She stood her own ground even under the most trying circumstances. Whenever I got into a retaliatory mode, she would remind me of one of her favourite fables: While a Mahatma was bathing in the river, suddenly a scorpion bit him. Like any normal human being, his reflex action to the painful sting was to pluck the biting scorpion and cast him away. As he saw the scorpion drowning in the fast-flowing water, the Mahatma extended his hand to pull the scorpion out of water. The scorpion bit him again. He again responded to the pain by casting him in the water. The scorpion began drowning again. The Mahatma saved him yet again. This went on and on. The scorpion too retaliated by biting him each time as he was pulled out of the water. People who were witnessing this interaction watched it in utter amazement, thinking that the Mahatma was crazy to endanger his life. One of the watchers finally asked the Mahatma why he was repeatedly saving the scorpion, knowing fully well that the scorpion could kill him. The Mahatma replied in his usual calm voice, 'It is the dharma of a scorpion to bite. That is what nature has bestowed on him. My dharma as a human being is to be compassionate towards all living beings and come to their aid in trouble. If a scorpion insists on remaining true to his dharma, how can I give up my dharma as a human being?'

RT: *A fascinating account. Thank you. What is the message that we should carry away?*

MK: It is a gross misrepresentation to describe servile and oppressed women as being Sita-like. My mother was Sita-like, but she was far from being submissive or slavish. It is good to remember that Sita was also Gandhi's favourite heroine. His Sita was the incarnate of a true *satyagrahi*, whose moral power intimidated even a mighty warrior like Ravana, who dared not touch her against her will even though she spent months in his captivity. The essence of *satyagraha* is that one does not fight back with the same weapons as those of the oppressor. It takes much greater strength to offer dignified non-violent resistance to oppression and injustice than to retaliate with violence. It requires supreme self-discipline and self-confidence to stay firm in one's own convictions and one's own chosen dharma as did my mother or the Mahatma of the scorpion story.

RT: *How do you relate to the idea of women's sexual liberation?*

MK: I feel that modern-day feminists use a lot of high-blown rhetoric of equality and women's freedom but are not necessarily able to live up to the demands of that rhetoric. This is especially true of those who challenge monogamous marriage as a patriarchal conspiracy. I have seen many of the so-called sexually liberated women imagine that they are proving their sexual liberation by moving from one sexual relationship to another, till they realize that the very men they engage with treat them casually or with scant respect. They may get away with it while they are young and attractive but they soon find that there are not many takers for them when they start ageing, whereas men much past their youth continue to be chased by younger women. Moreover, even those feminists who believe in sexual freedom go berserk when their partners get sexually involved with other women. A woman who wants a stable emotional life for her children needs a husband who is deeply committed to the family bond and takes full responsibility of the family. I would rather demand that my partner live up to Sita-like commitment rather than learn to copy irresponsible aspects of male sexual behaviour.

Real freedom for a woman lies in her ability to live without a husband's protection rather than accept humiliating terms for saving a marriage. There is nothing more humbling for a man's bloated ego than to know that he is dispensable if he doesn't behave honourably. There is no real freedom when a woman moves from one abusive relationship to another.

RT: *Do you see Sita coming out as a strong woman elsewhere in the epic?*

MK: She is the same dignified Sita throughout. She chooses her husband in a swayamvar from a whole array of princes. When Rama wants to leave her in Ayodhya when he is banished from the throne, she argues vehemently with him that her place is by his side and that their marriage vows bind her to be his partner in good times as well as in adversity. Her mother-in-law and all others try to persuade her to stay back in the palace, because as a woman she might find it hard to bear the harshness of life in a forest. But she remains adamant. She is loved and admired by all including Rama's family and devotees. She advises Rama on more than one occasion, and at one point even rebukes him for being motivated by anger with a visible propensity for violence, thus losing the compassion necessary for remaining just and humane. She retains her dignity and resilience even in Ravana's captivity even though he woos her with all the power at his disposal. And as a single parent in Valmiki's ashram, Sita is the beloved of all. It is noteworthy that she raises her children single-handedly without as much as disclosing the name of their father to Lava and Kusha. She does not plead with Rama to take her back, even though she is left abandoned in a forest. This is her way of saying, 'A husband who does not treat me well is totally dispensable.' In contrast, many of my very modern, liberated friends insist on using their husband's name for themselves and their children even after divorce. Sita never becomes Mrs Ramachandra. She remains Vaidehi or Janaki—the daughter of Vaid or Janaka even after her marriage. And she makes sure that her sons, though deprived of their father's care, grow up loved and nurtured by many others of her adopted family in the peaceful ashram of the sage Valmiki. Her two sons are thus willing to go to war even against their own father on her behalf.

Her final rejection of Rama leaves him forever diminished. She is considered superior to him. That is why her name comes before his, as in 'Jai Siya Rama'. Valmiki writes a whole epic to vindicate her. Men and women alike see her as being worthy of worship, rather than as an object of pity.

RT: *You would see Sita as very relevant to contemporary discussions on the status of women in India.*

MK: I would like to sum up by saying that the continuing hold of Sita on the popular imagination ought not to be interpreted as proof of Indians not having broken the hold of crippling traditions. Sita is wrongly seen by some feminists as a harmful role model which culturally enslaves women, conditions them into accepting subordination and maltreatment at the hands of men and leaves them without the courage to protest or retaliate. To see her suffering as a 'victim', or imagine her as lacking in selfhood, or to condemn her for her passivity and subservience is to negate the power of satyagraha.

We may not want to be Sita-like but we don't need to treat her as an adversary whose influence among women is to be countered. Most feminists identify with the aggressive militant goddesses such as Durga and Kali. Goddesses who are content with matrimony are viewed with disapproval, even if they are honoured as spouses, as was Parvati—and Sita too for most of her life. The broad thrust of feminist politics has been to encourage women to reject the Sita mould. As opposed to the mainstream society's efforts to reformulate Rama and make him worthy of Sita, the feminist project tends to be 'reform Sita' and make her forget Rama. This school of thought would like to see Sita emulate Ibsen's Nora and defiantly walk out on her husband to build a new life for herself or, better still, be an Erica Jong. If she has to stay within the traditional framework, she becomes acceptable only in a Kali-Durga *roop*. Why force Sita to act like Ibsen's Nora, or insist that Sitas and Radhas turn into Durgas and Kalis? Such monotheistic, one-dimensional, standardized behaviour is neither good for ordinary women nor for goddesses, not even, for that matter, for men.

THE DIARY OF SITA

NILIMMA DEVI AND A.K. ASHBY IN CONVERSATION

NILIMMA DEVI IS a noted dancer and choreographer who has devoted her life to the elegant art form of Kuchipudi—a classical dance style originating in seventeenth-century south India. Her choreography reflects, to some degree, a distillation of her identity—at once Indian and American—to convey social equity on a global stage for a diverse audience. Delving into Sita's myth has had an inherent logic and appeal for her. Devi embarks on her most ambitious foray—*From the Diary of Sita*—to confront what lies at the core of a woman's experience of personal anguish. What follows is a rare opportunity to talk to Devi and have her explain some of the choices she has made as a choreographer, as well as her thoughts on Sita.

A.K. Ashby (AKA): *You say you have grown up with the epic Ramayana. How did this affect your decision to create your dance drama* From the Diary of Sita?

Nilimma Devi (ND): I have grown up hearing my own mother sing of Sita. And as a child, I embraced her reverence for Rama and Sita without question. But in my twenties and thirties, I began to ask what it really meant to revere Sita. Yes, I resonated with Sita's radiance and her divinity as the daughter of Mother Earth.

AKA: *Did you ever resolve such visceral polemics—and if so, how?*

ND: That's one of the wonderful (unintentional) results of creating this production. I have found my peace with the Sita of tradition. See, poets and storytellers rarely show women doing what is believed to be 'heroic' (fighting, etc.). Rather, they are abducted or pawned or humiliated. Therefore, many women try to project Sita as a source of strength by saying that her silent stoic suffering is 'strong'. It is either that or one has to reject Sita. But now having done the research on Sita, and thought about it, I see it another way and am able to read between the lines of Valmiki and Tulsi, and understand that Sita was making choices all along. It is fascinating how the village women of India have been doing precisely this for hundreds of years—singing songs telling of a powerful Sita in various languages like Bengali, Marathi and Hindi.

AKA: *In what ways did you diverge from the traditional story?*

ND: Actually I didn't. The story remains as it is. Only this time, Sita speaks up. She describes exactly how she feels, what she thinks, and in the end, she makes her final choice. Thus for me, the traditional narrative revealed a mother lode of feminine energy once I allowed the Sita of my creative imagination to speak.

AKA: *Was it hard to communicate this to your American audience?*

ND: Yes and no. I have always attracted a diverse audience—non-Indian and Indian—so I had to assume that everyone was unfamiliar with the story of the Ramayana. While many may know of the Greek Homer's Iliad, few would know that Valmiki's Ramayana is the most pervasive epic across not only India but much of Asia. I outlined the basic story in the programme sheet. The dance itself was not weighed down with explicit narrative; instead I let the viewers draw their own meanings.

I did highlight certain episodes which I think are pivotal to Sita's character. Sita going from a life of royal privilege to one of forest privation—a choice requiring courage and physical endurance; and what happens later—the abduction by Ravana and Rama's demand of the fire test and abandonment. Destiny is brutal to Sita, yet it does not make her helpless. When Rama gives in to political pressure and abandons Sita, she exercises her freedom to choose once again. She freely enters Mother Earth's arms.

AKA: *Yes, but can't that action be seen as a negative choice—a form of suicide to enter the earth?*

ND: I don't see it that way. From the beginning, Sita is said to be the daughter of Mother Earth—she literally exudes the radiance associated with divinity. In my performance, I convey this quality with a lit brass lamp carried by a dancer. Sita uses that shining consciousness to endure, survive and finally transcend her suffering. What could be more freeing? She goes back to the ultimate source.

AKA: *What was the most memorable part of the production?*

ND: The music and dance both offered an opportunity to peel away the layers of Sita's persona. I was really challenged to merge the facets of dance, theatre, martial arts, shadow puppetry and music to convey the story. I think my favourite moment emerged out of my own childhood memories coming alive with the research reading. It triggered this dream-like inspiration of poetry composed with Anila, which seemed perfect for Sita's voice, so perfect, in fact, that I ended up recording it directly into the musical score.

Born of Mother Earth
I dance to the pulse of my gurus,
Vast oceans, venerable trees,
Rama, archer prince, pierced my heart
I followed him into exile
Abducted by Ravana
Rama came to rescue
Not me but his pride
I walked through flames to prove my chastity
But not my love
Yet Rama abandoned me to the forest
These mute memories
These tears of stone
Mother Earth called me
'Return Daughter'
I entered her depthless embrace
Everyone calls me 'Sita'
But I have other names too
Seema, Sara, Sophie.

O my mother
I shall be born again and again
And in every breath
In every voice
In every woman
I manifest
For I am free.

AKA: *What made the poem mean so much to you?*

ND: The poem accomplished two goals: one, it was a condensed narrative; and two, it was a nuanced interpretation. The poem evolved into a writing process that took on a life of its own when my daughter Anila became intrigued. We argued and agreed and were caught up in the energy of Sita. What does Sita feel and think towards the end? Does she find solace in grief or does she make a choice to end the cycle of sorrow? What does her final destination mean? Seeing the reaction of other women, I was doubly assured that Sita and her story has a message that transcends the limits of history. I have to say, however, that it doesn't always transcend the limits of gender. Two male musicians objected to my rendition, saying, 'But Rama is god; and he never meant to hurt Sita . . . why is this all about Rama's faults?' Before I could explain, the vocalist of our group—a quiet young woman—answered pointedly, 'But it is not about Rama . . . it is about Sita, that is why it is called *From the Diary of Sita* . . . remember?'

AKA: *What about the dance; after all you are foremost a dancer?*

ND: As the poem took shape, so did the dance movements. With the dance emerging in poetic/narrative episodes, I would see flashes: Mother Earth coalescing in fluid lines or Sita passionately stamping out a *jathi*. Other sequences sometimes took agonizing effort. Working on the deadline for the debut performance, I would literally fall into bed exhausted, invoking Sita, my muse. The core dancers were pushed to execute kinetic dichotomies—rapid fire rhythms, yielding yoga poses, powerful jumps and unfurling leg extensions. My superb martial artist was challenged to adapt to the Kuchipudi form and rhythm. Shadow puppets foreshadowed Rama's battle with Ravana, which was a mesmerizing martial combat with swords.

In the meantime, I designed and had four white linen panels made to be hung vertically from behind, from which the dancers would fluidly emerge and retreat back into. The panels, symbolic of a book, connected both the beginning and the end of Sita's story with its layers of meaning.

AKA: *What was it like to make the music?*

ND: Out of all the many theatrical fronts needing attention, nothing was quite as absorbing and challenging as the music. I had a superb cadre of diverse musicians—classicists with a gusto for creativity—who played the veena, violin, mridangam and *koto* (a Japanese stringed instrument). The striking pure notes of the koto became a haunting motif of Sita's voice. As the choreography evolved, rich notes of rhythm and song were correlated with the body movements. It was hard work and the risk was high. The music had to work for the dancers and yet sound good enough to stand on its own.

AKA: *How would you describe the performance in your words?*

ND: When all the elements came together, the performance took on a soulful vitality that captured my original sense of Sita. The pure notes of the koto had a quiet strength, so I had them echo while the poem was read and the audience sat in a darkened auditorium. Next came the dramatic entrance of a dancer leaping into powerful jathi. She ends with the statement, 'My name is Sita' and retreats behind a panel. A second dancer's eyes dart a glance through a small window in the second panel. Elaborate eye play gives way to another rapid jathi and the enunciation of 'My name is Sita' in Hindi: '*Mera naam Sita hai*'. The third panel exposes dancing feet and the statement 'My name is Sita' in French. Sita is thus depicted as a woman of the universe by making her speak different languages. The fourth dancer employs martial arts behind a backlit panel to create plunging shadows. The last dancer storms onto the stage lifting the Ramayana to the statement, 'She has other names too'. I wanted to suggest that beyond geography and language, Sita exists within every woman.

AKA: *What thoughts did you come away with after finishing the work and it's public performance?*

ND: In my work as a dancer and choreographer, I wanted to use the tools I had honed over the years to explore Sita. She is, without a doubt, one of the most potent symbols of Indian womanhood, and I wanted to probe that, see it blossom. It was the extraordinary labour of nurturing this choreographic 'infant' that gave me insight into Sita beyond tradition. *From the Diary of Sita* offers an image of a strong, eternal Sita; and the message seems to be resonating within me personally. It is wonderful now to see how it all merges into a larger tapestry—my history as it connects with India, with womanhood as a mother, as a daughter. I feel as though the layers of culture, time and language are just peeling away, revealing what truly lies underneath—an effulgent universal sisterhood.

You know, just the other day, I had turned on the TV and saw a group singing a beautiful African–American spiritual song. The words captured my heart, echoing what I had learned on this journey of Sita—'freedom never dies'. Sita proclaims at the end of my piece, '. . . for I am free . . .' Sita is every woman who sees truth, light and freedom underneath the shifting sands of life. The fierce courage of this divine daughter of Earth—who faces trial after trial and unimaginable heartbreaks—is ours. I truly believe this. After all, this is my story too.

LAYING JANAKI TO REST

MADHUREETA ANAND AND RINA TRIPATHI IN CONVERSATION

FILMMAKER MADHUREETA ANAND has recently completed a documentary film *Laying Janaki to Rest*, inspired by the idea of the contemporaneity of Sita. She inquired into the lives of women in various contexts of social existence, and asked them about their understanding of Sita. The resulting film, scripted by Madhureeta, was shown at a festival in Delhi with its focus on gender and sexuality.

~

Rina Tripathi (RT): *Why does Sita still have such a strong hold on the Indian psyche?*

Madhureeta Anand (MA): Sita's life finds an echo in that of every Indian woman, especially Hindu. This is due to the way we have been conditioned in social life. Intellectually we might be thinking differently, but our emotional and psychological states are conditioned. We know that children learn by example. Similarly, all examples of women around us, our mothers, sisters, aunts, are Sita-esque. When we are presented with real-life situations, we get defensive. The reason for being defensive is that the icon of Sita has been put on a pedestal and we are supposed to follow her example. Sita is a character that none of us can measure up to. Nobody in the world can be like her because she is an imaginary ideal. This is why Indian women constantly live under the impression that they are somehow incomplete. Women feel guilty because they have not been able to become Sita. On the other hand, no man in this country is trying to become Rama, Lakshmana, Krishna or even Dasharatha. Societal pressures thus do not work for men as they do for women. Now for me as a woman, in my life there is a very definite echo. Sita was trying to do her best but she was questioned for no reason at all. She could never prove her 'innocence' and therefore ended up alone with her children. Sita always held her head high and never went back. There are some variations of the Ramayana where Rama tries to call Sita back but she refuses. Sita was really on her own, and I related to this part of the Sita mythology. I found it so strange that a person like me who has travelled so much, done so much in life, read so much, could relate to Sita easily. I do not find echoes of my life in stories of other women, but find an echo in the life of Sita. There are parts of Durga and Draupadi in me but the events of my life were very close to what happened to Sita. I was married to a man who had a deeply suspicious nature and was sure that I was having an affair, which I was not. Instead of trying to question him, I spent years defending myself and saying that I am not like that. I spent years trying to prove my chastity but came to a point that I knew I could not prove anything. I had to seek separation. I am a single mother, and I have a young daughter. The problem with the times we live in is that women are becoming more and more successful. Women have to fight hard to achieve success. Men, on the other hand, have been told that it is alright for them to be just men, so that is what they are, just men.

RT: *How is Sita a contemporary figure? How is women's success in all fields changing the society?*

MA: There comes a point when women become so successful that society tries to find reasons to undermine them. Men feel threatened by this success. Our society is in a conundrum. We have two things happening simultaneously. On one hand, you oppress women, whereas on the other hand, our economy needs them to work. Here, very reluctantly society allows women to join the workforce, which has changed things for women. This is a new and strange situation that our society is facing. Men believe that they are superior just by virtue of being men. For women, however, it is a difficult transition, as if a group of people has been pushed to become stronger and now when they have become strong, the consequences of this transition pose a problem. In a patriarchal society, some drastic changes are bound to occur.

RT: *Do you think there are changes occurring that will challenge our conditioning?*

MA: Society has to take a collective decision on whether it will go on curbing women. Sexually, women have no liberty in this country. In my film, *Laying Janki to Rest*, I have portrayed three real-life cases. I talked to the women and found that the pattern of abandonment was exactly the same in all three situations. In one case the man wanted dowry, while in the others they wanted money. When they didn't get it, they started alleging that the women had bad moral characters. In one of the cases, where the woman's brother would come, with a box of *mithai*, to fetch her, to take her, to her parents' home, the people at her in-laws started accusing her of having an affair with him. In another case, the same thing happened with a caring brother-in-law. Since these women were usually closeted inside the house, they were suspected of having a relationship with the first man who came along. A certain gentleman I met pointed out that the practice of burning brides is very uniquely Indian. We burn our brides in a sort of agni pareeksha hangover. It is a direct link—you can shoot them or push them off somewhere, but instead you burn them. Of course, it is also convenient. You can make it look like a suicide. Incidences of women jumping into the fire in the name of committing *johar* and *sati*, they all come from that story of the agni pareeksha.

RT: *Do we see a strong Sita emerging by the end of the epic?*

MA: Sita's strength is her lack of fear while she is going into the forest, which shows her link with nature. A woman who has such a profound link is bound to be a very strong woman, but she is not shown as such. Instead, she is portrayed as a weak, subservient creature. We get glimpses of her strength in only a few episodes, like her questioning Rama when he berates her after she is rescued from Ashok vatika or when she refuses to go through a second agni pareeksha. Usually, the qualities of Sita that are brought forth are her loyalty to her husband and her purity as a woman. To me it seems that a particular Sita image has been perpetrated in this country. She is the only goddess who is so closely identified with the Indian woman's femininity. Durga typifies the idea of stability, while Draupadi's atypical situation is not easy to identify with in personal terms for most women. It is Sita who is seen as a role model for women, but she has been made unidimensional. It is time, in my view, to redefine Sita, destroy the image that society has cast her in and resurrect her in the image that we women know ourselves as. We are good spouses, mothers and daughters, but we are not the one-dimensional Sita!

RT: *What do you think are the views of the younger generation on Sita? What do they think of her; do they accept her as a role model?*

MA: The educated empowered girls who go to college—the 'hep' crowd—say, 'Look, we don't think Sita is our role model because she is too idealistic and we will never match up to her. If Sita had to give an agni pareeksha, why didn't Rama also give one because he too stayed away from her for an equal amount of time! Why did she go back to Mother Earth when she had children to look after?' These are the views today's girls have. When we speak to the boys, they say that it is difficult to find women like Sita these days. They themselves are not like Rama but 'modern' men are actually yearning for Sita-like women. Where then is the meeting point between the perceptions of men and women? Women are forging ahead while men are just left with the notion of being superior merely because they are male. What will this do to social relations?

RT: *Whom would you prefer to portray in film—Sita as a mother, Sita as a wife or Sita as a daughter?*

MA: I think I would prefer the role of Sita as a mother, because that phase was the clearest, strongest and most difficult in her life. As a wife and as a daughter, she was always under the control of somebody else. There is an engaging description of Sita's interaction with sage Valmiki in the forest. Valmiki tells her to go back to Rama, but Sita says that she would rather live on her own. Then Valmiki asks her to stay in his hermitage. She was a queen but she had brought nothing with her to the forest. Yet, she lived contentedly with her sons, and nurtured and educated them. For Indian women, Sita as a mother could become a role model. Being a single mother, I relate with this facet of Sita. She never felt the need to explain her life to anyone and was at peace with herself, which is really a woman's supreme strength.

RT: *Is there something to learn from Sita's life for contemporary women?*

MA: There is a lot that one can learn from her life. One may accept the struggles and come up with creative solutions. In the *Adbhuta Ramayana,* Sita herself kills Ravana but makes it look as if it was Rama who has killed him. I find this very endearing. When Rama and Sita are together privately, he recognizes who is stronger of the two. People who know this version realize that women struggle with the dilemma of whether they should rise to their full potential or not in a male-dominated society.

RT: *Does Sita portray the power of the male over the female?*

MA: Sita lives under the protection of her father first, then abides by her husband's wishes, and then lives for her sons in the end. In that sense, she is always under the influence of males like the typical Indian woman in a patriarchal society. She is hardly seen as an individual but more as a mother, wife and daughter. I am not sure if she can be a contemporary role model. She may not be our contemporary, but the irony is that she is, because how many of us dare to break out of the traditional mould? But we may recall that Sita, though fulfilling her duties, also asserts significant choices. She is not a passive character.

RT: *Does the role reversal take place and men also end up getting exploited and dominated by women?*

MA: This happens, but the number of such men is very small and society always supports men when they complain of harassment. If a woman complains that her husband is being unfaithful, she is ridiculed and told that all men do this and that she would have to accept the situation. If a woman is unfaithful and the man claims that his ill-treatment of her is due to her adultery, society, mostly, supports him. An ideal situation is one where both men and women are treated equally by society. It is not ethical to ill-treat a man, a woman, or a child for any reason, for that matter. What I want to convey is that the social construct so heavily favours men that no matter how many legal provisions we make, how many seminars we hold, how many books we write, it will continue to be so, not until we change our role models and our icons. Until we redefine the image of Sita, we are going to be stuck in the same social mores forever, because she is the goddess that all Indian women across the board most identify with.

The journey portrayed in the Ramayana is actually metaphorical; it is, in fact, a love story. The relationship of Sita and Rama is determined by public morality. We have almost no insights about their conjugal life. Sita though utterly loyal to Rama suffers deeply through her separation from him, and later through the public questions about her 'purity'. It is a sad tale that is relevant for Indian women today. If she is attractive, she is accused of luring men, if she is successful she is supposed to have used feminine wiles, if she cannot produce a male heir, she is 'guilty'. In common thinking by men, the woman should be 'like Sita', meaning chaste and obedient. But women in India can learn that there is another Sita in the same mythological tale—one who questions the standards and assumptions of public morality. I try to capture her in my film on Janaki and in my own life.

RT: *What was the response to your film?*

MA: After my film on Sita was screened, a man asked me whether I was trying to create a division among men and women, trying to create a male versus female paradigm, and someone in the panel answered that empowering women does not mean disempowering men. Another woman came up to me and asked for a copy of the film, saying that she wanted to show it to her husband to prove to him that the Sita whose example he cites was not actually like she has been portrayed in the epic. I had myself been caught up in the quagmire of trying to prove my innocence, trying to prove that I was not having an affair. I wondered at that moment whether that woman could ever develop a frame of mind whereby she could tell her husband, 'Listen, you are not like Rama, so why do you want me to be like Sita?' I strongly feel that with Sita being such a powerful influence on the Indian psyche, we need to transform the Sita myth and impart modern relevance to her, to ensure the progress of feminism in India.

SITA SINGS THE BLUES

NINA PALEY AND MALASHRI LAL IN CONVERSATION

NINA PALEY (b. 1968, in the US) is a long-time veteran of syndicated comic strips, having created *Fluff* (Universal Press Syndicate), *The Hots* (King Features) and her own alternative weekly *Nina's Adventures*. In 1998 she began making independent animated films, including the controversial yet popular environmental short film *The Stork*. In 2002 Nina followed her then husband to Thiruvananthapuram in India's southern state of Kerala, where she read her first Ramayana. This inspired her first feature *Sita Sings the Blues*, which she animated and produced single-handedly over the course of five years on a home computer.

ML: *We understand from interviews that your personal experience led to your reading Sita's story in a contemporary light. How can the film reach out to women in India across cultural differences?*

NP: That is a good question. I can't tell you how curious I am to discover how the film will be received in India—or if it will get shown there at all. Some people may love it, some may hate it. Every viewer brings his/her own experience and perspective to a film, and every interpretation is valid, be it critical or adulatory. We can only wait and see.

ML: *Sita has traditionally been revered as a figure of ideal wifehood, though new and critical opinions are calling attention to the denial of 'choice' in several episodes of her life. In particular, the agni pareeksha sequence calls for a review in terms of a feminist understanding of* *woman's agency and action. Do you think Sita in the Ramayana was a passive person, or do you believe that it was merely a patriarchal interpretation which highlighted the submissive aspects of her character?*

NP: The latter—I do not see Sita as passive. The agni pareeksha I see as a metaphor for grief. I wanted to kill myself when my husband dumped me, and the unbearable pain was like fire—I thought it was going to kill me and I'm still kind of amazed it didn't. Sita's walk through fire is actually an active expression of a heartbreak experience. In this way Sita is far more active than most of us. In fact, Sita is a model for expressing what we often repress. She loves Rama actively, without censure or shame or any limits. And when he breaks her heart, she expresses her pain with her whole being. How many of us mere mortals can do that?

ML: *What remedial measures did you take in your version to emphasize the strength of Sita?*

NP: I am not trying to take any 'remedial measures'; I am just showing it like I see it. I think Annette Hanshaw's voice is the best emphasis of Sita's strength: strength in vulnerability, honesty and yes, purity. Hanshaw's voice rings clear as a bell after almost a century, and its sweetness is devastating. Sita's ferocious love for Rama is an unstoppable force, a true source of power, if not empowerment. At the end, Sita's own power takes the fore, when she calls on Mother Earth to take her back into her womb. Here she displays supernatural powers exceeding those of any other mortal character, even Rama. But this is all there in the Valmiki text; I am not making it up.

ML: *Did the mix of technology that you used offer better results than conventional cinema or theatre?*

NP: I used animation because I'm an animator. I just wanted to tell this story, using the skills and sensibility I have.

ML: *Using shadow puppets is another highly effective device as it reminds the viewers of the popularity of the Ramayana in vast areas of Asia. Did the creative and production work involve researchers from South and South-East Asian countries?*

NP: The only researcher on the production was me! I was also the writer, producer, director, designer and crew. But it's not hard to find reference to shadow puppets. A friend bought me a few in Indonesia, and I found pictures of shadow puppets from Malaysia, Thailand, Cambodia and India in books and online.

ML: *I am intrigued by your choice of colours: Sita wears pink, and Rama is painted blue. This is a very elemental colour coding for the male and the female. Rama is described to be in the lineage of Vishnu and blue could be justified from that viewpoint. Sita's wearing of baby pink from the beginning to the end of her tragic story seems to make an ironic comment on the notion of female innocence as such. Do you agree? What would be your interpretation of the colours you use?*

NP: Sita is called 'The Ideal Woman' and Rama 'The Ideal Man'. So, in their designs I wanted to emphasize Sita's female-ness and Rama's male-ness in every possible way, to a ridiculous extent. In the West, pink is considered a colour for girls and blue for boys, and this did fit in nicely with Rama's blue visage in many traditional paintings. More than the colours, the shapes emphasize gender. Sita's hourglass shape is impossible to achieve; if I had made her waist any thinner, I would have had to bisect her. Likewise, I gave Rama enormous biceps and an impossibly broad chest. The characters' silhouettes unmistakably say 'female' and 'male'.

Ideal doesn't just mean a 'desirable role model'. It has other meanings, as in 'Platonic ideal'—an abstract essence. These extreme poles of masculinity and femininity are how I see Rama and Sita, and how I convey them in both the narrative and the art.

ML: Sita Sings the Blues *blurs the distinction between the tragic story of the epic and the comedy of modern lives, especially of women caught in the binds of marital conventions. Was that your intention?*

NP: To be clear, *Sita Sings the Blues* isn't a critique of marriage or sexist social conventions: it is an anguished critique of romantic love itself. I didn't love my rejecting husband because society told me to. What blew my mind while reading various Ramayanas in the midst of my own break-up was how primal and universal the problems of love are, and have always been. I do not see Sita as a victim of society. She was not 'forced' to be loyal to Rama. She could have stayed at the palace during his forest exile; she could have walked away when he rejected her in Lanka (when he declares, 'You are free to go wherever you want'; he also gives her permission to remarry). It was Sita's essential nature to love Rama, regardless of what the rest of the society expected of her. At the end, when she finally gives up on him, her life can end. The way I see it, she attains *moksha* at that point—liberation not only from her congenital love for a man who breaks her heart, but from all of life's sucker punches.

ML: *In India, some of the Rama Lila performances enacted at Dussehra attempt to impart a contemporary slant to the story but they may not innovate in any extreme form because the context is religious. Do you see your film as rewriting religion or creating a secular text based on religion? Maybe you have another category in mind that you wish to describe?*

NP: I'm certainly not rewriting religion. I understand that for Hindus, the Ramayana is a religious text, but the Ramayana belongs to hundreds of millions of non-Hindus too, and has for centuries. It belongs to Muslims in Indonesia and Malaysia, Buddhists in Thailand and Cambodia, and to everyone in India regardless of religion. My Christian friend in Kerala told me her family always exhorted her to 'be like Sita!'. The Ramayana was clearly important to her and her family, but was it a religious text for them? I don't think so. So a secular interpretation of the Ramayana is nothing new at all.

I didn't contrive this story, and I have no agenda in telling it except to express my own heart. *Sita Sings the Blues* is just my honest telling. It is modern and American because I am modern and American. It is funny and sad because I am funny and sad. It is what it is—I tried to get out of its way and let the story just tell itself. But it told itself through me, and that is why it is such a strange hybrid!

VERSIONS

THE ESSENTIAL ORPHAN: THE GIRL CHILD

NAVANEETA DEV SEN

'HOW CAN I have parents?' asks Sita in a Marathi song. And her cry reflects the sense of abandonment voiced by millions of Indian women through folk songs and traditional sayings. In our rural women's work songs, the girl child comes through as the essential orphan.

Take this Marathi song: 'Sitabai says, "What kind of a woman am I? I was given away to Rama when I was five years old. What sort of mother's love have I got? . . . Dear Plum tree, dear Babul tree, Sita is telling you the story of her life. Please listen . . . I was found at the tip of a plough/How can I have parents?"' The feeling of rootlessness and aloneness in which a girl child grows up is very clear, when a woman has no one to talk to about her sorrows, except to the trees in the wilderness.

Now let's go back to the sixteenth century, to Chandravati, the first woman epic poet in Bengali. Chandravati's Sita pours her heart out to Lakshmana, 'I have no father/I have no mother/I was found at the tip of a plough/I don't know who my parents are/Or who my brother is/Like moss in a stream/I float from shore to shore . . .'

In a contemporary Marathi work song, Sita echoes her 400-year-old Bengali self, 'I have no father, no mother/I have lived my life in forests, eating wild fruits/I have no sister, no brother/My soul has become an exile/Living in the wilderness.'

And in this contemporary Munda tribal song from Chhotanagpur, we hear Sita's sighs once more:

'On the grassy uplands, the ploughmen found me
They took me to the King's palace
. . . I grew up like an edible fruit
Though Janaka gave me in marriage to Rama
I didn't forget my sufferings . . .
Never have I known happiness . . .'

Why is it that all these women choose to sing of Sita as an orphan, rather than as a princess? The commonest epithet for Sita in Bengali (also found in Maithili) is '*janam-dukhini*' (born to suffer). These women's songs underline the fundamental insecurity of women and see the universal woman as the essential orphan. For a girl child grows up as a being without an identity, an ever-alienated self in exile.

The concept of the child as the essential orphan does not seem far-fetched once you are initiated into the positioning of the girl child in our culture. Our folk tradition gives us an overview, where details vary according to local custom and socio-economic status. A rural girl and an urban girl, a Dalit girl and an upper-caste girl, a slum-dweller and a bungalow-dweller do not have the same everyday cultural experiences, yet they do seem to share essentially the same cultural positioning in our proverbs. A quick look at proverbs gives us a greater understanding of the girl child's place in traditional Indian society. In this essay, I shall touch upon some Bengali proverbs, but there are parallels in other Indian languages, and readers will no doubt be reminded of similar sayings in their own languages.

Proverbs: Salt and Ashes

A rather unsophisticated but common expression of exasperation by a mother harshly scolding a girl child in a Bengali household was, 'Oh, why didn't I finish you off with salt in your mouth in the birthing chamber?' (*Oh toke anturh gharey mukhey noon diye mere phelini keno*?) Such detailed imaginative outbursts were especially reserved for the girl child. Mothers of course had little respect for themselves, let alone for their daughters; they hated their own gender.

Being a single child, I was an avid reader, and often came across this expression in dialogue in Bangla literature. And I wondered, how could anybody die eating *salt*? It's not poison! And why should a *mother* want to kill her daughter? I could not quite imagine my mother wanting to kill me off early. The vision of a witch-like mother, with pointed teeth and a pointed nose and sharp claws, poisoning her newborn, was repulsive and fearsome. That expression remained in my head as an unsolved mystery until I read Jyotirmoyee Devi's unnerving stories on female infanticide as practised by Rajasthani women. The ugliness and anti-nature attitude expressed in the proverb clearly shows how deeply patriarchy has distorted a mother's natural instincts, eroding her protective emotions. Be it to protect herself from the shame and torture of failing to produce a son, or to protect a girl child from a future harsher than death, it was the gross injustice of our cultural situation in which a girl child is born that made a mother feel it was better to kill her daughter at the moment of birth. The proverb clearly exemplifies the inhuman aspect of patriarchy that changes a mother into a witch. My guess is that most Indian languages have a proverb similar in spirit to this one.

Here's another proverb: '*Jaabat kanyaa taabat shoke.*' As long as you have a daughter, you have grief. Or '*Khaay daay paakhiti, baner dikey aankhiti* (The bird eats and drinks, but her eyes are fixed on the forest)', meaning bringing up a girl child is thankless for parents, for she is only waiting to leave for another family.

Interesting how the same proverb is also used by the girl's in-laws, the other way round, meaning the girl eats and drinks, but her loyalties are fixed on her parental home. So where does the girl child actually belong? Neither her parents nor her in-laws regard her as an integral part of their family. Each family unit feels her loyalty lies elsewhere. This makes the girl child a homeless soul. An essential orphan.

By placing the girl child in our cultural context pretty clearly, proverbs reflect the girl child's alienation. Take the proverb, '*Ma morle baap taloi*', meaning after the mother dies, the father becomes a distant relative. (*Taloi* is the father-in-law of a sibling.) Motherless girl children are unsafe, unprotected in the family, even if they do have a father. This proverb hints at the danger of child abuse, reminding us that a father is not always father-like to a girl child. She is an essential orphan, once again.

From her childhood, a girl in Bengal would hear encouraging proverbs like this very common one, '*Purhbey meye urhbey chhaai, tabey meyer goon gaai* (Let the girl be cremated, let her ashes fly, only then shall we sing the girl's praises.)' No matter how hard you try to please society, no matter how exceptionally good you are, as a girl, you will not be publicly appreciated. Appreciation only comes after a woman can hear it no longer.

Interestingly, in Bengali culture, several proverbs celebrate the birth of girl children. For example, '*Je beti seyana hoy, jhi biyaaiya aagey loy* (A clever woman gives birth to a daughter first.)' Boys are no help to their mother, but girls become trainee housewives as soon as they can walk, and offer a helping hand.

A rather lovely proverb opposes this view, welcoming a late girl child, '*Tin pooter parey jhi, aay aay rajlakshmi*! (A daughter after three sons, welcome, my princess!)', implying that when there are already three boys in the family, a change is welcome.

Female infanticide was obviously not unknown in Bengali culture, but it was never as common in Bengal as in Rajasthan, Uttar Pradesh, Punjab and Haryana where the sex ratio has changed drastically due to this inhuman practice. And has led to another inhuman practice, that of girl trafficking. This is where West Bengal and Bangladesh have come in grandly. Teenage girls from West Bengal and Bangladesh are regularly sold off by their parents as 'wives' to bridegrooms from Punjab and Haryana, who often use them as domestic servants as well as child-bearers. Sometimes also as second wives to show off their money. Brothels all over India, especially in Bombay, are another point of disposal of these girl children, both rural and urban, who come looking for a good break or lucrative domestic service in the rich man's city.

We Indians happily cohabit widely varying time zones. We send a Kalpana Chawla to NASA in the USA and gang-rape and lynch Surekha, a Dalit woman, with her three children in Maharashtra, all roughly around the same time. Similarly, we manage to balance awareness of gender rights with outdated cultural expectation. Today, girl children in urban middle class families are very gender-conscious. Even girls growing up in urban slums are far more aware of their rights than before. But religious customs live on. Like the values embedded in women's prayers.

Vrata Kathas: Praying for Death

If we take a look at the prayers in the Bengali *Vrata kathas*, we can clearly see how a girl child grows up—unprotected, unwanted, lonely in a crowded household, a mere tool in the patriarchal machinery. Like many other little girls in my time, I too had performed these vratas in my childhood along with my cousin sisters, under the guidance of my aunts. And what did we pray for? We chanted this mantra, 'I hope and pray that my in-laws' granaries overflow with golden grain, and that my husband lives forever and my children live in luxury on milk and rice. As for me, let me leave a son in my husband's arms and die in peace as a chaste woman, my head in my husband's lap, and my body dipped up to my neck in the waters of Ganga.' Whenever my aunt made me chant these lines, I wondered, 'But why? Why must I die, and that too with half my body drowned in the river?' But I never dared to ask my aunt.

In another vrata, the girl child makes ten clay dolls and prays for a better life in her next birth. 'After I die this time I shall be born as a doll,' she prays, 'and get a husband like Rama. After I die this time I shall be born as a doll and get a father-in-law like Dasharatha! After I die this time I shall be born as a doll and get a brother-in-law like Lakshmana! After I die this time I shall be born as a doll and be a *sati* like Sita . . .' It went on. She cannot expect to achieve any of her wishes in her present life, of course. The child says this mantra not once, not twice, but ten times, '*Ebaar morey putul habo Ramer mato bar paabo! Ebaar morey putul habo Dasarath-ke shasur pabo! Ebaar morey putul habo Lakshman-ke dewor paabo! Ebaar morey putul habo Sitar mato sati habo . . .*' She asks for death and rebirth to correct the big mistake of being born as a girl child. She wants a doll's life, only then will it be possible to get a husband like Rama and the rest of package deal that comes with him and *satitva*.

Popular vrata kathas like these initiate the girl child into traditional womanhood. They teach a child to be a woman according to the accepted patriarchal values, to be giving, to be self-sacrificing, to produce sons, to worship the husband, to nurture the children, to serve the in-laws and help them to prosper. And to ask for nothing in life except a peaceful, early death, to avoid the pain and indignities of widowhood. All her prayers are for other people. It's a completely self-negating attitude, culminating in a death wish. Could there be a more negative upbringing for a girl child? Dignity, it seems, can be attained only through death. *Purhbe meye urhbe chhai, tabe meyer gun gaai.*

Dignity as Chastity

The question of the inner dignity of a girl child did not arise. It did not form a part of a girl's social training. We were only taught physically restrictive things. There were many no-nos—never laugh aloud in public, never talk loudly, never look into a man's eyes while you talk, never comb your hair in public, etc. Girls got pretty much the same advice in other parts of India as well. Take this Telugu wedding song:

> Don't visit your neighbours after sunset
> Don't go to the washerman in the evenings
> Never walk the street with your hair open
> Don't laugh showing all your teeth
> Don't look around when you are in a crowd
> Keep your eyes downcast in public
> Never step upon the rice husks
> Strewn on the kitchen floor.

And now the most important advice of all: 'Never offer flowers to any man other than your husband.' The flower may also have a rhetorical meaning here. This song is sung at Andhra weddings even today, since the mother's advice reads like a book of etiquette for the middle-class girl child anywhere in India.

As soon as we started showing signs of womanhood, girl children were taught to be careful, to avoid such undignified acts as listed above, to keep all our precious body parts, from head to foot, safely away from the greedy touch of men. It was not dignity but chastity that mattered.

The Child Bride

Even today, the responsibility of finding a suitable match for their daughter is the worst worry of Indian parents. The fear is reflected in this Maithili song about looking for a groom for Sita, which goes like this:

> Princess Sita is scrubbing the floor
> Her sari slips off her shoulders and her mother the queen tells the father
> Up, up, King Janaka! What are you doing here?
> Go, get a groom for Sita.
> She is ready for a husband.
> So Janaka gets up, puts on a clean dhoti,
> ties his turban on his head, takes his peasant's staff in his hand
> and sets out toward Munger and Magadha.

Clearly, here the royal matchmaking involves a good Bihari peasant father looking for a groom for his dutiful daughter, adept at scrubbing floors.

In another Maithili women's song about looking for a groom, Sita, still a child, is sweeping the courtyard. She comes across a hefty bow, and lifts it with her left hand while cleaning under it with her right. Witnessing this, Janaka faints, as he had never been able to lift the bow himself. Then he bursts into loud laments, '*Ab Sita rahali kumari, yo!* (Now Sita will remain unmarried, woe!)' Since a girl has to be weaker than her husband, where could such a strong girl ever find a husband?

To be worthy of her, Sita's suitor must be able to string that bow! A swayamvar *sabha* is called and suitors arrive from all over. The same story appears in Maithili, Bengali, Telugu and Marathi, with variations. But only in the Maithili version does Sita play an active part in the process. For example, when one suitor after another fails to string the bow, Sita's parents are in a panic, lamenting, '*Ab Sita rahale kumari, dhanusha na tootale he*! (Now Sita will remain a spinster, the bow remains unbroken!)' But a desperate Sita climbs to the rooftop and shouts, 'Oh, Mother, is there no one strong enough in this world who can string the bow and keep my father's vow? (*Unchi jharokhe chadi Siya Chahundishi chitvathi he/Mai he, nai koi duniyame bir Pita-Pran rakhata he*?)' A bad-tempered Lakshmana is most annoyed when he hears this. 'Why is she so desperate?' he grumbles. 'Rama will come in his own sweet time and string that bow.' But Sita wasn't taking any chances.

Another Maithili song begins without any preliminaries, with Sita going up to her father importantly. 'Listen, Father, I have something to tell you,' she says. 'How much longer do you plan to keep me unmarried? This is not right behaviour! (*Sunu Baba araji hamari yo, kumari katek din rakhava? Iho ne uchit vyavahar yo*!)' Thankfully, Lakshmana didn't hear this conversation. Of course, Janaka promptly got the astrologers over for matchmaking.

In spite of such songs, the worth of the girl child is routinely ignored and they are still married off early. As women sing about getting the girl child ready for her wedding, we hear the lament for a very young girl, not yet ready to start an adult life, being sent away into an alien surrounding. Take this Telugu song: 'The tiny girl is only as tall as seven jasmine flowers/She can stand neither the heat nor the rain/ . . . Such a lovely child is being given away in marriage (to Rama) today.'

Or this wedding song, from Bangladesh: '*Alpo alpo dhailo re jal,/ Sitar haibo sardi jwar/Gamchha diya tuilo kesher jal go* (Pour the water a little at a time, let's dry her hair with a towel, or little Sita might catch a cold and fever.)' As Sita's aunts give her the pre-nuptial ritual bath with turmeric, their song exposes the paradox of child marriage. A mere child who is not yet physically capable of taking care of herself, is being forced to take up the social responsibility of wifehood.

Films, Literature and Life

We see the various faces of the girl child in Indian literature down the years. Just looking at modern Indian women writers from Bengal, you have a wide spectrum: from Jyotirmoyee Debi, Ashapurna Debi (especially *Prothom Pratisruti*) to young writers who reflect a different reality today. Her changing face is reflected in cinema as well. Probably Indian cinema's most memorable girl child is Durga, of Satyajit Ray's *Pather Panchali*. Durga was a child in every way, but also a little mother to her younger brother, and cared for her neglected grandmother. But Durga dies of pneumonia, herself a neglected child. In a recent Bengali poem, the poet says, 'Durga, if you were born in the same village today, you would have had some kind of training to save yourself, you might have been a teacher in the village school, or maybe an *anganvadi* worker, but you would not have died of pneumonia, untreated, at twelve.' Yes, times are changing; the girl child's position in our culture is changing too. We have to think positive.

Durga was not Ray's own creation, she was created by author Bibhutibhushan Bandyopadhyay. Similarly, in *Tin Kanya*, it is Rabindranath Tagore's girl characters that Ray depicts so beautifully. Noticeably enough, girls do not appear in Ray's own children's stories. But in *Goopi Gayen Bagha Bayen*, which was his grandfather Upendrakishore Ray Chaudhuri's story, he introduces two girls. How? Two princesses are brought in as potential brides for the heroes, with the famous sentence, '*Rajkanya ki kam parhiyachhe*? (Is there a shortage of princesses here?)' It is clearly an expression used for commodities and not for human beings. It is out of place, therefore funny. We all laughed at first, but then, if you are a woman, it soon stops sounding funny to you. A girl child is always a commodity, even if she is a princess.

Fairy Tales and Other Stories

In fact, she is all the more a commodity if she is a princess. That is what our fairy tales have taught us. The princess is a damsel who gets distressed and waits to be rescued by the prince. She is not a free agent, not an active participant, she is merely a cause for trouble, the peg to show off the prince's princely qualities, and ultimately serving as a passive prize.

This used to bother me as a child, so as soon as I had my own little girl children, I started writing fresh fairy tales for them, where the problems are generated elsewhere in society, and it is always the princess or the queen who saves their country, the people, and often the king and the prince as well. The source of their strength, however, is not physical prowess. They are not princes in saris. Although they are trained in riding and fencing, they do not need to use conventional weapons to conquer their enemies. Their source of strength lies in their head. They are courageous and intelligent, they can *think* their way out of trouble. Similarly, in all my adventure novels for children, it is a twelve-year-old girl who has these adventures and solves the mysteries.

And I have a series of stories about my family, about four women of various ages: an elderly widow (the grandmother), a youngish working woman (the mother), and two schoolgirls. No male family members. In these stories, the children are free agents, they think and act on their own, they have a friendly yet respectful relationship with their mother and grandmother, and their views are taken seriously.Though the only bread-earner in the family, the mother does not impose patriarchal values on the family, the grandmother is the one who rules the household from her sickbed. She is the eldest and the wisest, looking after all the three younger women. No typical girl children rules apply in this family, although the kids are caring, they take care of their grandma and the pets, and continuously advise their mother in her worldly activities since her actions are often full of flaws.

For example, at midnight the mother decides to learn to ride the moped from her daughter, who is herself only a teenager, and hilarious activities follow. The whole neighbourhood wakes up and gets involved in the great feminine act, and when Ma fails miserably, it brings grief to some but relief to all. There are many stories like this, not fiction but real stories from my own life, where I use real names. These were written in the late 1970s and early 1980s, long before chick-lit began in the West.

In such stories, we can see the changing world of the girl child. It is a so-called 'broken home,' but not a sad or dysfunctional one. It is full of laughter and warmth, full of activities, absurdities and love. One thing the girl children clearly display in these stories is self-confidence and dignity. Women in this household think, talk, play, read and laugh. They all enjoy life. In all my literary works, the cultural positioning of the girl child is consciously altered.

In every serious art form today, in painting, literature, cinema or theatre, sensitive artists—especially women—are trying to find a dignified, respectable place for the girl child without moving away from social realities. In spite of the proverbs and the vrata kathas, the perpetuation of patriarchal values and sexism through television serials and advertisements, our girls can reach for a dignified existence if only we want them to.

THE PORTRAYAL OF SITA IN TWO BENGALI RAMAYANAS

MANDAKRANTA BOSE

A MAJOR EFFORT of contemporary scholarship in the culture of India has been to re-examine the Ramayana as a model of social relationships and personal conduct. Such initiative makes it necessary to question the common view of Sita as the epitome of wifely devotion, which is understood as absolute submission to her husband. Her readiness to always put her husband before herself, accepting whatever suffering her wifely loyalty brings her, has secured her fame as the perfect wife, an ideal held up before girls in traditional Hindu society and sometimes even outside that society. Yet while Sita's loyalty to Rama is indeed central to the narrative tradition of the epic, her portrayal as the epitome of wifely submission is highly questionable. The Sita we encounter in the fountainhead of the epic's narrative tradition, the Valmiki Ramayana, is by no means meek or silent; on the contrary, she is a woman who not only knows her mind but also speaks it, often against the authority of her husband.

My source for this view is Valmiki himself. For brevity's sake, I shall cite only two crucial episodes in the story as he tells it. The first occurs when Rama is about to go into exile for fourteen years and instructs Sita to stay behind so that she may look after his ageing parents and escape the hardships of a forest sojourn. It is at this point in the Ayodhya Kanda that Sita first displays her assertiveness by insisting on following Rama into exile. Although what she invokes here is the wifely duty of always following her husband, it is surely ironic that she does so by flouting her husband's express wishes. That she invokes scriptural authorities to argue her case suggests both learning and tenacity, and a character profile distinguished by independence.

As an interesting aside, I may mention that in a medieval version of the epic known as the *Adhyatma Ramayana*, Sita clinches her argument by saying that none of the many Ramayanas she knows tells of Rama going into exile without Sita. In yet another late Ramayana, the *Ananda Ramayana*, Sita takes a similarly determinist position when she says in the Sara Kanda (the second kanda) that even at her swayamvar, she knew he would be going into exile and had vowed to follow him. In much the same vein in Krttivasa's Bengali Ramayana, Sita says that her going into exile with Rama had been foretold by an astrologer, which makes it her fate. Doubtless these variants emphasize Sita's loyalty to Rama, but they also underscore her resolute character, which seems to give the lie to the image of meekness that has come to dominate popular views of Sita.

The second episode occurs after Rama's victory over Ravana in the Yuddha Kanda. The demon king is dead, Lanka has fallen, and Sita is brought out of her garden prison to be presented to Rama. At this moment, when anticipation runs high of a joyous reunion, the story delivers the crudest shock imaginable as Rama rejects Sita for having lived under another male's control and advises her to attach herself to some other man. Magnanimously, he tells her she may choose anyone: Lakshmana, Vibhishana, Sugriva, or whomever she fancies to live with. Rama's reason is that as the scion of a royal family, he cannot allow into his home a woman who has been living in Ravana's establishment unchaperoned.

Sita's response is telling in both its substance and its immediacy. Instead of swooning or breaking into tears, she at once launches into a sharp and public rebuke. Rama, she says, is speaking like an uneducated, uncivilized person of low-birth (*prakrta*). Her harsh words and her readiness to voice them are hardly characteristic of a submissive woman but of one moved by an offended sense of propriety and self-respect. Also telling is Rama's silence. There is no rebuke from him for Sita's plain-speaking, nor any command to his followers. Rather, it is Sita who decides what is to happen when she commands Lakshmana to light a pyre because she would rather die than suffer such undeserved shame.

I am by no means claiming that Valmiki portrays Sita as an authoritative figure. The general lines of the narrative make it clear that she conforms to the ethos of the warrior culture and plays the role assigned to women, and here as in the pre-exile situation, she invokes the duty of a loyal wife. My point instead is that she articulates her reasons as an independent person. Still more strikingly, she derives her reasons from principles of social good and dynastic necessity, which she places above the patriarchal law of the husband's absolute authority over the wife. If there is irony in the fact that in order to serve her husband, Sita disobeys him, it only underscores our need to release her from conventional readings.

How this independent, articulate, and decisive Sita that Valmiki created became transformed into the exemplar of uncomplaining acceptance is a fascinating process of literary manipulation serving religious and social ideologies, which calls for a separate discussion. For the present, let us note that the Sita imagined by Valmiki was not altogether lost in all retellings of the epic, as we see in some of the Ramayanas from eastern India. Here I shall look only at a small sample of Bengali Ramayanas. The most influential of these is Krittivasa's fourteenth-century Bengali Ramayana, but also worth consideration are two later versions, both abbreviated, one by Candravati in the sixteenth century and the other in the eighteenth century by the father–son team of Jagadram and Ramprasad.

As I have noted above, when Rama is going into exile, Krittivasa's Sita chooses to accompany Rama against his wish. In the other episode that I have cited, Krittivasa not only follows Valmiki in narrating Sita's affronted response to Rama in the Lanka Kanda but expands on it by having Sita say that Rama, of all people, should know his wife and not humiliate her publicly by treating her as an *itara nari*, a woman of low birth. She adds, 'Why do you treat me as a *vesya* (prostitute) or *nati* (dancer) and try to give me away?' Thereafter, Krittivasa scales down Sita's protest and shifts the demand for setting up a pyre for her to Rama, whose command to Lakshmana is to 'let Sita burn in the fire so that I can get rid of the shame she has brought upon my family' (Lanka Kanda). But note that though Sita submits to the fire ordeal, she does so not because she accepts Rama's judgment but out of her grief at her betrayal by Rama.

This assertion of an independent self, expressed as grief, forms Sita's character most movingly in Candravati's Ramayana. While her Sita does not protest against injustice, she realizes with intense grief, not only her own fate but the fate of all women. This Ramayana, dismissed by critics through the nineteenth and twentieth centuries as an incomplete sketch, has been only recently recognized, by Navaneeta Dev Sen and the present author, as a deliberately designed narrative that hinges on women's experience as understood through the lives of Mandodari, Sita, and Candravati herself. Candravati notes how social power is fundamentally tilted against women and how women can do nothing but accept their lot. This is hardly surprising because Candravati was a product of the sixteenth century, by which time women had lost their voice completely and had been brought up to accept Manu's infamous *fiat* that never in her life may a woman have independence. That Candravati's Sita is only too aware of the injustice inherent in being a woman and yet sees no way out of submission to the dictates of society makes one wonder how throttling was the experience of a woman in a society where her voice is raised only to be silenced immediately. Yet, the absence of overt protest does not mean that injustice is mutely accepted. Though apparently passive, the central figure, whether it is Mandodari or Sita or Candravati, nevertheless acts through her words as witness to the systemic oppression of her society. The issue here, I would suggest, is not one of submission but of fatalism.

An entirely different, indeed contradictory, representation of Sita occurs in the Jagadrami–Ramprasadi Ramayana. This father-and-son team follows the conventional storyline on the whole until the very end, where they spring an extraordinary surprise by adding on a new section that they call Puskara Kanda. This episode, derived from the older *Adbhuta Ramayana*, is a flashback triggered by an incident in the main body of the story wherein Sita smiles knowingly as Rama boasts to his courtiers of his prowess in vanquishing the ten-headed Ravana. Asked to explain her dismissive smile, Sita tells the story that forms the Puskara Kanda. She reminds Rama of the time after Ravana's death when Rama faced a greater demon, the thousand-headed Ravana. This rakshasa proved to be too much for Rama, who fell unconscious in battle, after being overcome by Ravana's might. At that point, Sita assumed the form of Kali, the destroyer goddess, and it was she who killed the monster and rescued Rama from his clutches. The point of the story, drawn from the *sakta* philosophy, is that the ultimate energy of the universe derives from the feminine principle of its composition and is thus truly to be assigned to various forms of the Great Goddess, of whom Sita is a manifestation.

Given that Valmiki consistently presents Sita's strength and independence, and that several re-tellers of the story similarly viewed her, it is remarkable that she should have been transformed into a model of obedience and dependency. The main responsibility for this lies with Tulasidasa, whose *Ramacharitmanas* wholly reconstructs Sita in the image of what we have come to generally see as the delicate maiden of medieval romances, whose only strength lies in her self-abnegation and unquestioning obedience to her husband, and whose voice is raised only in declaring her fidelity to him. This tradition of Sita's portrayal has dug itself so deeply into public consciousness in India that the older view of her independence and strength has been forgotten.

We must, however, note that Sita's sufferings at Rama's hands have been so hard to stomach even for Rama's devotees that since Valmiki's time, every reteller of the Rama story has had to invent some rationalization to blink away their discomfort. Sita's humiliation is explained away either by shifting the responsibility for it away from Rama, or by invoking some unknown design of the gods, or—most inventively of all, in the *Adhyatma Ramayana* and followed in Tulasidas's version—by revealing that the Sita abducted by Ravana was not Sita at all but a mere image devised by Rama himself to keep the real Sita unpolluted. It is only in some Ramayanas from eastern India that we find an actual criticism of Rama. To my knowledge, the most explicit criticism of Rama occurs in the nineteenth-century Bengali version, only a partial one, by Dasharathi Ray. After Sita's rescue from Lanka, when she is forced to undergo the fire ordeal, the god Agni leads her out of the pyre, and as he does so, he says to himself, 'Now I see how it works:/The day Rama's reign begins/This is the justice the poor and weak will receive!'

But such occasional sparks cannot prevail against the general acceptance of Sita's submission. Ultimately, the effect of representing Sita as totally compliant is to weaken Sita to the point of incapacity for not only action but even speech. This is how Sita is known today. Thomas Coburn alerts us to this by reporting Sudhir Kakar's finding that irrespective of gender, the vast majority of Indians see Sita as the ideal woman because they know of her as an uncomplaining and obedient wife. It is an image that has been finally carved in stone by the hugely popular televised *Ramayana* of Ramanand Sagar (1987) as it constructs her. The Bengali Ramayanas that I have cited are exceptional in assigning, in their very different ways, a self-conscious personhood to Sita.

The story of Rama and Sita has been rewritten over the centuries since Valmiki's time. At least 300 Ramayanas are known to have been written and in every one of them, Sita stands as a role model not only for an Indian woman but also for women of many Asian countries where the story of the Ramayana is popular. In most of them, Sita is submissive and voiceless. Is the Sita of the later Ramayanas, then, merely a product of patriarchal control strategies? Or, is the ideological framework rather that of the *bhakti* worldview, which sees Vishnu/Rama as the centre-point of existence, necessitating the total submersion of all else in Rama? This may explain why Sita's abject surrender appears in Tulasidas's Ramayana, a wholly bhakti narrative, and not in Valmiki's, for Valmiki builds his epic on the need for upholding dharma as a social good and draws upon the deterministic philosophy of karma as the explanation of history. But even if we were to accept the bhakti interpretation in reading the later treatment of Sita, we would be hard put to disregard the gender issue, since it is only Sita who is subjected to utter humiliation, repeatedly so, and specifically on grounds of sexual purity. The odour of patriarchal management is hard to ignore in the reconfigured myth of Sita.

The influence of the myth is great in the Indian cultural world, but even more so in the Indian diaspora, particularly in Western countries, such as the UK, Canada, and the United States. They celebrate Sita as the ideal woman precisely because she is known to them as the most subservient, unquestioning, and voiceless wife of Rama. This is partly because Rama himself has evolved since Valmiki's time, from a heroic warrior born as an incarnation of Vishnu into Vishnu himself. Valmiki's Rama was a mortal, subject to mortal predicaments and errors of judgment; the Rama worshipped today is not a mere mortal but the Lord Himself, whose actions are inscrutable, beyond question, and have to be taken on faith—just as Sita does. How, then, may the devotee not admire this Sita? And why, then, would they not bring up their daughters to be like Sita? Thus, it is by robbing Sita of her voice that victimhood has been made palatable for women—indeed their highest destiny—through literary manipulation.

SITA IN PAHARI LOK RAMAIN

MEENAKSHI FAITH PAUL

IN THE HIMACHAL, the elders of the family usually sang and narrated the stories of the Ramain to the other family members, over days and weeks. Sometimes, a famous folk singer or Ramain storyteller was invited to the village. Then, the narration of the *katha* was accompanied with the fervent beating of tambourines and drums. That zest has dimmed in recent years, due to the popularity of TV and the migration of youngsters to the towns. Moreover, good folk singers are either very old or scarce today and the people's interest in and patronage of this art is waning.

At one time, it was a sacred duty to listen to the Ramain. During the festivals of Diwali and Shiva Ratri in the Mahasu area, that is, in the Shimla and Solan regions, it was a common sight to see villagers dancing around a large bonfire. Holding hands to form a garland of dancers, they swayed slowly and rhythmically to couplets and quatrains from the Ramain. In other districts also, the *Rama katha* was narrated and sung around Diwali and Rama Navami, as well as during weddings and harvest festivals. In the hills, elaborate ceremonies mark the travels of local deities, often linked to Ramain performances.

Lord Rama is seen as an ideal by the people of the Himachal. As an individual, student, son, husband and king, he is the standard against which the people measure themselves. Idioms and figures of speech with Rama in them are extremely prevalent.

It would not be a hyperbole to say that it is equally natural for the people of the Himachal to be attached to Sita or Janaki—two common names in the hills. Sita is as deeply embedded in the imagination of the people as Rama. She is perceived as a mountain lass, with different areas giving her their own costumes, habits and idiosyncrasies. She is seen dressed in a *chola*, or a *ghaghra*. She banters and argues with her brother-in-law, Lakshmana. She refuses to fetch water unless she is given new clothes and a golden pot. She rebukes Rama for playing dice while the golden deer is destroying her precious kitchen garden, in raising which her fingers had become raw.

In all such instances from the Pahari Ramains, Sita is either the energy or the agency of destiny. She is instrumental in positioning all the persons and events into place to facilitate the final confrontation between Rama and Ravana. It almost seems that she engineers the road that both should tread. Also, Sita emerges as a strong woman in the Ramains. She knows her mind and is not afraid to voice her opinion. Sita takes womanly pride in her looks and in being well turned out. She is aware of her status and position, and displays self-esteem and dignity. She is delineated as a determined, hardworking woman who can take on anything that the world may offer. Also, she is not overshadowed by the larger persona of Rama. Rather, she stands tall in her own right and is an equal partner in the marriage. In many kathas, it is clearly indicated that Sita allows herself to be carried away by Ravana for the greater good of humanity. She is neither duped by nor helpless before him. In the overall perspective, she is more Aditi than Prakriti. Therefore, after Rama, Sita and Lakshmana settle in Chitrakoot and till she withdraws into Lanka, Rama takes on an unassuming role and Sita takes centre stage.

The oral traditions of the Ramain have been documented and preserved in a crucial and ground-breaking volume, the *Pahari Lok Ramayan*, published by the Himachal Pradesh Art, Culture and Language Academy in 1974 during the 400th year national celebrations of Tulsidas' *Ramacharitmanas* (1974). The book neatly categorizes different streams of the Ramain prevalent in the various districts of Himachal Pradesh. It is an effective classification, though it must be borne in mind that oral Ramains differ, not so much according to administrative units, as by rivers and mountain ranges that border cultural shifts.

In the Ramains of Kullu, Shimla–Solan (Mahasu) and Una districts, Sita is said to be Ravana's daughter. The *Mahasuvi Ramain* also gives an interesting reason for Sita's abduction—her culinary skills. According to this Ramain, Ravana does not desire Sita for her beauty or grace. Rather, he perceives her as an excellent cook and, by extension, a good wife and homemaker. These qualities are highly valued in the hills, where a woman's charms are always secondary to her competence in running the household. This invention also provides another reason for Ravana not forcibly seducing Sita. Apparently, he didn't desire her as much as the food she could lovingly cook for her husband! Hence, her inviolability is ensured through the incest motif. And her abduction is made possible through the device of destiny, for a reverse Oedipus-like fate is written in her birth chart, to which Ravana must succumb.

Mandodari's Passion

This story is popular in the Una region. Ravana, the king of Lanka, levied taxes on all the people. Once upon a time, some sages and saints happened to pass through his kingdom. Ravana asked them also to pay up the levy. The sages had no money to offer the king. So in lieu of cash, Ravana extorted some of their blood as tax.

Now, Ravana was also a learned man and he knew that the blood of sages and saints had miraculous powers. So, Ravana poured the blood into a pot and put it safely away in a cupboard. He then wrote a line of warning on the cupboard: Whoever touches that which is kept inside, will be reduced to ashes.

After this, Ravana went away to do penance.

Some time later, Ravana's wife, Mandodari, began to miss her husband. Restless with passion that Kama Deva had aroused in her, she took a long, aromatic bath. Then, she set off in search of Ravana. When she reached him, Mandodari asked her husband to satisfy her craving. But, Ravana was too engrossed in his meditation to respond to her advances. Hurt by his cold-hearted rejection of her charms and of her longing, Mandodari returned to the palace. She was so agitated she wanted to die. 'I will kill myself somehow,' she said to herself.

While thinking of a suitable way of dying, Mandodari came across the cupboard in which the blood-filled pot was hidden. She read the words written on it and thought, 'I'll eat the thing inside and so, die.'

Impetuously, she opened the cupboard and picked up the pot. She drank up the blood right there and then. But God had other plans, for, instead of dying, Mandodari became pregnant.

In time, Ravana finished his penance and returned to the palace. Mandodari saw him approaching at a distance. Fearful of what he would say when he saw her heavy with child, she quickly closed and bolted her door from inside.

Ravana came to the door and knocked on it. Her heart pounding, Mandodari asked from within, 'Who is it?' 'Your husband, Ravana,' he replied. 'You cannot be my husband,' Mandodari retorted. 'My husband has such a mighty voice that when he speaks, even wild animals abort in fear. Your voice is nothing like that! If you really are my husband, speak in that same thunderous voice.'

On hearing Mandodari's words, Ravana roared with all his might. The resounding voice, at once tightened her womb and she instantly delivered her child. It was a baby girl. Mandodari quickly wrapped the infant in a cloth and hid her in a corner. Then, she opened the door and sat down on the floor, to indicate that she was menstruating. When Ravana entered the apartment and saw her sitting on the floor, he believed her ruse and went away.

After Ravana had left, Mandodari sent for a trusted minister. She placed her baby daughter in a wooden casket and gave it to him saying, 'Brother, take this casket to a far-off place and bury it there.'

The minister took the casket and crossed the sea with it. He travelled a long distance and reached King Janaka's kingdom. There, he buried the casket in a field. No sooner was the casket buried than it stopped raining in the land. A twelve-year-long drought and famine struck Mithila, Janaka's kingdom. The king was very anxious and tried hard to bring rain back to his kingdom. One day, his guru, Uatanand said to him, 'Majesty! Surely a murder has been committed in your kingdom; that is the reason for the famine in the land. Now, if you have a plough made of gold, yoke a white and a chestnut ox to it; then plough a field yourself with the golden plough while the queen follows you, sowing seeds. Only then will it rain in your kingdom.'

Janaka heeded his guru's words. He got a golden plough made, yoked a pair of oxen, one white and one chestnut, to it and began to plough a field. The queen followed him scattering seeds. As Janaka ploughed in a furrow, the ploughshare hit the casket buried there by Mandodari's trusted minister.

The king quickly uncovered the box and opened the lid. Inside was the most beautiful baby girl he had ever set his eyes on. The king and the queen joyfully brought the child to their palace. That very minute, the rains poured down all over the land. Joy and prosperity spread all around Mithila. The girl grew up as a much-loved princess. She was called Sita because she was found in a furrow ('*sin*').

The Birth of Sita

An unusual version of Sita's birth is related in the *Mahasuvi Ramain.*

All Lanka rejoiced—
A daughter was born
To the ten-headed one.
But wise men said—
It'll so transpire
She'll marry her sire
And cause his death.

Ravana and Damodari (Mandodari) had a daughter. The whole kingdom of Lanka was joyous and celebrated the birth of the princess. Ravana sent for the court astrologer to prepare his daughter's horoscope and foretell her destiny. The soothsayers said, 'This girl's stars predict her marriage with her own father. She is unlucky for him and will destroy him.'

Ravana was furious at this prediction and ordered that the girl be put to death at once. But a mother's heart is tender. Damodari secretly had a golden casket made. She wrapped her daughter in fine silk and placed her in it together with gold and silver. She then commanded that the casket be set adrift in the sea.

The casket floated a great distance and eventually reached a place where an old fisherman and his wife had cast their net to catch fish. When they pulled in their net, they found it was very heavy. They saw the rich casket caught in it and began to fight over the box. The fisherwoman, even at her age, was stout and strong, and more than a match for her husband. Finally, they got tired of fighting and decided to open the casket together.

When they opened it, they found the beautiful princess richly clad, and the gold and silver beside her. Taken aback, they realized she was a king's daughter and reasoned that if it became known that they had taken the casket and the baby girl, the king would have them crushed in an oil press. So, they quietly buried the casket in King Janaka's field.

God so willed that the very next morning King Janaka came to plough the land and discovered the golden casket in a furrow. The childless king was surprised and overjoyed to find a beautiful baby girl smiling at him from the casket. Rejoicing, he brought her home as his daughter.

Sita's Role in Ravana's Destiny

The fame of Sita's cooking is narrated in *Ramkatha ke Lokprasang.*[1]

It is said that once Ravana wanted to impress his wife, Mandodari, and challenged her to test his powers. Mandodari asked him to fetch her a lotus growing on the bank of the river. Ravana was angry at her petty demand and ignored her. Next morning he thought of indulging his wife and so quietly sneaked away from the palace to get the lotus. At the riverbank, he casually reached out for the flower. But, the flower moved down and away, leading Ravana into the underworld. There he was asked by several deities of the netherworld to either make a golden ladder leading to heaven or to marry Rama's wife, Sita. Ravana thought the construction of a ladder to be suitable work for the court carpenter, so he decided that a mighty king like him would abduct Sita because that was the 'work of a man'.

Ravana sought the help of his uncle, Marich, in this plan. As they sat thinking of a way to carry off Sita, a crow flew down to a coping of the palace. He had a piece of fried *bara* in his beak. The savoury bara steeped all of Lanka in its aroma. Ravana said to Marich that he wanted to see this rare bara held by the crow. So, the sorcerer, Marich, called the crow to him and caressed him gently. He asked the crow where he had got the bara from and what it was made of. The crow didn't answer because his mouth was full.

Ravana, however, wanted the crow to speak so that the bara would fall down and he could eat it to savour its taste. So, Ravana asked the crow who the greatest king and the noblest queen were, and which kingdom had the best grain and water. The crow was afraid of Ravana and to please him replied that Ravana was the greatest king and Mandodari the noblest queen, and that Lanka had the best grain and water. As soon as the crow opened his beak, the bara fell down and Ravana picked it up and ate it. Then the crow was angry and said the truth to his face: 'Ramachander is the greatest and Sita the noblest. The grain of the plains and the water of the hills is the best. The righteous king gave this crow a bara and the evil king has snatched it away.' The crow wailed that he had brought the bara all the way from Chitrakoot where Rama and Lakshmana were performing King Dasharatha's *shradh* and Sita had made the delicious bara with roots and vegetables.

When he heard this, Ravana became even more attracted to Sita. He and Marich immediately set off in search of Sita and Rama. After travelling several days, they reached Chitrakoot at night. They stopped near a *bauli*, a stepped fresh water tank, at some distance from Rama and Sita's hut. Marich cast a spell on their hut and then the two lay down to rest. The next day was Rama's birthday. Fresh water was required for the *puja* and it had to be fetched from the bauli. Under the spell cast by Marich, Lakshmana felt unusually lazy in the early hours of the morning and did not want to bring water like he did everyday, so he made an excuse that Sita should fetch water because it was her husband's birthday. Sita was annoyed at Lakshmana's behaviour. She retorted that she had never before gone to fetch water so she would not go that day, either.

Sita argued that people would tease her if she went to bring water. For, if she walked slowly, while carrying the heavy pitcher, they would call her haughty, if she walked fast they'd say she was impatient. If she walked in measured steps, like a peacock, they would say she didn't know how to walk at all. She added, that if she took a clay pot people would call her a potter's wife, if she carried an iron pot they'd turn her into a blacksmith's wife and if she took a golden pot they would make her a goldsmith's wife. To end the quarrel, Rama had an eight-metal pitcher made for her. It was placed in a golden *kilta*, a cone-shaped basket, and silver straps were fitted on it to secure it to her back. He dressed her in a flowing, tunic-like *chola* of stars and placed the moon on her forehead for light.

Arrayed in such splendour, Sita agreed to fetch water from the bauli. As she drew near, Marich and Ravana saw her coming in all her glory. Ravana was afraid and asked Marich what they were seeing—was the vision a demon or a summer's flood? Marich informed him that the vision was Sita, for whom he had crossed the vast ocean. Then Ravana hid in a shoe and Marich turned himself into a golden deer before entering the water of the bauli. As Sita bent to fill her pitcher she was enraptured by the deer and tried hard to catch it. The deer was playful and frisky and eluded her. So, she ran back without filling water and asked Rama to catch the deer for her. Rama advised Sita to forget the deer because nature did not make deer of gold. 'It is probably a demon trying to trick you,' he said. But Sita turned on him saying he was being lazy and cowardly. She stormed:

I'll break your bow
And your five arrows!
Either bring the deer
Or I'll die, you hear?

In this way, she forced Rama to leave in search of Marich, disguised as the golden deer.

Sita in the Folk Imagination

The people of Himachal imagine Sita in her simple domestic roles, yet as a woman endowed with mystical capabilities. She is one among them but also divine, she shares in their daily chores but also transcends them. Words and songs are attributed to her in the easy familiarity that is established. The household presence of Sita mata is an everyday inspiration for the hill folk.

VERSIONS OF RAMAYANA STORIES IN TELUGU FOLK LITERATURE

D. RAMA RAJU

THE TELUGU PEOPLE worship Sita and Rama with devotion. They feel that it is their good fortune that this divine couple spent some time on the banks of the River Godavari in Andhra during their exile. It is said that while the brothers, Rama and Lakshmana, fetched water from the Godavari, Sita prepared the beds and watered the saplings and creepers in the front yard of and around the *parnasala* (hermitage), their forest above. At that time the river heard the chatting and whisperings of these three and absorbed them into the innermost recesses of its heart. Till today, the murmurs of the Godavari fill the ears of the Telugu people, enhancing their knowledge of the secrets of the Ramayana and Rama's story.

Ramayana-based stories and folksongs multiplied widely among the Telegu people. I have come across more than twenty-six songs that narrate the complete story of the Ramayana. There are more than fifty songs that narrate some part or the other of the Ramayana story. And there are more than fifty songs that are concerned with Sita alone.

Ramayana folksongs in Telugu may be classified under four groups:

1. Songs that deal with Rama-katha either completely or almost completely.
2. Songs that describe a couple of major events or minor incidents from Rama-katha.
3. Songs that are woven around the personality of Sita and her life, though they may not be directly connected to Rama-katha.

4. Songs connected with philosophic, religious, ritualistic and social events which refer to the Rama-katha. Children's songs including lullabies, and songs of *arti* also come under this group.

Among these, some songs are adapted from the Valmiki Ramayana, some from the *Adhyatma Ramayana*; some are influenced by the Ramayana in regional languages; some bear influences of Jain and Buddhistic traditions, and some are pure creations of the folk genius. The Telugu people have identified themselves closely with Rama and Sita. Incidents from Sita's life—her play, her songs, her abduction, her fire ordeal and her exile, are experienced as their own. Such were the empathetic feelings and emotions of the country folk that a plethora of tales grew around her name.

1. The songs that narrate the complete Ramayana story contain many incidents that are not found in the Valmiki Ramayana. The tale of Jambumali, the story of Sulochana, the incident with Kalanemi, Sukra's advice to Ravana, and the latter's sacrifice in the nether lands are some such incidents. They have even been borrowed by Telugu classical poets like Bhaskara and Ranganatha. Besides these, there are many more tales current in Telugu folklore which these classic poets have no doubt included in their works.

Before I narrate the beauties of the folk versions of the Ramayana, I venture to assert that the innocent folk have conceived of Ramahood as the divine aim of devotion. They believe that 'godhood' can easily be attained by adopting the course of devotion and piety. To suit their ends they have reconstituted and reconstructed the thematic arrangement of the story. Their lack of sophistication helped them to take these excusable liberties.

The following song belongs to the first category: *Kusha and Lava charitra* (The story of Kusha and Lava).

This is a long ballad describing the Purva-Ramayana story in brief and the Uttara-Ramayana story in detail. The Telugu people have their own saga of Uttara-Ramayana. It has many interesting episodes and incidents. Only a few are cited below.

The ladies of Ayodhya came to see Sita after her return from Lanka. Sita talked to them lovingly. She spoke to her friends and acquaintances thus: 'Hullo, sisters and mothers! Did you think of me during my exile? O charming lady, I am told your youngest daughter gave birth to three children. She was only in her teens when I went to the forest. Please bring her tomorrow without fail. Alas, my dear friend, I heard that your elder son is living separately. Shantha told me all about your daughter-in-law. You selected her. So you have reaped the fruit to your heart's content.' When these ladies were returning to their houses, after talking to Sita, they said to each other, 'How kind and loving she is. She did not forget us though she was in exile for fourteen years.'

One day Rama and Sita were playing dice. Rama and Shantha were partners against Sita and Lakshmana. Rama lost the game and Sita demanded the bet price. Annoyed, Rama retreated to his bedchamber. Sita did not follow him. He waited for some time and asked his brother to fetch his bow and arrows, turned them into handmaids and enjoyed their attentions. One maid fanned him while another offered him betel and areca and yet another pressed his feet. Hearing the clamour that ensued, Sita peeped in to find out what was going on. She was shocked to see Rama in the company of other women. She addressed Rama sorrowfully. 'My father gave me to you in the belief that you would be true to me for life. But your true character has been exposed in this way!' The ladies in disguise retorted to Sita, 'Janaki, who are you, after all? We are his eternal companions. During your absence in the forest he was happy with us. You entered his life only when he broke Shiva's bow, but we were with him from the beginning.' Being thus insulted, Sita began to cry. Shantha intervened and reconciled husband and wife.

These two incidents depict the love and affection of Rama for Sita. The following episode is a tale devised to justify Sita's abandonment.

One day, inspite of Sita's disapproval, Rama was going on a hunting expedition. At that juncture, Surpanakha, the evil rakshasi who survived the Rama–Ravana war, entered Ayodhya disguised as a female hermit in order to wreak vengeance on Sita. She got access to Rama's presence by boasting of her powers. Impressing Rama with her magical skills, she gained entry to the palace. Inspite of Lakshmana's warning, Rama sent her into the palace to entertain the royal ladies while he went hunting with his brother. Surpanakha entertained Sita with her skills and as a reward demanded Ravana's picture be drawn by Sita. Sita drew only the toe of Ravana as she had seen only that much of him. Surpanakha left the palace, completed the picture and compelled Brahma to pour life into it. Finally she left the picture in Ayodhya before going away. The picture came to Sita and grabbed her saying, 'Let us go to Lanka.' Sita was annoyed. The royal ladies tried to destroy the picture by throwing it into the fire, the well, etc., but it survived and continued to harass Sita. At last she swore by Rama and put it under her bed-cushion. The picture remained silent. Meanwhile, Rama and Lakshmana returned to Ayodhya. But neither Sita nor the other royal ladies informed them about what had happened during their absence. At night, while Rama slept by the side of Sita, the picture suddenly reappeared, knocked down Rama and repeated the same words to Sita. Suspicious, Rama ordered Lakshmana to take her to the forest and kill her. The folk version puts forward this strong reason of jealousy for the abandonment of Sita.

Jain and Bengali Ramayanas are also said to contain this episode. There are similar folksongs in Tamil and Marathi.

According to the orders of Rama, Lakshmana took Sita into the forest to kill her. When he lifted the sword to do so, it turned into a garland. At the second blow, the earth shook and he missed his aim. At the third attempt, the Goddess Earth appeared before Lakshmana. Lakshmana left Sita, killed a hare and took its blood to Ayodhya as proof that he had done the deed.

A variation of this story is found in a Marathi folksong. In it, Sita drew the picture of Ravana not at the request of Surpanakha but at the request of Kaikeyi who still entertained ill-will towards Rama and Sita, and therefore tried to drive a wedge between them. She completed the picture and stealthily hung it in their bedroom. Lakshmana carried back an artificial hand that dripped blood as proof of having killed Sita. This was made by an Andhra carpenter Nagaya, brother of Kokasa Vadiya of Elure. Meanwhile, in the forest, the hermit boys led Sita to the hermitage of Valmiki. In Ayodhya, Rama performed the obsequies for Sita. But Lakshmana informed Urmila his wife that Sita was still alive, and she passed on this information to Shantha. On a aupicious day Sita gave birth to a boy in the hermitage. Bharata, leading a military expedition, witnessed the birth while passing through that region. One day Sita entrusted her son Lava, who was sleeping in the cradle, to Valmiki and went to pluck flowers. In the garden she saw a monkey breast-feeding her baby and came back at once, unnoticed by Valmiki, to breast-feed her own child. When the sage could not find Lava in the cradle, he created another baby with a blade of Kusha. Lava and Kusha grew up together and received education and training from Valmiki. One day they asked Sita about their parentage. Sita narrated her story. Lava and Kusha pledged that they would reunite her with Rama. There ends the song. Besides many interesting and novel episodes, this song contains descriptions of many rituals and ceremonies performed at the time of confinement, delivery, birth and death.

2. The following songs come under the second category of Ramayana songs. The first is *Putra kameshti*. It begins with Dasharatha's rule and his desire to beget children and ends with the wedding of Rama with Sita. To a great extent the story is in consonance with the Valmiki Ramayana but with a deviation at the end. According to Valmiki, Rama sees Sita only after breaking Shiva's bow, whereas according to this song, Rama and Sita love each other prior to it. Great poets like Bhasa, Kamban and Tulsidas have also depicted the pre-marital love between Rama and Sita.

Rama and Lakshmana followed Vishwamitra to Mithila to witness the *dhanuryaga*. In the pleasure garden they encountered Sita along with her maids. She saw Rama looking like a *balayogi*, performing evening *sandhya*, and made obeisance to him. The dialogue that took place between them is quite interesting.

Sita: Where have you come from? What is the purpose? What is your name and who is your guru?

Rama: I am the disciple of Vishwamitra, I have come to witness the dhanuryaga and my name is Dweller-in-the-Hearts-of-Yogis.

Sita: Why have you become a sanyasi? Your face radiates royal lustre.

Rama: It is so with Vishwamitra. He was a heroic kshatriya in the beginning but became a *brahmarshi* afterwards.

Sita: Is it proper for a yogi to contest for a dhanuryaga wedding? Tell me the opinion of your guru.

Rama: My guru will graciously perform my wedding if the bride is offered with devotion.

Sita: Janaka offers Sita to the hero who lifts and strings the bow, but not to others.

Rama: Why is the bow that used to be worshipped now brought out to be stringed? What is its weight?

Sita: While Sita was playing, her ball went underneath the bow. She lifted the bow and pulled out the ball.

Rama: Oh, if the weight is so easily lifted by a girl, what is it for a mighty hero?

Sita: Many mighty kings and emperors could not lift that bow of Shiva and fell while trying.

Rama: Did you not hear in the assemblies that what is not possible for the mighty king is child's play for the yogi?

Sita: If it is possible for you, is it proper that our Sita should wed a yogi?

Rama: Sita who is born and brought up in a furrow should not wed a prince at all.

Sita: I am Sita. Pardon my wrongs. Get me married to Rama.

Rama: This is impossible. I cannot do it. You approach and serve the great sages for that.

Sita: You are capable of protecting those who seek your refuge. I prostrate before you, kindly save me.

Rama: Take the pledge to alleviate the troubles of the meek from today. Rama will become your husband. He is nowhere but before you.

Bashful, Sita runs away from the presence of Rama.

The second song is *Urmiladevi nidra* (Urmiladevi's sleep), a popular ballad sung by women throughout Andhra. All classical writers of the epic, from Valmiki down to the latest, have entirely forgotten the role of Urmila, the bride princess of Lakshmana. But the Telugu women have treasured this great princess in their memories. While the village bards gave the highest place to Sita, they did not forget Urmila's place in the grand epic story. When Lakshmana followed his brother and sister-in-law to serve them, Urmila requested Lakshmana to permit her to accompany them. Her offer was considered an obstacle by Lakshmana. He quoted some sacred injunctions such as the following:

'The younger sister-in-law shall not tread.
The same ground traversed by the eldest brother-in-law.
She shall not be within earshot of him.
How can I take you, to follow them?'

He told her to stay in the palace. Urmila, the chaste wife, confined herself in the palace and obeyed her lord. Now rises a question regarding the magnitude of this sacrifice. Is Sita greater, who followed her lord against his will to the forests, or Urmila, who remained behind forlorn when her lord left her? Let us not consider the travails of Sita during her captivity in this context. The course of the Ramayana would have been different if Urmila had followed the other three. Lakshmana, in his absolute obedience to his elder brother, Rama, was insensitive to the fate of his wife. How Urmila suffered the acute agony of this enforced loneliness can only be imagined. The lady went into a comatose state of sleep. 'From then onwards she lay in coma on her couch.' That was the manner in which Urmila survived fourteen long years. She thought of her lord and lay in sleep.

When Lakshmana returned home, what was his primary duty? He ought to have approached his better half. But no—during the coronation, he got busy waving the whisk for the king, Rama. He forgot about his wife. Women alone can fathom and comprehend the psychological state of women. One day, 'Rama, after coronation, was seated majestically on the throne. Bharata, Shatrughna and Lakshmana rendered due services. Hanuman sat at Rama's feet and massaged them.' At that moment Sita approached her lord Rama and said:

> 'O Lord of Lords, I have a request to make, please listen.
> When we were leaving for the forests,
> Our dear brother-in-law volunteered to be with us.
> His bride Urmila also wanted to follow him.
> Lakshmana issued a mandate to her to stay on.
> From that moment dear Urmila is sleeping
> On the couch in deep coma,
> Now at least, please relieve Lakshmana
> And allow him to meet his dear love.'

At her request Lakshmana was permitted to meet Urmila. It was only then that Lakshmana must have learnt about his wife's state. Instantly did Lakshmana repair to the bedchamber of Urmila. Instead of soothingly waking her up and offering apologies to her, this prince began to address her thus, sitting on the bed by her side:

> 'Oh my dear, this moon-like lover has come
> To serve your beautiful face.'

Lakshmana behaved roughly and impetuously. The lady, who had closed her eyes for a period of fourteen years, felt the sudden presence of an intruder in her private chamber. She remonstrated:

'O Sir, who are you? Why this outrage?
Wandering in lanes and bylanes,
Why did you commit this mistake?
Why did you intrude into this solitary chamber?
If my sire King Janaka learns about this
He will order your punishment.
If my sister and her husband know about this,
Danger to your life is imminent.
If her brother-in-law was here now,
He would not allow you to survive.'

Thus she gently warned him. Her shyness, her chastity and other noble virtues are obvious in these lines. Lakshmana was bitterly chagrined. She further remonstrated over her misfortune:

'I have brought ill-fame to the great dynasty,
What can I do now?
Being born of a reputed family,
I have brought disgrace to it.'

She thought she should give sound ethical advice to the intruder:

'Indra became a physical wreck because he
Desired another's wife.
Ravana met with genocide because he made
Overtures to another's wife,
Kichaka met with disaster for loving another's wife.
How could you deliberately indulge in such an outrage?
Have you no sisters?
Have you no mother like me?'

Thus did she read him a tirade on the despicable custom of courting others' wives. The reference to Kichaka is an anachronism, but the rural folk have in their memories several mythologies. The precepts uttered by Urmila were posited as ideals for women, to be followed scrupulously.

The revealing and recognition of the identity of Lakshmana and the conversation that ensued between husband and wife have been finely described. Urmila prostrated herself at his feet, overcome with emotion:

'It was at a capricious moment that our sire
King Janaka gave me to you.
Men focus their attentions in a particular direction at a particular time and are indifferent to those who love them.
Paying attention elsewhere, men
Belittle their loved ones—such are men.'

Urmila continued her diatribe. Lakshmana understood her feelings. He told her that during the exile, he had served his brother and Sita without eating or sleeping. They both regretted their separation, attributing it to past actions in a previous life. Perhaps they had been responsible for separating espoused partners.

The dowager queen Kaushalya and other elders of the royalty calmed them, gave them auspicious baths and feasted them. Urmila was glowing radiantly. Her sister-in-law Shantha said:

'The lustrous sheen of a golden image was hiding in her face till now,
Let her not be struck by an evil eye,
Let us perform auspicious rites to allay the dangers of such sight.'

Shantha, who had an impish nature, joked and teased the reawakened bride Urmila. Poor Urmila kept silent. But Sita took her side and retorted with quick repartee. She said to Shantha:

'My brother Rishyashringa was tempted by you
And that anchorite was head over heels in love with you and followed you.'

This silenced Shantha.

Urmila's bedchamber was beautifully decorated. Lakshmana sat by her side and began to help her in her toilet. He dressed her hair, plaited the tresses and adorned them with flowers. While he was doing this, her thoughts were on the tragic fate that had befallen her sister, Sita. She inquired:

'When you of leonine strength were there, how could Sita be captured?

> When you rulers of earth were present, how could Sita be abducted?'

Lakshmana narrated the whole experience to her. The retold tale brought sorrow to Urmila. She relayed the story to her sisters in the palace. They felt sad while listening, but were soon happy at the thought of Sita's safe return home. The ending of the song promises blessings to the listeners:

> When these songs of Urmila's separation are sung or heard by people,
> They will be benignly transported to the Abode of Vishnu
> And they will attain the ultimate release.

A third song is *Lakshmanadevara navvu* (Lakshmana's motiveless smile). In this song we see the psychological understanding of the folk people. To picturize in words, classical writers indulge in literary adornment and figures of speech. But the folk is more concerned with episodic setting and thematic emphasis. This trait can be discerned in this song.

After Lanka, Rama returned to Ayodhya with Sita. All the gods, sages and friends attended the coronation. When all were assembled,

> Laughed, laughed and laughed the great Lakshmana,
> This raised doubts in the minds of those that assembled.
> He laughed uproariously,
> At the loud laughter the king felt humiliated.

This laughter made everyone introspective. A series of chain reactions have been ascribed by the folk poet to everyone present at the royal assembly. Shiva thought that Ganga, the fisherman's girl on his head, was the cause of the laughter. Vibhishana thought that the cause was his fratricidal crime to secure the kingdom of Lanka. Sita thought that the laugh was directed at her for the uncivil and rude speech she indulged in with Lakshmana when she heard Maricha's false alarm. She felt embarrassed. Rama thought that the laugh was due to his having restituted Sita who had been a captive of Ravana for long. Likewise Sugriva, Jambuvan, Hanuman, Bharata, Shatrughna and every dignitary present in the coronation hall thought Lakshmana was laughing at him alone. This one incident produced a series of reactions in individuals. Out of a single act, multiple reactions were set in motion. Like the phrase *astameti gabhasliman* (the sun has set) very often quoted by the rhetoricians in order to convey different kinds of suggestive meanings, here the laughter had compelled everyone to search their minds. They hung their heads, bitterly humiliated. Rama's anger grew to a pitch as he felt that the whole assembly was being insulted. He drew his sword from the sheath to behead Lakshmana. But Vashistha and Vama Deva intercepted and stopped him. They said that Rama should not punish Lakshmana without a proper inquiry. It was Ramarajya, that is, Rule of Law and nobody could pronounce a punishment without a proper inquiry or just cause. Therefore, Rama asked Lakshmana to explain the reason for his laughter. He in his turn bowed to the king his brother and explained:

'I have an explanation, my lord!
In the forest I was the sentry with bow and arrows.
One night, when you were asleep inside the parnasala,
Slumber overcame the whole living world from the ant to the lion.
I was the only one awake, watching over you and the hermitage.
The goddess of sleep was afraid to approach me,
She did not dare,
She made rustling sounds on the banks of the Godavari
And began to wail.
I approached her and asked her the reason.
She said "I am the Goddess of Slumber,
The eight elephants that watch the cardinal points,
The seven rishis of the Great Bear,
And the seven seas are now under the spell of sleep,
I rule over Vaikuntha.
All the birds, animals, mountains, rivers,
Trees and plants and human beings submit to me.
No human being can gain victory over me.
But my power is nullified before you.
This is against nature,
I have lost my suzerainty before you,
It is an insult to me and my supremacy."
Then I prostrated before the goddess and said,
"I am duty bound, I must keep guard over my brother and his wife.
I am a watchman to my brother Raghurama and his wife Sitadevi.

I am watchman to this parnasala,
I have come all the way from Ayodhya to serve them.
Thou should *now* to the city of Ayodhya,
There is the spouse who has been left there alone by her husband.
She should not be alone like that,
Both by day and by night envelop her with sleep.
Leave me to my ever-vigilant state,
After the return, when my Lord gets coronated in Ayodhya,
When he is happily surrounded by his ministers and guards,
You may come and possess me,
Till then, kindly spare me, O celestial one of sleep."
I thus importuned her.
She acquiesced and left me.
Today, during the full session of the royal assembly,
She appeared before me and began
Dancing on my eyelids.
That is why I laughed, my Lord.
Excuse me for my indecency and improper behaviour.'

Hearing this tale, Rama's heart melted. The selfless sacrifice made by his brother was brought home to him. Compared to the noble service rendered by Lakshmana at the altar of fraternal feelings, his own petulant action mortified him. He raised his arm with the drawn sword and tried to cut off his own head in order to make amends. The high priests Vashistha and Vama Deva prevented him. As a punishment the high priest suggested:

'O Ruler of the Earth: this is improper for you.
Allow Lakshmana to sleep on a royal couch,
You shall massage his feet.
This retribution is enough in the circumstances.'

Rama agreed. Lakshmana was on his couch, ready to sleep. Rama slyly entered the chamber lest any noise disturb his sleep. If Lakshmana awoke he would have prevented his elder brother from massaging his feet. Lakshmana was asleep no doubt, but the touch of Rama's palm distracted him. The first touch kept him silent. The next pressure of the palm was felt like a touch in a dream. The third made him open his eyes. He realized that it was no dream but reality—that the king was indeed massaging his feet. He rose up at once and prostrated before his eldest brother:

'With the touch of your foot Ahalya was purified,
Your foot rests on the head of the philanthropist Vali.
All the celestials pray at your feet
They massage your divine feet.
O Lord, you shall not touch my feet,
You must pardon me for sleeping unawares.'

Lakshmana offered his homage at the feet of Rama. Not only he but all the folk who have created this tale and its listeners seek the sacred feet of Rama. Rama raised his brother and said:

'Just as the moonless night is always dark,
So too is the royal assembly, bereft of you.'

The folk mind has created this incident, assigning vigilance around the clock to Lakshmana and deep slumber for fourteen years to his forlorn wife at the palace as a compensatory distribution of energies.

One cannot aptly describe the exuberant mood of Rama. He proposed that his three younger brothers should observe that night as one of consummation, a honeymoon night. In that royal household, Shantha always had the whiphand over things. (Even now in Andhra households, the daughter of the house has an eminent position.) Rama was curious to see the wives of his younger brothers. But in a royal household the young wives never appear before elders—and certainly not before the king. So he hid himself behind Shantha and Sita, and with Shatrughna by his side, stole a glance at the young brides. His paternal affection for them was unbounded. When the last of the brides passed by, Rama asked Shatrughna who she was. He kept silent and did not say that she was his queen.

A similar situation was introduced in Bhavabhuti's play *Uttararamacharita*. In the picture-gallery scene Sita showed Lakshmana Urmila's portrait and asked who she was. Here Rama pointed out the bride to Sita and in order to please Shatrughna, praised her charms. Shatrughna immediately replied:

'Brother Rama, you shall not say so,
Sita is the First Goddess of Wealth,
She is the Mother Goddess of the Worlds.'

That night was a honeymoon for all the bridal couples in the palace. Sita escorted Urmila to the bedchamber of Lakshmana, and Mandavi to her bridal couch to join Bharata. Sita gracefully walked into her own chamber to meet the Lord.

Instantly Rama saw the Goddess of Wealth approaching.
With ripples of laughter on his face he said,
'At the sight of green grass in summer, cows feel happy;
For the loyal wife, the sight of her lord gives happiness.'
During that night,
Like sugar dissolving in milk
Rama and Sita entwined themselves.
Like molasses Bharata and Mandavi were together.
As jaggery is mixed with fennel (jilakarra),
Lakshmana and Urmila met at amorous play.

But the youngest of the brides, Srutakiru, did not move towards the nuptial chamber of her lord. Shatrughna, waiting in vain, complained to his mother Kaushalya. She escorted the hesitant and bashful bride to her son's bedchamber. The bride was still in her teens, a mere girl still addicted to play and playthings. Kaushalya said to her:

'You shall now conduct your play on your lord's couch.'
The youngest bride was on the move
In the corridors of the palace
Her brightness tarnished the well-polished metal pillars
The lustre of the diamond lights brightened many-fold.
The sun rose but these happy bridal couples slept on.
Hanuman was requested to raise a fanfare to announce
The dawn. Trumpets blew.
The grooms were startled awake.
On the face of Bharata there were marks of turmeric,
On the forehead of Lakshmana there were marks of kumkum,
On the cheeks of Shatrughna there were strokes of collyrium.
Their brother-in-law Rishyasringa was there.
Embarrassed, they felt that he might ridicule them for their over-indulgence.
They refreshed themselves.

Thus erotic pleasures have been suggested naively and yet subtly in this folk ballad. Another feature of folk psychology could be noted in this poem—simple naturalness. An illustration serves the purpose.

Hanuman is a demigod both for the scholars and the common folk, but the latter enjoy joking about Hanuman. After all, he was a monkey, given to impishness. Their naturalness in describing the following incident disarms the scholarly rhetoricians. A grand royal feast was arranged the day following the honeymoon night. (The menu of the banquet is not detailed lest the listeners feel the descriptions are unreal, being far from their own world.) Rama was sitting with his friends, relatives and other guests. The party began to sing and narrate their experiences at Lanka. They forgot to invite or fetch Hanuman, who was momentarily forgotten by everyone assembled there for the feast. Hanuman entered the hall, murmuring. Rama realized his mistake in not extending an invitation to his great devotee and friend-in-need. It was too late for regrets. He decided to propitiate him and offer him his apologies. It was his duty to appease the neglected guest and induce him to partake in the feast which was half over. He approached the monkey chief:

'You are one of us, we kept silent.
You are the supreme friend, sit by my side.
It is because of you that I could secure Sita,
It is because of you that I am able to dine with my brothers,
Dear Hanuman, pay heed to my *apperd*,
Sit by my side, oh supreme friend.'

Hanuman's chagrin intensified. He was not so simple as to swallow the shallow explanation offered by Rama. But how was he to give vent to his anger? He replied:

'Am I your equal, to sit your side?
I am not the "Supreme friend".'

Thereby he sarcastically reproached not only Rama but all those who sat by Rama's side. But as he was a devotee of Rama, the remnants of his master's food were most precious to him.

He saw the well-filled plate of his master.
He snatched it away and went up a tree and settled himself there.
This joke is immensely popular with the rural folk.

He made a round of a mouthful.
He kept it on the branch,
Then threw away the golden plate as unwanted excess.
But his anger was not alleviated.
Rama went to the tree and
Implored him to come down.
He extended his hand and invited
Hanuman to alight from the tree.
The anger subsided. Hanuman seemed to be appeased.
Like a pet parrot he alighted on the arm of Rama
Rama placed him on the ground below, and adorned him with a pearl necklace.
Hanuman with this necklace round his neck remains the favourite demi-god of the rural folk, and at the same time a lovable creature full of pranks.

3. *Sitadevi anavahi* (Sita's identification) is a song that comes under the third category, that of songs woven around Sita.

When Hanuman starts out to search for Sita he asks Lord Rama how to identify Sita and convince her that he is a messenger from Ramachandra. At that time Rama describes Sita's beauty and narrates some interesting incidents from their marital life. The description of Sita is superb. Not only Hanuman but ordinary human beings like us can easily identify Sita, through these identification marks that glorify her beauty.

'O Hanuman, I will tell you how to identify Sita, listen.
Her dark tresses are undressed; they are matted and very long.
She looks as if she has taken an oil bath, though she has not.
She looks as if she has smeared raw turmeric, though she has not.
She looks as if she has applied collyrium, though she has not,
She looks as if she has applied a beauty spot, though she has not,
She looks as if she has put on ornaments, though she has not,
She looks as if she is chewing betel leaf, though she is not,
She looks if she is decorated, though she is not,
She looks like a gem tied in a worn-out black cloth
She looks like the water in cold winter
She looks like the Veda studied on Padyami day,
Shorn of all her glory and brilliance.'

This is the description of Sita's physical beauty and charm, which has no parallel. Now I will quote a couple of memorable incidents pertaining to the conjugal life of this divine couple, born of imaginative folklore.

The first incident pertains to their wedding. While Sita was playing *vamanaguntalu* with her friends in the wedding hall, Rama desired to have a look at her and subsequently came to the hall. Sita's friends first saw him and began describing his beautiful eyes full of longing to see Sita. They said to her, 'O Janaki, Rama has come to see you. His eyes are beautiful, his eyes are charming; they are shining like lights. He is like the Lord of Love.' Sita bowed her head in shyness and slipped away to her mother's chambers. She stood near her mother with head bowed. In the meantime, her mother realized that Rama was approaching. She too said, 'O Sita, look, Sri Rama is coming to see you. Sri Rama is coming to talk to you.' Sita, still shy, bowed her head and stood still. Rama says that this is an incident he will never forget. He asks Hanuman to narrate this episode to Sita so that she may believe him to be a messenger from Rama. This incident depicts Sita's innocent and childlike bashfulness which is very dear to the folk mind.

Rama narrates further. 'O Hanuman, there is one more incident. Don't forget to narrate this to my Sita. One day while she was combing her long hair she saw her own image in the mirror standing in her bedroom. She asked me, "Who is this lady with such a beautiful and charming shape and gait?" She then rushed towards me and said, "O Rama, O Ayodhya Rama, you are deceiving the world. My father gave me to you thinking that you are ek patni vrata. You are now unmasked. Is it fair to keep such a bewitching and enticing woman in your bedroom?" Knowing her innocence I inwardly laughed at her ignorance. I caught her by the hand and told her, "My darling, you are very angry because you saw that lonely lady without her husband. Will you be pacified if I show you her husband?" Then I ordered a life-size-mirror. After cleaning it well, I placed it in front of her. She saw two people—a man and a woman—in that mirror. When I reassured her that they were only Rama and Sita, she fell at my feet. O Hanuman, remind her of this incident without fail.'

This also describes Sita's innocent and charming beauty of which she was unaware, especially when she was alone without Rama at her side. This is a chaste and pious delineation of Indian womanhood.

Rama narrates another incident which occurred during their exile. One day when they were wandering at Chitrakut, Sita prepared for her bath. She smeared her body with raw turmeric and went to the pond to take a dip. But she returned almost immediately, complaining to Rama her lord and the descendant of the solar race that there was something strange near the bathing pond. The mischievous moon was playing in the pond, with innumerable bees flying over it, making it impossible for her to bathe. She asked him to accompany her so that he could see for himself. Rama was perturbed and followed her to the pond. When they reached, Sita pointed to the 'moon and bees'. Rama was amused and told her that the 'moon' was her own face and the 'bees' were locks of her hair. When she realized her mistake, she bashfully bowed her head. 'Therefore, Hanuman, you must narrate this incident to Sita so that she may know you to be my confidante,' Rama told him.

There are scores of such beautiful incidents that illustrate the folk versions of the Ramayana stories in Telugu. Only a glimpse has been provided in the above essay.

SITA'S TRIAL BY FIRE AND BHOJPURI WOMEN'S SONGS

SMITA TEWARI JASSAL

FOR AN EXPLORATION into the meaning of Sita for the peasant women of the Bhojpuri-speaking region, a good starting point is the Rama Lila of Ramnagar, near Benaras. It is enacted over a period of thirty-one days, with the theatrical action taking place on five makeshift stages. Peasant women, at once audience and pilgrims, often choose to give the stage-Sita company, rarely leaving her side as she sits in captivity in the Ashok garden of the demon king, Ravana. While the audience moves with the actors to the sites where the action is being staged, it is the way that women choose to express solidarity with Sita, and their complete identification with her plight, that lingers on, with all its poignancy and pathos, even after the festival is over, that invites questions about the deeper meaning of Sita for the peasant woman's consciousness.

Contrast the passive stillness of these women at the staging of Tulsidas' *Ramacharitmanas* at Ramnagar to the imagery of Sita's trial by fire, a recurring motif in the *jatsaar*, or the peasant women's 'ballads of the millstone', undoubtedly the most tragic genre of Bhojpuri folk songs. Like Sita who had to furnish proof of her chastity, the heroines of the jatsaar are also put to various tests by fire. In the ballad of 'Satmal', which tells the story of a sister of seven brothers, the heroine appears wearing a gold necklace that glints as it catches the rays of the sun while she serves and offers water to her close affines. One by one, each of them inquires about the source of the necklace. In turn, each is told that it is a gift from her brothers. Finally, at the suggestion of her unconvinced husband, and in a turn of events evocative of Sita's trial by fire, Satmal must take the ultimate test in a vat of heated oil. The ballad states:

Rama charhi gai dharami karahiya ho na
Dhadhaki aginiya Satmal koodiein ho na
Khaulat telwa mein Satmal koodein ho na
Dhadhaki aginiya bujhee gailee ho na

In the centre the vat of truth is ready
In the flames leapt Satmal
In the burning oil she leapt
And then the flames died down.

As the vat is being prepared, she sends a message home but by the time her brothers arrive, it is too late—Satmal has already jumped into the hot oil! Now the husband reproaches himself for harbouring destructive suspicions against his chaste wife. Regret and remorse take over as he wonders where he'll ever find a wife as pure as Satmal.

In Valmiki's Ramayana, the motif of trial by fire is as much about Rama's test and transformation in consciousness regarding his own divinity, as about Sita. The song of Satmal offers a glimpse into the anguished mental state of a husband, who like Rama, must succumb to the censorious pressures of patriarchy instead of offering his wife protection against it. And just as Agni, in the Ramayana, is scorched and extinguished by the greater *tej* (inner fire) of Sita who emerges unscathed, so also is this heroine unharmed by the flames as they die down on her entry into the cauldron.

A return to Mother Earth or to surrender to elements like fire is a compelling motif in these women's tales, which is invoked to underline the need to transcend 'this-worldly' concerns or even to unleash the 'superhuman' potentialities of women. In another women's ballad, 'Tikuli', the protagonist becomes the object of her elder brother-in-law's sexual attentions, and is lured away by him into the woods where her husband lies dead. She invokes Agni with the plea that fire should envelop her before she loses her virtue. The ballad goes:

Sat ke to haile saami
Are ghar ki biyahuwa nu re ki

Anchra se aagiya hey oothle
Sami mukh tarle nu re ki

If indeed I am a chaste
And wedded wife
Then from my bosom cloth should rise
The fire offered to the husband's pyre.

Scarcely are these sentiments uttered than fire indeed rises to engulf Tikuli and save her from the impending violation—a fate that must surely be perceived as worse than death. With minor variations, such solutions occur repeatedly in the jatsaars, for which the term 'singing bitterness' seems apt. The last lines of another ballad that evoke the same mood, applaud the decision of the woman protagonist, who chooses to avoid shame by willingly taking her own life rather than entering into an illicit relationship. The lyrics of this ballad are:

Jo ham hobai sat ke raniywa ho na
Hamra achre se dhadhake aginiya ho na
Are hoi jaate dunu jan satiyva ho na
Jab lag jethwa agni le kar aaave ho na
Are rama tab lag duno jan bhaile satiyva ho na
Are rama kaal ke bitin budhiywa rakhlis ho na
Are bhaiya se gaili aur bahuiyo se na

If I am indeed the queen of chastity
Let the fire rise from my upper garment
And devour us both
And while elder brother went to fetch the fire
Both were burnt to ashes
(They said) this young one had her wits about her
But he lost his brother as well as his brother's wife.

Alas, in these tales, suspicions about women's purity can only be laid to rest after a heavy price has been extracted from them. It is through such ordeals that women's chastity is confirmed and threats to the patriarchal order contained. Through the act of death staged in the ordeal by fire, women, like their ideal Sita, not only avert the misfortune of an illicit or threatening relationship, but also secure for themselves an elevated status that in reality is denied to ordinary rural women.

Women of all castes sing these folk songs in an endearing manner, with a great deal of pathos and conviction, without the slightest hint of recognition of the extent to which they themselves may have imbibed the values of patriarchy or indeed, how they might be complicit in their own oppression. The endorsement that the songs receive from peasant women is also reflective of the extent to which they have themselves internalized a specific 'male' view of their sexuality.

How then are we to explain the apprehensions inherent in the following intriguing and rare wedding song set? It articulates an alternative voice and viewpoint, among the hundreds sung across caste divides, that celebrate nuptials by evoking Rama and Sita as the ideal couple.

Tilak chharhhai Baba ghare chali alien, Aama dehariya dhaile thhar
Kahu kahu Raja ho Ram ke suratiya, kavna nacchtare avatar ho
Kaa ham kahin Rani Ram ke suratiya, Ram surajwa ke jot
Ram ke jyoti dehin adit chhapit bhailen, mohi rahlen pasuram
Pheri avaou Baba tilak ke dinawa, balu ham rahbon kunwaar ji

The engagement settled, father returned home, mother waited at the door
Tell us about Rama's beauty, under which auspicious star did he take birth as divine
How shall I describe Rani, Rama's beauty, his countenance [like] the rays of the sun itself
The sun was made in Rama's likeness, none other than Him that Parsuram adored
Break off the engagement, father, I'd much rather stay unmarried.

Was it Sita's tragic fate and impending ordeal that prompted this daughter's unusual request to break off an engagement with maryada purushottam Rama, that 'most exemplary among men'? In the context of the fire ordeal, the price would indeed seem too high to pay for ordinary mortals, especially as wedding songs often underline the impossible standards set by the unattainable ideal, Rama. Here is a typical wedding song:

Purub khojalon beti pacchim khojlon, khojlon orissa jagarnath
Charon buvan beti bar eik khojila, katihen ne milen siri Ram

Searched the east, searched the west, as far as Orissa and Jagannath
In all four directions, daughter, searched for a groom but nowhere did I find Sri Rama.

The theme of chastity, and women's understanding of Sita as symbolizing it, is foregrounded in the following meditation on that extraordinary moment when Queen Mandodari, the wife of Sita's abductor, Ravana, pays Sita a visit. The song begs understanding at many levels:

Siya ji se milane Mandodari chali aayii
Aare suraj joti ke lahanga pahine
Chandra joti thahrai
Sooraj joti jab Siya ji ke dekhlasi
Sudhi-budhi sakal bhulai
Jo tuhun rahalu satya ke Sita
Anka bhataar sang kaahe chali aayi
Aare ham to rahli satya ke Sita
Tohre rajwa dekhe chali aayi
Atana bachan jab sunali Mandodari
Nayan se neer dharai

Mandodari came up to pay Sita a visit
In her grand and dazzling finery.
It turned as cool as a moonbeam
In Sita's fiery luminous presence, like the sun
Was struck speechless with awe and wonder.
'If you were indeed so chaste and pure, Sita
How come you went off with the husband of another?'
'Chaste and pure I ever was
Merely came to see this kingdom of yours.'
On hearing these words
Tears rolled down Mandodari's eyes.

The song notes the transformation in the consciousness of Mandodari, when she is confronted with Sita's divinity and awe-inspiring presence. When Mandodari sets out to confront Sita, it is once again Sita's fire of chastity that first 'melts' down her pride, then evokes reverence and humility. A question hovers over Sita's abduction, and there is a conundrum about whether or not such a fate might in any way diminish her. But the way Sita handles her misfortune and conducts herself is nothing short of exemplary. Pathos and empathy are highlighted in these lines. Hence, instead of the challenging mood of rivalry suggested at the beginning of the encounter between Mandodari and Sita, what we witness is a shedding of layers of artifice in a final expression of feminine solidarity and understanding.

In contrast to the 'fierce feminine' imagery of the jatsaars that evoke Sita's trial by fire, is the following song that enumerates the range of beings from the human and animal worlds which witness the abduction of Sita. In their link with Rama's pain, they secure a hallowed place in the sacred universe, except for one species, a pair of chatak birds. So engrossed were they in lovemaking that they failed to see the abduction. Consequently, the birds could not inform Rama about the direction taken by Ravana's chariot.

Lakari chirat tuhun loharwa chokarwa
Eihi rahihe dekhuwa Sita ho jaak
Hamahun to seli Rama Sita ke palangiya
Sita ke Ravanva hari le jaak
Kapara dhowat tuhun dhobin bitiya
Eihi raahi dekhuwa Sita ho jaak
Hamahun to phichin Rama sita ke chunariya
Sita ke Rawanawa har le jaak
Eihi paar jatwa ho, oh paar jataaiya
Eihi rahihe dekhuwa Sita ho jaak
Hamahun to rahin rama apana Chakuwa jare
Ham naahin dekhuwa Sita ho jaak
Din bhar chakwa ho joriya milhiya
Saanjh beriiya rahiha ho cchipaaiy

The woodcutter's son, fashioning wood, says,
'Along this road, I saw Sita being taken away
I sewed Sita's cot

Saw that Ravana abducted Sita along this road.'
The washerman's daughter washing clothes, claims,
'I, who wash Sita's *chunari*
Saw Sita abducted by Ravana.'
On this side, Jat and on the other side, Jatni
Saw Sita being abducted along this road.
'So engrossed was I in my *Chakwa*
I didn't see Sita go by.'
So, all day long the chatak birds may pair
But at dusk must pine for each other in vain.

Indifference to Sita's plight, even as an oversight, is a lapse for which the birds are held guilty. In the last two lines, the terrible curse of separation that the species will have to bear for eternity, is spelt out. Lack of empathy for Sita's misfortune, indifference and the inability to bear witness to her abduction, results in a lack of unity, eternal yearning and separation. In brief, the judgement pronounced in the song is nothing short of a cosmic sentencing.

Empathy with Sita then, is a value that the peasant women understand and deeply experience in their own lives. From wedding songs celebrating the marriage of the ideal couple, Rama and Sita, to those describing scenes of Sita's devotion and domesticity, and even in the pedagogical jatsaars, it is the peasant women's own selves that stand reflected. Hence, for the women as 'spectator–pilgrims', the unique opportunity to spontaneously express solidarity with Sita at the Ramnagar Rama Lila could be described as affirming, even transformative. For all its poignancy, however, this particular expression of peasant women's agency remains confined within the process of patriarchal production.

SITA IN THE ORIYA RAMAYANA

G.K. DAS

AT THE SIXTH International Oral History Conference held in 1987 at St John's College, Oxford, the subject deliberated upon was 'Myth and History'. Astute exponents of oral history rightly expressed reservations about the historian's traditional preoccupation with 'reality' and concrete 'fact', and dismissal of 'myth' as an ingredient of history. In that context the Ramayana, much of which is based on oral history and has often been read as '*itihas*', becomes a controversial text, for not every individual, location, or action described in it was real or a fact.

Archaeologists, on the basis of evidence, have confirmed some locations that figure prominently in Valmiki's epic. It has also been asserted by learned scholars like R.C. Dutt in *The Great Epics of India: Ramayana*, for example, that the narrative actually 'relates to the ancient traditions of two powerful races, the Kosalas and the Videhas, who lived in North India between the twelfth and tenth centuries before Christ'.

The text, whether Valmiki's or Kamban's, Tulsi Das's *Ramacharitmanas* or Balarama Dasa's *Jagamohan Ramayana*, is a composite construct, to the making of which myth, folklore and history together have made significant contributions. A literary (or culture-related) text cannot be fully identified with any specific genre of written *itihas* (history) or *puran* (myth).

From the time of Balarama Dasa (16 AD), who is known to have given *diksha* or spiritual initiation to Sri Chaitanya at the instance of Raja Prataprudra Deb and was designated by the latter as the Supreme

Guru, to that of the modern icon of Oriya 'Yatra' literature, Baishnab Pani (1882–1956), some fifty different versions and varieties of the story of Rama are said to have been written in Oriya. One can observe that in this rich and eclectic tradition there are two eminently distinguished portrayals of Sita, the beleaguered queen of Ayodhya, and the vivacious and innovative woman. Let me illustrate this by discussing four different versions of the story of Rama written by Oriya poets at different points of time.

These four versions are: the *Jagamohan Ramayana* or Dandi or the 'Dakshini' (southern) Ramayana of the Vaisnavite poet Balarama Dasa; the *Vilanka Ramayana* in two different versions written by Sarala Dasa/Siddheswar Dasa; the Ramlila, which is an improvised, or written script based on amateurish popular performance of the story of Rama; and the vast body of hymns, songs and dance-drama based on selected episodes from the story of Rama and Sita.

JAGAMOHAN RAMAYANA

Balarama Dasa's work remains an all-time classic. It is recited in the Oriya household, despite the occasional archaisms in the expression, as a sacred and popular text, especially in the month of Kartik. Following basically the Valmiki Ramayana, but also departing from it by virtue of its strong local colour, the *Jagamohan Ramayana* portrays both Sita and Rama as divine constructs of ideal womanhood/manhood. Sita is portrayed as an embodiment of beauty, purity, wifely chastity and devotion. Traditionally, the Oriya woman has looked at her as the exemplar of femininity. Eminent modern scholars like Mayadhar Mansingh and Surendra Mohanty both see her as a paragon of Oriya womanhood: a 'grihalaksmi' as well as her husband's companion, embodying incomparable grace and a rich feminine sensibility combined with an unflinching sense of devotion to her husband, family and relations. To the ideologically committed feminist, however, Balarama Dasa's Sita may appear as a glorious victim because of her blind love for her husband even when she knows that Rama was brutally unfair to her in asking her to undergo the 'chastity' test twice in 'public interest'.

There are two interpretations as to why Balarama Dasa's Ramayana was titled *Jagamohan Ramayana.* The term 'Jagamohan' in temple architecture refers to the small '*pidha*' (platform) temple in front of the main temple; next to it is the '*natya mandap*' where temple dances are performed; next to that is the '*bhoga mandap*' and then comes the sanctum sanctorum. Balarama Dasa was a frequent visitor to the Jagannath temple in Puri where sitting in the Jagamohan he is believed to have composed parts of his Ramayana, which is why his work came to be called *Jagamohan Ramayana*.

Another explanation given is that the word 'Jagamohan' which lexically means 'universally charming' was probably thought appropriate as a title for Balarama Dasa's widely popular kavya. (See Sitakant Mahapatra, 'Jagmohan Ramayan of Balrama Dasa: Inheritance and Innovations' in Avadesh Kumar Singh (ed.) *Ramayana Through the Ages*, 2007)

Vilanka Ramayana

Based in significant ways on the Sanskrit text *Adbhuta Ramayana*, also attributed to Valmiki, the *Vilanka Ramayana* is believed to be the work of Orissa's 'Adikavi' Sarala Dasa of the fifteenth century, writes Mayadhar Mansingh. Some later scholars, no less competent, like Banshidhar Mohanty and Krushna Charan Sahoo, however, hold the view that the real author of the *Vilanka Ramayana* was one Siddheswar Dasa of the post-sixteenth century period. Incidentally, Siddheswar Dasa was also another name of 'Adikavi' Sarala Dasa. The main text of the *Vilanka Ramayana*, the authorship of which is still a debatable matter, is an epic of lesser merit than Valmiki or Balarama Dasa's monumental work. Posterior in time, it is a narrative of the 'thousand-headed' demon, ruling the land of Vilanka, who wants to avenge the death of his fellow-king Ravana by killing Rama, but is eventually defeated and destroyed by the active intervention and ingenuity of Sita. It shows Sita not only as a super strategist in conflict and war, but as a woman with an innate mental as well as physical superiority to the might of the thousand-headed Ravana or of Rama himself.

During an interesting dialogue between Rama and Sita following the war, Sita claims the credit for having killed the tyrant and oppressor of gods and angels, Vilanka Ravana. The relevant text (translated) is as follows:

Janaki told her lord not to swear,
she it was not he who killed
the thousand-headed demon
of Vilanka, who would never
be vanquished but for her.
'You only killed the ten-headed Ravana.'

When the war between the warriors on the side of demon king of Vilanka is in progress, frustration and despair shroud the camp of Rama at one stage because of the apparently unconquerable mettle of the tyrant. Once, by a mere clap of Ravana's hands, Rama was blown away and thrown at a distance. Hanuman shoots at the tyrant five lakh arrows first, then another seven lakh and yet another ten lakh but his efforts are in vain. Sita becomes furious at that sight. Lakshmana too is defeated by the demon king of Vilanka. Finally, it is agreed upon that Sita alone would be able to vanquish Ravana.

When Rama hears this he feels hesitant to ask his consort, who, being a woman, he had thought to be delicate of nerves, to come to their rescue. None can convince or persuade him to take Sita's help in winning the war. A disturbing silence and uncertainty prevail in Rama's camp. Finally, Rama is persuaded to ask Hanuman to approach Sita for help. Sita immediately rises to the occasion and to a personal as well as a patriotic cause. She assumes an extraordinary and never-seen-or-known-before (*apurva*) image and appears on the battlefield. She knows that fighting the demon with the usual war-weapons is no good, for in war success alone counts, for the end justifies the means. Even Sri Krishna in the Mahabharata says so and urges Partha to fight and destroy the wicked and the inglorious.

With remarkable presence of mind and pragmatism Sita decides to use a new fighting skill with which to confront the thousand-headed tyrant. Using the five-arrowed weapon of Cupid, the '*panchasar*' of Kandarp, she shoots at the demon and unsettles him. Hit by the 'panchasar' the mighty king of Vilanka, tyrant and oppressor of gods and angels, melts and approaches Sita with the humility of a mendicant. He begs for her love and implores the 'pure woman' or 'sati' to be his wife, and forsake Rama. At this moment Rama, with his bow and arrow in hand, cuts the tyrant's head with a sword and goes on to separate five hundred of his heads. The demon king of Vilanka thus meets his end at the hands of his enemy and due to the wise, prudent and all-seeing intelligence of Sita.

At the end of the narrative the gods and angels sing in jubilation and celebrate their freedom from tyranny. They bring an iron plough for Sita and Rama with which the triumphant couple plough through the kingdom of Vilanka, symbolizing the equality of the high and low. The plough is symbolic. Associated with the birth of Sita, its 'levelling' role at the end of the narrative heralds a new age that will be free from inequality and oppression. The act of ploughing is also associated with fertility to which the Sita of *Vilanka Ramayana* is linked. She comes through in the text as a unique representation of Indian womanhood striving for a balance of her various capabilities.

The Rama Lila

The 'Rama Lila' tradition in Orissa is age-old. Celebrated annually on the occasion of the birth of Rama, it is immensely popular. Women, men and children in the villages especially, participate in it with a deep sense of involvement. The nine-day performance enacts the story of Sita and Rama and gives people an experience of re-living the myth year after year. To them the deities are actually present before them during the celebration. Choruses of jubilation and tears mark the celebration; jubilation on occasions like the marriage of the prince and princess; tears on account of their 'vanavas' or exile from the kingdom of Ayodhya for fourteen long years, or Sita going into the burning flames or her leaving the world and being received into the bosom of Mother Earth.

Hymns and Songs

The narration of the 'Rama Katha' in the form of hymns and lyrics composed by poets is an all-India phenomenon. The most popular among these composers was Tulsidas. His songs are sung nationwide and modern singers of Rama *bhajan*s like D.V. Paluskar and Lata Mangeskar hold immense appeal for people of all ages. In Orissa, the tradition of hymns and devotional songs written on the story of Sita and Rama is largely contemporaneous with the tradition initiated by

Tulsidas. In fact, a moving and widely known composition by Balarama Dasa, the author of *Jagamohan Ramayana*, belongs to an earlier period. It is 'Kanta Koili', a touching poem in which Sita imprisoned in Ravana's Ashok van laments her separation from Rama. In her sad loneliness, Sita is narrating her tale to the cuckoo and hoping that a message will be carried by the bird to her Lord, and he would fight Ravana and rescue her.

This tradition of Ramayana literature which was carried on in Orissa in later years was strengthened with the works of a number of poets who followed Balarama Dasa. Some of the highly gifted and popular poets in this tradition are: Achyutananda Dasa (16th century AD), Arjuna Dasa (16th century AD), Salabega (17th century AD), Dina Krushna Dasa (17–18th century AD), Upendra Bhanja (17–18th century AD) and Gangadhar Meher (1862–1924). Bhanja's well-known kavya *Vaidehishavilas* and Meher's *Tapaswini* are both among classics of Orissa's remarkably original and innovative *kavya*s devoted to the story of Sita and Rama.

Both the poets Upendra Bhanja and Gangadhar Meher have written the story of Sita and Rama in a highly individualistic fashion. Bhanja, the older of the two, himself belonged to a princely family of southern Orissa. He wrote in an ornate and Sanskritized style, using a measured metrical pattern. His *Vaidehishavilas* is an erudite work, not easily understood by the common reader. But it is amazingly popular with the common folk who sit for hours on a summer day listening to his poetic narrative being recited by a learned speaker or a group of Pala singers. Pala is a popular art form that consists of a poetical presentation by a group of five or six people who sing and explicate to a large public audience a mythological or actual story from history. Bhanja was a great devotee of Rama. His images of Sita and Rama as presented in the *Vaidehishavilas* are remarkably romantic and vital. They are portrayed as a youthful and immensely attractive couple exuding divine splendour and grace. In the description of their wedding ceremony the poet's attention is evocatively centred on Sita. To Bhanja, love was a divine passion and the body its holy source. There can be nothing vulgar or obscene about the human body or in love. Accordingly, Sita in *Vaidehishavilas* is shown as a woman of flesh and blood as well as a divine spirit. Bhanja saw no contradiction between the divine and the human, that is, a human of the purest kind: pure of heart, in feeling, thinking and action. Bhanja's Sita is one of the world's most adorable creations: full of womanly charm, gifted with a quiet yet robust sexuality and divine passion.

Gangadhar Meher, author of *Tapaswini*, the story of Sita's exile, was from western Orissa's district Sambalpur. He belonged to a family of weavers. Growing up in a humble home, he was temperamentally modest. His love for working-class people gave his writing its plain core of substance and its day-to-day spoken idiom. Written in an unadorned lyrical form, it excels in invoking sympathy for Sita in her exile. Nature too seems to be in sympathy with her. A delicate and romantic woman, Meher's Sita strongly resembles Kalidasa's Sakuntala in the poetic play *Abhijnanasakuntalam*, which is one of the most widely translated, read and performed works of India. Meher believed an ideal woman to be an embodiment of sweetness and grace as also a fusion of natural and human piety. The Sita of *Tapaswini* is a perfect image of such womanhood.

Early Traditions

In medieval Orissa, when Sarala Dasa and Balarama Dasa wrote, Vedic learning was common among the Brahmins. Both Sarala Dasa and Balarama Dasa say in their kavyas that they were unlettered and ignorant. But it was an expression of authorial humility rather than a fact. The *Sarala Mahabharata* and the *Jagamohan Ramayana* in fact show astute knowledge of the Vedas, Puranas and other kavyas written in Sanskrit, such as Vyasa's Mahabharata and Valmiki's Ramayana, although both the Oriya kavyas have strong local colour and flavour infused by the two exceptionally gifted and pioneering authors. The Oriya texts were composed by the 'Sudra' authors in protest against the hegemony of Brahmins and the Sanskrit language, to provide the vast majority of people of the lower classes access to the sacred texts, a privilege that had been denied to them in the past.

As we have seen, Balarama Dasa's *Jagamohan Ramayana* portrays Sita as a woman of supreme grace and power. This was the representation of Sita not only in the *Rig Veda* and the *Atharva Veda*, it apparently was a historical fact. Several old inscriptions bear testimony to the fact that women in medieval Orissa played an important role in administration. Some queens of the Bhauma Kara dynasty occupied the throne in the absence of male heirs, according to a well-researched monograph, *Life in Medieval Orissa* by Ayodhya Prasad Sah. On occasion, it goes on to point out that the queens were empowered to register land charters and women of royal households were trained in the art of government and given certain privileges.

To sum up, Orissa's long and rich Ramayana tradition shows that Sita, one of the greatest creations of the Indian imagination, is both the glorious victim as well as the triumphant woman. If the *Jagamohan Ramayana* and other versions and variations of Ramayana written in the Oriya language and the myth and folklore associated with the story of Sita and Rama are any guide, womanhood in India/Orissa in the past was both traditional and surprisingly avant-garde.

CREATIVE INTERPRETATIONS

READING PICTURES: SITA IN VICTORIAN INDIAN PRINTS

AMAN NATH

'The British, too, were divided on this issue of sensuality and Puritanism. Some of the British, especially in the early colonial period, admired and celebrated the sensuality of Hinduism. Others, particularly but not only the later Protestant missionaries, despised what they regarded as Hindu excesses. Unfortunately, many educated Hindus took their cues from the second sort of Brit and became ashamed of the sensuous aspects of their own religion, aping the Victorians (who were, after all, very Victorian), becoming more Protestant than thou.'

Wendy Doniger

AS INDIAN MYTHS passed through the colonized cleansing of Victorian England, Indians began to view themselves through the colonizer's eyes. While posturing and portraiture began to reflect the influences of the photo studio, compositions too became rather like arrangements for group photographs.

The coy, double-standard morality which wavered between suppressed instinct and public rectitude is evident in this *Sitaram Samvad*. Only the *nayak* and *nayika*—the heroic subjects of this romance—look at each other as Kama, the god of love, has just shot his arrows. Observe the gaze of the others, turned away, to comprehend the prudish morality of the moment, almost as if no one has seen them. Sita has turned her neck and her waist is in pivot. As if to look was to flaunt, to say too much.

Dutiful Sita held firmly by Rama, in total possession. Already Raja Ravi Varma (1848–1906) had cast his mould for that pan-Indian, head covered, sari-clad woman. Lakshmana, the obedient brother of Rama, looks vacantly away, for his is only a shadow role.

Lakshmana continues to be absent in his presence because Sita flouts the rules of public morality to lean romantically on her husband's shoulder. Normally this would be a closed-door, after-dark gesture. The boatman who ferries them across is busy reciprocating the task of transportation—rowing his lord from one bank to the other, much as Rama will row him across to heaven for this good deed.

In a curious representation of Rama, Sita and Surpanakha *nasikachchedan*, from the Chitrashala Press, Pune, the 'demoness' turns her back to Rama and Sita for an inspection of her feigned innocence. Both Rama and Sita look relaxed and no threat seems to lurk in the air.

Anant Shivaji Desai's pastoral representation of an Indian forest landscape in Western guise has all the European lessons in perspective, light and shadow, and academic detailing. Actress-like in her posture, Sita plays the non-suspecting, about-to-be abducted nayika, the golden-deer disguise not even evident to the viewer of this work.

Sitaharan or the abduction of Sita, as depicted in the rather luminous print from the Chore Bagan Art Studio, creates a diagonal divide in the composition for the initiated viewer. This unnatural gap is the *lakshman rekha.* The fluent eyes, which were observed in the oleographs and lithographs from Maharashtra in the west, have been carried over to this depiction made in Bengal, in the east.

A saddened Sita whiles away time at Ravana's Ashok vatika. The clear academic modelling shows in the realism of everything which surrounds her, including the studio model's stool and the terracotta pot which recalls an urban nursery rather than vatika or grove. Even the sari, worn well and stylistically modelled, is not one of a vanavas or forest exile, but embellished with an eye for fashion. The props of animal skin and wandering hens bring a domestic courtyard to mind.

This coronation oleograph of Rama, painted and printed abroad—Austria, in this case—gives Rama's skin a silvery blue lustre as he is Vishnu's incarnation. But the faces draw attention—all are similar, grim, un-Indian with an uncertain regard like self-conscious actors trying to look away from the camera lens. Sita sits on Rama's left (the side traditionally offered to men), just as Parvati does. The awkwardness continues with her right arm possessively owning Rama—as no Indian woman claims her man. The *bhakti bhava* of Hanuman also presents a sorry picture.

As a closing counternote to the Sita–Rama sequence, a traditional depiction of the Shiva–Parvati concept of ardhanarishwara, the androgynous ideal of human and divine partnerships. As ardhanarishwara, the composite male–female yin–yang of Indian mythology, the Shiva–Parvati concept has few equals that can improve on its symbolism. To complete this liason and crossover, the vahanas or vehicles of Shiva and Parvati have been inverted, as also the water from the mouth of Ganga, placed within Parvati's hair, counterposes the heat of the flames.

THE DAY OF THE GOLDEN DEER

SHASHI DESHPANDE

WHY DOES HE not speak? He stands silent and withdrawn, his gaze turned inwards. The horses, the chariot, the charioteer, all of them silhouetted against the slowly darkening sky, are quiet and still, like figures in a dream. The birds, except for their soft rustling sounds, are mute too. Even the river at my feet seems caught up in this fearful spell of silence and slithers past in a subdued whisper.

Foreboding? I can swear that there had been none; but now the ominous hush brings on a sudden onset of fear.

And then the silence breaks.

'I must speak,' he says, harsh and abrupt.

No, I want to cry out, *don't say it, I don't want to hear it.*

It is too late. There is little enough for him to say and it is soon done. I hear the words, but for a while, they mean nothing; there is just blankness. Then, in one moment, the knowledge of what he has said surges over me, inundating me like a river in flood. A moment of such fearful agony that I feel I will disintegrate. Have I not gone through this, have I not lived through such a moment before? Yes, I have, on that day, the day of the golden deer, when I had felt the iron hands of the seemingly gentle hermit grip me. Now I feel them again, alien hands on me, cruel, hard and hurting. With an effort greater than I have ever made in my life, I take hold of myself. And, in a voice so calm that I can scarcely recognize it as my own, I ask him, almost in a whisper, 'But, why, Lakshmana? Why?'

I wait for a reply. I wait patiently until I know that there will be none. And then I have to speak myself, 'And is that all? Is that all the message you bring from your brother to me, his wife?'

He has been looking steadily at his feet all the while. Now, he raises his head and looks at me, for the first time, I realize, since he came to me, asking me to get ready.

I was sitting idle then, absorbed in my own thoughts, in the movements of the child within me, movements as light as fluttering leaves. At his words, I got up eagerly, so eagerly that I stumbled and would have fallen, had not one of my women held and steadied me.

'Go out?' I asked Lakshmana, suddenly lifted out of a placid contentment into happiness. 'And there? Near the river? Your brother suggested that, didn't he? I know he must have; he can look into my mind. Yes, just now, before you came, I was thinking of the few days we lived there and how happy we were then. We were happy, were we not, Lakshmana? Now, when they speak of it to me, they say, "It must have been a terrible time." They speak of all the days of our exile as days of sorrow. They don't understand. When we were together, the three of us, we were happy. You felt that way too, didn't you? And free. Free, as if when we walked out of the palace, we left all the unhappiness behind. I can remember that.'

But Lakshmana's face . . . why did he look that way? It suddenly occurred to me that my words brought back to him the terrible news that came to us when we were there. The news of their father's death. Contrite, I began to correct myself, when I noticed that it was a frown of impatience. Yes, of course, Lakshmana, eager to do any duty imposed on him by his brother, was impatient for us to go.

'But I am keeping you,' I said apologetically. 'I will get ready at once.' I suddenly turned back as I was leaving the room. 'Is the king not coming with us?'

'No, he is busy.'

'Busy? Too busy to spend some time with his wife?'

Trying to conceal my wistfulness, I adopted a light tone. But Lakshmana did not respond. Again I thought—what is it? Is he angry? No, not that. But, what is it then?

'You must remember he is a king, a king with many duties,' he said, as if speaking of a man who was unknown to me. Why was he speaking in this formal way? I thought it very strange. 'A very great king,' he added, the tone that of a man trying to convince someone.

Me? Or was it himself he was trying to convince? But I did not pursue the thought. I hastened to get ready, to come here to this place. To listen to *this*?

I stand mute, willing him to go on. Surely there is more? But I will not speak, I will let him speak; it is for him to tell me, not for me to ask. Stammering, nervous, confused, Lakshmana finally completes what he has to say. Excusing his brother. Telling me why the king has to do this. Only then do I open my mouth to ask, 'And since when does a king listen to the gossip of common people?'

'Queen,' he begins, giving me my formal title, as if reminding me of my position, when I blaze out, 'Queen! No, don't call me queen, I am no queen if the king casts me off. I am nothing. No,' I correct myself, 'I go back to being what I was. The daughter of King Janaka. No, not even that. I am just Sita.'

I can see that my anger astonishes him. What had he expected? Tears? Reproaches? Entreaties? Yes, they are all there, waiting inside me, clamouring for release. Wanting me to cry out—not to this man, who is only a messenger, but to the man who has sent the message—'*I am innocent, I am blameless. How can you do this to me? I have your child in my womb. My child . . .*'

My child . . . No, I cannot, I will not say these words. I know in an instant how I am going to endure. If I grieve, if I cry or complain, I am indeed lost. Nothing can uphold me now but anger; I have to hold on to that.

'No, no!' he cries out wildly. Something has shattered his fiercely controlled composure. What does he see on my face? 'Don't!'

'Don't what?' I ask.

'Don't hate him. He is suffering too. I saw his tears.'

'But I did not. Why could he not—why did he not tell me this himself?'

'You know why—how could he bear to see you suffer?'

How suddenly it springs into my mind then, that patient, vengeful ghost, as if it has been waiting all these years to haunt me at this moment. Vali! Who was it who had told me how Vali had died? Killed, I had heard, by my husband when Vali was locked in single combat with his brother Sugriva. I had not believed it then. My husband killing an unsuspecting man that way? No, it was not possible. Now . . .

'You remember, Lakshmana, how your brother killed Vali?'

A shade comes over his eyes. 'Yes, that was wrong. But it had to be done. For your sake. He would do anything for you—you know that.'

'And now this thing that he is doing to me—for whose sake is this?'

How simple things are to a simple man! He has no hesitation in answering, 'Why, for his people.'

A man who will abandon his wife to please his people? Why not? I should have seen the seeds of this in him even then. Long back, on the day I had come to Ayodhya as a bride. When I had seen the people lining our path only to look at him, when I had heard the people cheering over and over for him. He had turned to me then, with glowing eyes, a radiant smile on his face. I was too young then, too foolish, perhaps, to realize what his eyes were saying to me—"Do you see how they love me? Do you hear them?" I know it now what I did not know then—that a man can get drunk with the wine of too much love and admiration. Now, when it is too late for the knowledge to help me, I understand that it can become a passion too, this desire to be loved and admired.

'They are alike,' I am speaking almost to myself, 'the two men who have made my life what it is. They have ruined my life—with their passion.'

He hears me and his face flushes with anger. I can see relief too. For now, he thinks, I am wrong; he can prove me wrong; now, at last, he can defend his brother.

'Passion! How can you say that . . . how can you say such a thing about him . . . about my brother . . .?'

'You don't understand,' I interrupt his angry stammering words. 'It is not that kind of passion I am speaking of. That passion is simple. His passion, to be always in the right, never to do any wrong, is worse.'

But Vali . . . I think of that dead man again. What happened after Vali died? What did he think, how did he justify himself after he killed Vali? Why had I never spoken of these things? Why had I never asked him? Was it because I was afraid of what I would learn?

'It is because of this passion of his that I had to stand on trial to prove my purity. Once was not enough, no, when he knows as well as I do, what I am.'

'But you are a queen—and for a king . . .'

'I am no queen—only a woman who wants to live in peace with the man she loves. With the children born out of their love. Instead . . .'

Suddenly, the anguish in me spurts out like a jet of blood from an open wound. Savagely I close it up. Not yet, no, not yet. Laboriously, I pull myself out of that hell of pain to hear him speaking.

'He has no doubts, you know that. He knows you and what you are. But he has to do his duty, he owes his subjects that.'

Was it I who laughed? It has to be my laughter, for Lakshmana's face is grave. No, he is shocked, shocked by the laughter which was obviously mine. He looks as if something has pierced through the armour he had girded himself with when his brother sent him into this battle.

'Duty—yes, I knew that word would come. Yes, he is dutiful, I know that Lakshmana, and righteous too. I never doubt that. But tell me this, Lakshmana, what happens to those who are crushed under the chariot of his righteousness?'

He stares at me as if he cannot comprehend my words. I know he would like to defend his brother against my words, but how do you defend a man against the accusation of being dutiful and righteous?

'If it were not for his duty . . .' he begins and stops in confusion, knowing that he has used the word before, remembering that I have scorned it.

It is not just scorn. I hate the word, I have hated it since the day my husband said to me, after the battle, 'I had to do it, I had to let you go through the fire, I would have failed in my duty if I had let my love for you stop me from doing it.'

And it had hurt me then that he had shown me, not his grief at having to be cruel to me, but his pride in having done his duty. Even now, this time, if he had come to me himself, if he had told me that he was abandoning me and why, if he had revealed to me his grief at having to do this thing, why then . . . Why then what? What difference would it have made? I don't know. But I know this—that when one human suffers for another, there is a strange link between them. I realized this the day the man who had ruined my life had come to me and wept, showing me his grief, his anger, his weakness. And I had wept, yes, I had wept for him.

He had come to me when the end was near—though I, isolated from what was happening outside, had not known it then. But I had guessed, from the change in the way the women treated me, from their new air of fearful respect towards me. And when I saw him, with bloodshot eyes, dishevelled hair and unsteady steps, I knew. Yet, for a moment, I thought he was drunk. Even then, I had not been afraid. For some reason, after the first few moments, I had never been afraid of him.

'You!' he had said the moment he came to me, dramatically pointing a finger at me. His huge body was swaying, as if shaken by a violent wind. 'You have been the ruin of me.' And then, it had burst out of him, almost like a sob, 'My—my—Indrajit is dead.'

In a moment, the flaming sunset of his eyes had turned misty with tears. But he had conquered the tears instantly, as if he could not, no, he would not shed tears for his dead son in my presence. He had advanced instead, his large hands held in a menacing half-curve. I had not retreated, though the women with me had made small, frightened sounds. Where would I retreat?

'I should do it,' he had muttered, 'I should squeeze the life out of you. You have ruined me. But . . .' And he had stopped, as I had known he would, his hands groping, falling down finally helplessly by his sides. 'I can't do it, no, I cannot.'

It was then that I had realized his tragedy. And after he had gone, I had wept for him. Blade of grass? No, there never was any blade of grass between us, though they all speak of it now. There was just my will. And this feeling of his for me that would not let him force his will on me.

'Duty?' I repeat Lakshmana's word, offering it back to him. The word seems heavy, laden with all my sorrow. 'Yes, his duty has been my only rival, after all.'

'But for a king,' Lakshmana speaks with a weary patience, like an adult to an obstinate child who refuses to understand, 'for a king, duty comes first. And he—yes, he is a great king. I wonder when the world will see the like of him again. Never, perhaps.'

'Yes. A great king. But do you know, Lakshmana, how many ordinary people have to be crushed so that one man can become great?'

Strangely, he is no longer angry. He looks at me with what seems like compassion instead.

'It is no one's fault,' he says. 'I would do anything to save the two of you from sorrow. If there is anything that I can do now . . .'

He looks down at his hands, hands that had cleared paths for us, had built a home for us, hands that had fought and killed for us. But how can any hand save us from our own selves?

'It is fate,' he says heavily, after a long pause. 'Who am I, a mere mortal, against fate? Even the gods cannot save us from that. All this that has happened—it is his fate. And yours.'

Fate—I knew the word would come. But I will have nothing to do with it. I cannot believe in it. We cannot escape the consequences of our actions, of our wrongs, that way. That is the easy way out. It is not fate that shapes our lives, but our wills, our actions. It was not fate that left me unprotected that day, the day of the golden deer. It was my fault, the result of my weakness, the weakness of my great love, too great a love, for my husband. It was this that had made a coward of me, making me afraid that he had been hurt; it was this that had made me say those cruel words to Lakshmana, which finally drove him away from me. I can still remember the reluctance with which he went, the shame and anger on his face before he turned away. I had been very clever in using the right words that would impel him to leave me and go look for his brother. Yes, it was my fault and mine alone. And earlier, when my father-in-law, I remember it now, had cried out in anguish against the cruel fate that made him exile his own beloved son, I had thought rebelliously—fate? How can it be fate? This is the result of your own weakness, the weakness of a doting old husband for a young and beautiful wife.

No, I can't blame fate for anything. And this time, there is nothing to soften the agony, either. That time, when I had been abducted, I had known it was my fault—my fault for sending my husband after the golden deer, my fault for sending Lakshmana after him. But now I can't blame myself; I have done no wrong. The wrong is his and his alone. It is because of his weakness, his belief that he can never do any wrong, his desire that he should never be seen to do any wrong, that I have to suffer. He believes that his image as the righteous, the perfect ruler should not be tarnished. That is his god. And he has sacrificed me to it.

People will talk about us because we are a king and queen who have had more drama in our lives than most people have in theirs. Perhaps this episode, a small part of our story, will be forgotten. It is possible that people will not believe it; *it cannot have happened*, they will say, *he could not have done such a thing*. Or else, they will revere him even more, as the king who put duty before self, before his own happiness.

And because I will remain silent—yes, it is true, I will say nothing, I know that they will say I submitted, that I endured and forgave. Perhaps I will forgive him, after all, not because I am a virtuous or a devoted wife, not because I am good and merciful, not even for the sake of our shared life, our memories, tears and laughter, but because I pity him. For what is he but a victim of his own idea of himself? He is still chasing it, the golden deer of perfection, while I . . . No, for me, the day of the golden deer is over; I know it is nothing but a mirage, a delusion.

Across the river I can see the dark forest we had entered so many years ago. Now I must go into it again—and alone. The demons we fought last time are nothing compared to the demons I will have to fight now: the demons of fear, hate, self-pity and bitterness. Yes, and anger too. Only when I have vanquished these will I emerge out of the forest of exile once more.

I stand up, and now the whispering of the river is even more hushed, as if it knows it is all over. He looks at me and I see he has realized it too. For a moment, his hand comes up, an instinct to stop me perhaps. Then he controls himself and the hand falls down by his side. Seeing his face, I know how his brother must have looked when he gave him the message for me.

'Is there anything you want me to tell the king?' he asks me, the messenger once more. Getting back into the armour of formality.

Anything to tell the king? Words fill my mind, such a loud jangle of them that I feel dizzy with the clamour. Then they vanish and I am left with blankness. What have I to say to the king? Nothing. There is nothing. Yes, finally it is all over.

But he is waiting for me to give him some message to take back; he has to take back something. And can I let him go empty-handed after all these years of knowing him? Yet, what can I say? What is there for me to say to the king?

Nothing. But there is something I have to tell my husband. I was wrong in thinking that I had surrendered the golden deer. I have not, not entirely. Now, it is time for me to do so, to give up the idea of perfection in any man, in any human.

'Tell my husband,' I say, 'tell my husband that he could have done something worse. He could have forgiven me.'

It is finally over. Nothing left now but to walk into the forest, to face the terrible years that are waiting for me.

JANAKI

VIJAY LAKSHMI

IF ANYONE TELLS me that education makes people wiser, I say, 'Trash.' If anyone tells me that riches and big bungalows give people happiness, I say, 'Humbug.' People think I'm crazy. Or else, why would I be sitting under a neem tree, repairing bicycles for peanuts, when I could get a good job? They're ignorant, of course. They don't know what I know. They don't know that having a lot doesn't mean you have it all. My employers, Sudhir and Janaki Thakur, had everything people dream about—a fancy home, two cars, friends, fame, money. Sudhir Saab was a big manager in a textile firm. Janaki Memsaab was a successful lawyer. I was twelve, a dropout from school after the fifth grade, when I left my village, and came to Jaipur to find work. The death of dadi, my grandmother, had left me an orphan for the second time in my life. The first time was when floods that washed away our tiny village, nine years ago, had swept off my parents too. But this is not my story. This is the story of the people I loved the most. Of Janaki Memsaab and Sudhir Saab, a couple I called Sita and Rama. Of a woman I truly adored.

Janaki Memsaab had hired me to help around the house—make tea, purchase groceries, clean Saab's car, and attend to other light housework. She was recovering from a miscarriage. Although there were other servants—a cook, a cleaning maid, a driver and a gardener—I was the only live-in servant. A year later, after the cook left, I took his place. Saab and Memsaab trusted me. They treated me like their own child. Unfortunately, they didn't have any children of their own. Even though I read the *Hanuman Chalisa* everyday and prayed to my god, my Hanumanji, to bless them with a child, my prayers went unanswered.

A few months after I started working at Saab's house, Janaki Memsaab decided to send me to school. She didn't want me to end up washing dishes or cooking all my life. I would leave for school in the morning, come back in the afternoon, water Memsaab's plants and flowers, make tea for her and Saab when they came back from work, and do my homework sitting under one of the flowering trees. We had so many of the smiling trees then—*semul*, *gulmohar*, acacia, you name it and we had it. And then there were the fragrant shrubs. *Champa, chameli, juhi.* But I loved *raat-ki-rani* the most, for its fragrance grew intense as the night spread its dark wings wider.

I still remember the sweet scent that had wafted into Saab's study when I went to close the window that evening. We were waiting for Memsaab to return from Delhi before nightfall.

'It's my first case at the Supreme Court,' she had told me the day she was to leave for Delhi. I was chopping onions to make omelettes for her and Saab. 'I must win this case, Mungu,' she said. 'You will,' I told her, wiping the tears caused by the onions from my eyes. 'You know so much, Memsaab.' She was sharp. Memsaab was. Or else, how could her picture have appeared twice in the local newspaper when she won two famous cases? 'I will pray to Hanumanji,' I said.

She had flashed at me her beautiful smile that lit up the kitchen as if the sun had burst in through the window.

'I'll be back the day after tomorrow,' she told Saab who was gulping his tea. He was in a hurry to leave for his office to attend an important meeting, as usual. He put down his cup and took Memsaab's hand in his. 'I wish you'd fly or go by train. I don't like you driving alone on the Delhi–Jaipur highway, especially after dark,' he said. 'The truck drivers get drunk and reckless then.'

Saab was given to worrying too much. That's what Memsaab always said to me. 'If he had time, your Saab would start counting the minutes between when I finish arguing a case and come home.'

Once she had made up her mind, Memsaab was not one to listen to anyone. She had smiled at him. 'Worry bug! You know I'm a very careful driver. I have never had an accident.' 'True,' Saab replied, weighing his words carefully. 'But you know—why don't you stay overnight in Delhi and come in the morning?'

'I want to be home, Sudhir,' she cooed, pressing his hand between her palms. 'Why should I spend a night in some stupid hotel?' Saab didn't say anything. How could he? But his brow was still furrowed as he drove off to work.

Memsaab left a little later, promising to be back in time for dinner the day after next. 'Come back soon,' I told her as she got into the car. I didn't like the house when she wasn't there. It seemed too big and too dismal. I didn't have to cook much, for Saab would hardly eat anything in her absence. He would spend all his time shut up in his study, working. I whiled away my time reading, or watching TV.

The evening she was to return, I prepared a meal that I knew both she and Saab would enjoy. Saab's favourite stuffed *karela* and memsaab's favourite *makhani dal*. The very thought of her arrival made the walls laugh with pleasure. The sun had just set, though its red-gold light still lingered on the treetops. After their routine clamour among the leaves, the sparrows had settled down for the night. I could hear the sound of a film song floating in the air. Saab had gone straight to his study after returning from work. 'I want to finish everything before she comes home,' he said, picking up a biscuit from the tea tray I had placed before him. 'If anyone calls, I'm not at home.'

'Yes, Saab.' I knew how to protect Saab from the unnecessary calls. That evening, however, I couldn't protect him from *honi*—the mistress of the inevitable—which appeared in the form of the vicious dhobi, the washerman. I was shelling pistachio to garnish the *kheer* when his wife started screaming.

Smack. Thud. Screams. And curses. The dhobi was beating her again. The peaceful evening was torn to shreds. '—you'll die the death of a leper,' the dhobin was yelling, '—become a beggar with no one to take care of you.' 'Shut up, you *churail*.' '*Hai Rama*—mad dog is drunk. He will kill me—O *Bhagwan*, my children will be motherless.'

I was afraid Saab would explode now. He detested the violent squabbles between the couple. In fact, he would have had the dhobi's tin-shed that stood across the street dismantled, if Memsaab hadn't interfered. 'He's a stupid, illiterate man,' she had said. 'What can you do about his behaviour?' In fact, she and all the other ladies of the neighbourhood liked the small shop that the dhobi had set up. They could instantly get a sari, a shirt, a blouse ironed out and ready. The dhobi picked up laundry from the homes every morning, washed it at the river and brought it back for the dhobin to iron. It would be delivered the next day when another bundle of dirty linen was collected.

'Wish you'd drown in the river where you wash clothes,' the dhobin's voice was ripping my eardrums. 'I won't shed a tear if a crocodile ate you up . . .' 'Ho! Ho! There are no crocodiles in the river, woman,' the dhobi laughed. 'If there were, I would have thrown you in long ago.' I could hear the servants from the neighbouring houses giggling. They must have sneaked out to enjoy the spectacle periodically provided by the couple. 'What else can you do? Only a wicked man will wish his wife ill and . . .'

'Mungu!' Saab bellowed above the noise. I left a pistachio half-shelled and ran to the study. 'Can't you ask them to shut up?' he said, as soon I reached the door of his room. 'Yes, I will, Saab.' I turned to go.

'Bastards,' Saab struck his fist on the table, sending a whole pile of papers cascading to the floor. I collected the sheets and put them back on the table. 'What's he beating her for, today?' 'Nothing Saab. All useless, all *bakwas*.' 'What is it?' 'He's mad Saab. *Ekdam paagal*.'

'That he is,' Saab muttered, pushing back his chair and getting up. 'I'm going to talk to the fool.' 'Don't Saab,' I said quickly. 'He's drunk.' I had to stop him. I knew that the dhobi's talk was would send Saab into a frenzy. He wasn't good at controlling his rage.

The dhobi was shouting again. 'You shameless woman, you.' 'He sounds real mad, as if she had run away with another man,' Saab said. 'What is it, Mungu?' 'It's the picture you took of her with Ramesh Babu that . . .'

Saab didn't let me finish my sentence. He had started laughing.

Ramesh Babu was Saab's friend from his school days. A filmmaker settled in America, he had come to India to make a documentary about fishermen in Kerala. He had stayed with us for four days, before going on to Kerala. Those four days, he talked and laughed so much that you could hear the whole house shaking with mirth. He was a restless man. Since Saab was very busy writing a report then, it was Memsaab who kept him company. She took him shopping. She sat and talked with him late into the night, while Saab worked. I had never seen her laugh so much. When Ramesh Babu left, it seemed as if the sunshine had walked away with him.

'Come visit us before you fly back to New York,' Saab had said. They were eating dinner, and I was serving them *chapatis*, hot from the oven.

'I wish I could,' he said. 'But I have just two weeks in which to finish this project.'

'Come on,' Memsaab said. 'You can extend your stay.' 'Next time, I promise.' 'Okay, next time,' Saab had said. 'We'll all go to Mt Abu. No more reports to be written. No more briefs to be prepared.' He had winked at Memsaab.

I am sure *honi* was watching them from a corner and laughing, as my grandmother used to say.

The day before Ramesh Babu was to leave for Kerala, I remember too well. Restless as usual, he had started taking pictures at random. It was Memsaab on her knees among her roses—snipping dead leaves, pruning twigs. Or, it was me scouring a pan, chopping vegetables, praying to Hanumanji. It was the trees. Flowers. Birds.

'I want to take a natural picture of you two,' he had said to Saab and Memsaab, without giving them a chance to tidy up. He made them sit under the red canopy of the semul, which was in full bloom then.

The picture was now sitting on Saab's desk. Memsaab looked funny with a smudge of dirt on her cheek, her hair teased by the wind. Saab was dignified as usual. Dressed in his loose khadi kurta and pyjamas, he sat next to her, his arm half lifted to embrace Memsaab's shoulder, a smile hovering at the corner of his mouth, when Ramesh Babu had clicked the camera. I wished he had waited a few seconds. The picture would have been complete then. Saab's arm would have been around Memsaab's shoulder and his mouth would have curved into a smile. But some things are destined to remain incomplete.

Ramesh Babu had been putting away his camera when the dhobin appeared with her two children. 'One picture of my children, Babu,' she had begged.

Ramesh Babu had asked her to hold the baby in her arms and place her hand on her two-year old child's shoulder. 'Stand here, beta,' he had told the child, 'and give me a big smile.'

He focused the camera, then thrust it into Saab's hands, 'You take the picture,' he said, leaping to the dhobin's side.

The dhobin had started giggling, for the tall, lanky man with a scar on his chin, glasses slipping down his broad nose, and the lower lip jutting out must have looked incongruous—even to her. Saab had caught them at that instant. Ramesh Babu laughing with his grey head thrown back, the scar on his chin glaring in the sunlight. The dhobin, short and dumpy, had covered her mouth with a corner of her sari to stop the bubbling laughter. The round-eyed child staring into the camera had stuck the index fingers of his hands into the corners of his mouth to stretch it into a huge smile. It was a beautiful day with the sun still mellow, the wind still gentle, the roses still blooming. It was the month of March.

'What's wrong with that picture?' Saab asked me, leaning back in his chair. 'She stood next to a strange man,' I explained. 'That's not quite proper for a woman, he says.'

I was relieved that the dhobi had grown quieter. Maybe he was taking a swig from the bottle. 'Let me shut the windows, Saab.' I walked over to the open window. That is when the fragrance of raat-ki-rani wafted in. It's still with me. Even now. Often, while I'm sitting under the neem tree, repairing a broken bicycle, it drifts across to me. As I returned to the kitchen, I heard the dhobi's drunken babble surface again.

'—he can let his wife run around with another man, I won't. Rich people have their own foolish rules.'

I had to go stop him, I thought. He was going too far. If Saab were to hear what the dhobi was saying, he would kill him. I knew Saab's anger. 'Help me Hanumanji,' I said to the small idol I had placed in the kitchen, and stepped out.

The dhobi was sitting on an overturned dustbin, staring at the moon. He held out the bottle to me when he saw me approach. I asked him to shut up and go home. 'So the small monkey has learnt to leap,' he jeered at me. 'You yap too much, you fool,' I told him.

He was too drunk to pay any attention to me. The more I scolded him, the worse he got. He took another swig from the bottle, looked at our house, and made an obscene gesture. 'My wife is not your Saab's wife who can—you know—go around with another man. I am not blind like your Saab. And you know what? She tells my wife to leave me because I beat her.'

He was staring above my head. I turned around to see Saab standing at his window. Had he heard everything? My heart began to knock like the engine of a lorry about to conk out.

I turned to the dhobin who was nursing her baby. 'Tell your husband to stop drinking and babbling. He should know how to behave himself.' 'He never listens to me.'

'If he doesn't, then I'll ask Memsaab to have him jailed.'

'Jailed. Huh?' the dhobi perked up. 'Me? She's no Sita herself . . .'

I didn't hear the rest. I kicked the bin in my frustration and ran back to the house.

'Just you wait and see, you son of a pig,' the dhobi's voice pursued me. Once inside the house, I decided to check on Saab.

He was sitting in his chair staring at a document.

'Do you need anything Saab?' I asked. I wanted to hear his voice. I wanted to make sure he wasn't angry, that he hadn't heard everything.

'I'm fine.' His voice was like hot iron pulled out of a furnace. 'Just waiting for your Memsaab.'

'I'm sitting in the verandah. If you need anything . . .' He dismissed me with a wave of his hand.

I decided to have it out with the dhobi the next day, after he had sobered up. I knew he would recant. He would cry. He would promise never to touch a drop of liquor. I wished Memsaab would come home soon. She had the knack of setting everything right. She knew how to resolve cases in court. She knew how to make Saab smile.

But honi must have been smiling in the shadows again. 'O Hanumanji,' I prayed, 'I will fast every Tuesday. I will offer you a *prasad* of fifty-one rupees. Let there be peace in this house.'

The fragrance of raat-ki-rani and soft moonlight had drenched the verandah when Memsaab pulled the car into the driveway. I scrambled to fetch her bag. She looked tired after the long drive, but she smiled at me. 'I'm hungry, Mungu,' she said. 'I want to eat.'

'Dinner's ready. I'll have it on the table in a minute,' I said. 'Good. Where's he?' 'In his study, I think.'

'Why doesn't he have the lights on?' she muttered as she walked towards the study. I saw her step in and close the door behind her. I hoped Saab's anger had dissolved by now. She was home. She was safe. We were safe.

I was carrying the dishes to the dining table when I heard Saab's angry voice. He had never shouted at Memsaab. He had never sounded so angry. I didn't want him shouting at her. She was tired now. He could at least wait till she had eaten and rested before starting up a row. I could hear Ramesh Babu's name bouncing between them.

'—with that man who calls himself my friend.'

'You're out of your mind. Ramesh is . . .'

'You went to Delhi to be with him, didn't you?'

'He left . . .'

If I were to announce dinner, I thought, they would have to stop. Once they had eaten, they would be able to think coolly. I was halfway across the hallway that led to Saab's study, when the door flew open and out came Memsaab. Her face was red, her eyes blazing.

'Memsaab, dinner is ready,' I said. 'Feed it to that beast,' she said. 'I'm going away.'

'Of course, go away,' Saab had rushed out too. 'Why should you stay with me? Go to your lover. Go. Get out.'

I had always respected Saab, but at that moment I loathed him. I could have taken him by the shoulders and shaken him, and told him that he was no better than the dhobi, but I was small in every sense of the word.

Memsaab didn't answer. She didn't even look at him. She picked up the car keys and walked out of the house.

'If you leave now, you're never to come back. Do you hear? Never to come back.'

Memsaab shook her head and got into the car.

'Memsaab. Wait.' I ran after her. I wanted to go with her. But before I could reach her, she had rocketed out of the driveway. All I could see were the angry tail-lights of the car. Then darkness closed in.

I didn't ask Saab if he wanted to eat. I didn't want to see him. I didn't want to talk to him. I sat down on the verandah steps, chanting *Hanuman Chalisa*, waiting for Memsaab to come back. I have no idea what time it was when I heard Saab shouting into the telephone.

'What?'

'No.'

'Where?'

'How?'

'I'm coming.'

His voice cracked. He slammed the phone and called me. I could barely understand what he was saying, but I gathered that something had happened to Memsaab. I watched him race out, get into his car, and drive away. Those few hours were the worst of my life. I didn't know what had happened. I didn't know where Memsaab was. It was almost dawn and the birds had begun their morning chorus, when Saab came back. He looked as if he had added a decade to his age overnight.

'Where's Memsaab?' I asked.

He shook his head and collapsed into a chair. I saw him bury his face in his hands. His body shook with dry sobs. I didn't feel any sympathy for him. Later, I learnt that Memsaab's car had crashed into an oil tanker and caught fire. She was still alive, still untouched by the fire, when they pulled her out of the burning car. On her way to the hospital, however, before Saab could reach her, she died. Why she was going along the highway, I'll never understand. Perhaps, she had lost her way. I don't know. All I know is that I was orphaned for the third time.

There was nothing for me to do, but to hand in my notice to Saab and leave his service. He didn't ask me why I was going away. He didn't ask me to stay. He said he would give me a good reference. I had turned away without a word. I was done with working for the educated and the rich. The dhobi had tried to talk to me. One look at his tobacco-stained teeth bared in a sheepish grin, and I lost my temper. I shouted at him to go to hell.

For a living now, I repair bicycles. I patch up punctured tubes. I tighten brakes. I fix broken spokes. I straighten wheels. Thanks to a stream of young boys and girls on their way to, or from school, I make enough for two square meals a day. Sometimes, while my hands are straightening a spoke or tightening a bolt, my thoughts fly back to a fragrant evening soaked in horror. Then a young voice hauls me back. 'Hurry up, please. I'll be late for school.' I look at a pair of eager eyes fixed on my face. 'It's done,' I say. 'You'll be on your way in a jiffy.'

SITAYANA

MALLIKA SENGUPTA

WHEN SITA ARRIVED at the forest of Naimishkshetra, it was a sunless morning. The sky was overcast. Thousands had assembled to witness the marvellous event of Sita taking the oath of purity. No queen had given such proof of her alliegiance in public in the past, nor had any king repeatedly made his consort swear by her chastity merely on the basis of suspicion. Many men have deserted their wives out of mistrust. But none was comparable to the way Ramachandra was to make his wife affirm her purity before the vast gathering to set an example for all women.

The Brahmins were especially effusive in praise of Rama's decision. Lakshmana, who was sitting beside Rama, spoke to Shatrughna in a low voice, 'I tremble to think of what is going to take place. I still remember how Janaki had fiercely rebuked our elder brother in a similar situation earlier.'

Shatrughna replied, 'Heaven knows why our elder brother is dragging Janaki through all this again. Whatever peace the troubled lady had in the last few years is about to be shattered.'

Lakshmana said, 'Behold how the Brahmins are gleefully rejoicing. They themselves keep several wives over whom they have little control. The youthful girls fall for the young disciples and these loose-skinned pundits compose derogatory verses on women to relieve their spite.

'And responding to their indulgence and instigation, our elder brother has filled his own life and Janaki's with discord. I feel intense grief on beholding Lava and Kusha. The twins of the Iksha clan have grown up without knowing what a father or paternal love means, nor have they known the comforts and luxuries of the palace. Today they will have to witness the moment of their mother's extreme humiliation.' Lakshmana continued angrily, 'See, even the sun's rays had not beheld Janaki before. And then she lived with the ascetics in the forest away from the civilization of the city. And now she is being summoned before the gaze of thousands of common men on foot, without regal attire. We had not considered what garments or jewels the only queen of the most revered king of the whole of Aryavarta would wear when she comes to meet her husband after twelve years. Shame on our wealth, our fame! Look, she comes, lean as a bamboo staff with unhurried steps. Is she Janaki, the one who follows Valmiki, draped in humble attire, unadorned, bereft of her previous radiance? Is she Janaki, the one who looks as doleful as Brahma's follower Vedshruti?'

Besides Vashishtha, Vama Deva, Javali, Kashyap, Vishwamitra, Dirghatama and a thousand other Brahmins, were present Kshatriya kings and noblemen, Vaishyas, Shudras, and the sinewy rakshasas who had come from afar and stood still as mountain-peaks to watch the event. On seeing Janaki, a commotion of applause, blessings, and lamentation ensued.

Valmiki himself took Janaki by the hand and led her to Rama. He said, 'O king! This is your devoted wife whom you had abandoned near my hermitage for fear of public censure. She has spent a sanctified life for the past twelve years abiding by ecclesiastical laws. Now I have brought Janaki, who is like my daughter, according to your wishes.'

On beholding her ordinary garments and guessing at her emaciated frame, Rama had turned away his gaze. This woman was not the Sita whose beautiful form was etched in his memory. Deprivation and age had taken their toll, it was as if the shadow of the former Sita stood before him. On beholding Sita's lustreless appearance, he felt that his honour was at stake before all the monarchs who were present. Rama's discontent rose to the surface.

'Sita!' he called out.

Sita's gaze touched him despite the privacy of her veil. Her face was no longer delicate, rather it bore a masculine determination. Her complexion was no longer as fair as *champak* flowers, but had a coppery hue. This woman was a stranger to him. Was it for her that he had abstained from remarrying all these years? Rama spoke in a stern voice, 'I have summoned Sita to dispel all doubts. I have not taken another wife out of deep compassion for her. Now she must take the oath of chastity to assure me of her loyalty.'

Valmiki said, 'O king, I, the tenth successor of the line of Pracheta, who do not remember having ever told a lie, declare that Sita is blameless, that Kusha and Lava are the sons of your lineage. If I lie, let Janaki's sins defile me and render useless the virtues accumulated by my penance.'

He stopped short and glanced at those assembled around him. Then turning to Rama again, he said, 'You yourself had abandoned Janaki for fear of public condemnation despite being aware of her chastity. Now you must redeem this injustice. I have brought her here after judging her rectitude with my mind and five senses. If you continue to harbour misgivings, Sita will take the oath of her purity.'

Rama did not speak directly to his wife. To Valmiki he said, 'Reverend Sir, your words are convincing. Yet public censure is too severe. So let Sita take the oath of purity as you have suggested. This will satisfy all those assembled here. Sita too will be regarded as the paragon of virtue for all women.

Sita stood unmoved.

Shatrughna was restless.

Kaushalya felt uncomfortable behind the screen.

Mandavi, Urmila and Shrutakirti trembled on imagining what they would have done under similar circumstances.

Lakshmana abruptly stood up as if to speak, but sat down again fearing Rama's ire.

Sita observed each and every face. She was filled with a deep distaste. She knew that this unquestioned servitude of the brothers towards Rama was not an outcome of mere personal preference. As the king was pre-eminent in his monarchy, so the sway of the eldest was indisputable in the royal clan. This rule was not necessarily followed by everybody everywhere. But in the House of Raghu, it was stringently maintained. Rama had accepted exile to respect the wishes of his father without protest though Dasharatha had not uttered such an order himself. Rama had himself obeyed the rules and his brothers were taught to do the same. In this clan, the women were given little importance. Sita herself was, at one time, unquestioningly devoted to

Rama. Today, after long deliberation, she had learnt to think on her own, and had comprehended the tyranny and thoughtlessness of Rama's maxims. What she as a woman found unjust was not considered so even by competent men such as Bharata, Lakshmana and Shatrughna. Rather, they had accepted their elder brother's injustice. What a shame!

Shatrughna spoke up at this juncture, 'What is the use of an oath, Your Majesty? Devi Janaki is as flawless as a mirror, and you yourself and those assembled here know that.'

Sita could restrain herself no longer. With head upright, she spoke in a firm voice, 'Before whom will I take the oath, Shatrughna? Before that lord who had secretly deserted his pregnant wife? That lover who lacked the courage to deliver the news of exile but put the responsibility on Lakshmana's shoulders and himself remained concealed like a coward? That husband who did not bother to enquire if his children had a safe birth? That king who left his wife and sons to beg at the Brahmin's hermitage? He had commanded my exile without any fault of mine; but for what offence did he punish his sons? If a woman asks for justice on these grounds from a king who is famed worldwide for his wisdom, will Rama be worthy to sit on the throne of that judge?'

The assembly was stunned. Overcoming initial astonishment, Rama said with anger, 'Fie! Janaki has stripped herself of shame, the adornment of women.'

Sita simmered with resentment, 'And where was the king's adornment of public welfare for which the son of Dasharatha abandoned me? Where was his sense of duty when he killed an innocent Shudra at the instigation of the Brahmins for practising austerity? Is a Shudra not a subject? Are women not subjects? Fie on such kingly ethics. Fie on the rule of Rama!'

The Brahmins began to create an uproar. They were outraged at such audacity in a woman. Noticing this, Rama said sternly, 'Janaki must take the oath of chastity. Only then will I allow her into the palace because she is the mother of the children.'

Lakshmana said, 'O king! I had myself witnessed how Devi Janaki had honourably passed the trial by fire. Besides, the pledge taken by sage Valmiki is good enough. Why must we have more bitterness?'

Rama was unconvinced. Resting his eyes on Sita, he said, 'True, Sita was tested before the gods in Lanka and I took her back. But the same issue of public denunciation for which I forsook her may arise again. Besides, I do not know anything about her occupations during her twelve years of exile. If Janaki takes the oath, my former love for her will be renewed.'

'What oath, O king?' Defiance flashed in Janaki's eyes. Its incandescence pierced Rama. Still he wished to quell that blaze. He fixed his wrathful eyes on hers and repeated, 'The oath of chastity, of the purity of a woman's body . . .'

Sita looked at him sharply.

Rama was confounded for a moment, and then commanded, 'Take the oath, Janaki . . .'

Sita replied unshaken, her eyes fixed on his, 'No . . .'

A breathless silence descended upon the assembly.

Rama stood up from his throne in agitation, 'What is the meaning of this, Janaki?'

Sita said, 'The idea of the oath fills me with loathing. Will my body be free of guilt if I take it? What is sin, Your Majesty? The sin is not of the body; the knowledge of sin is a psychological one. I have no awareness of it. If Ravana had touched me when I was helpless, the fault lies not with me . . .'

'Sita, be silent,' Ramachandra cried in anguish. 'Only say if your chastity was preserved . . .'

A subtle smile played on Sita's lips. She appeared unnaturally quiet. Nothing seemed to matter to her at the moment. She surveyed the assembled crowd. The baffled and amazed Aryans looked like trees struck by lightning. As if jesting was her last revenge, Sita said, 'Let's suppose I had lost the golden coin named chastity in Lanka twelve years ago.'

'Sita!' Ramachandra cried out and collapsed on the ground, covering his face contorted in agony with his two hands.

Sita drew near him. Kneeling beside him, she quietly said, 'The loss of chastity is a mere accident, a physical assault just like your and Lakshmana's entrapment in the coils of the Nagpash in the battle of Lanka. The body of the woman does not alter after an assault, nor does her mind.'

Ramachandra raised his eyes and looked at her bewildered.

Sita continued, 'You have done grave injustice to me and my sons merely on the suspicion of what may have happened in Lanka. There can never be a proof. Today, if I take the oath of chastity, will you give us back those twelve years of our lives, Your Majesty?'

Rama looked like a frozen statue. His hands reached out to the sky like that of a drowning man.

Vashishtha came up and stood behind Rama.

Translated from the Bengali by
Sanjukta Dasgupta

SITA'S LETTER TO HER UNBORN DAUGHTER

CHANDRA GHOSH JAIN

Dear Paakhi,

Yes, I always wanted to call you a little bird. Why a bird? So that you would have wings to fly and soar, high up. Higher than the clouds. Beyond anyone's reach. Nobody could catch you or pin you down. Probably you may get a chance to speak to the wispy clouds, the ones that dissolve so mysteriously. Some of them might even take you along their eternal journeys across the skies. Paakhi, you may even fly close to that great orange-red orb in the sky. Feel its searing heat. I am sure my little angel will make friends with the great Sun God. Maybe even the Sun God will envy your freedom. The magical sunbeams will be partners in your adventures. Like a sunbeam you flood my life with light and colour. My darling daughter, yet to be born; how many dreams I weave for you. You will get to see the many-coloured rainbows. Paakhi, you might teach them to do a tap dance with you. My little bird, don't be afraid, as I was when I was young, of the loud rumbling of thunderstorms or the lightning that might come in your path. I would cling to Amma's sari and hide my face in her lap. I would close my eyes and think that by burying my head deep, my troubles would go away.

From this collage of fantasies your round face emerges full of laughter. Paakhi, you have the eyes of a doe and they are filled with endless mirth and gamine mischief. Unlike mine, that are always scared to admit even Hope. The grey blue pupils clouded permanently in a silent grief were the objects of endless admiration at some point of time. But why am I talking about myself? Your eyes are grey-black, but they also have shades of mysterious blue and purple in them. Depending on your mood and fancy more blue or purple. Yes, yes, I can hear your gurgling laughter trying to coax my straight lips into a smile. I can see your dimpled smile, the divine voice that will hold me enthralled forever. Do all mothers dream like this? Did Amma also yearn for me as I do for you, Paakhi? I was obviously not the favorite. Karan, my little brother was everyone's darling. Tall, slender, quiet and dreamy, he epitomized the concept of an obedient son. While I would be engaged in endless arguments with Amma, Karan would slip off. Emerging only when the storm was over.

'Why did you name me, Vaidehi?' I must have asked Amma a hundred times.

'What's wrong with the name? We all want to be like Sita. She is a Devi and worshipped by all,' Amma was clearly irritated.

'But Vaidehi was an orphan. Found at the tip of a plough. Abandoned, alone,' I persisted.

'Men also have names like Sita Ram, Sita Raman, the revered gods of our epics. Would you have preferred to be called Surpanakha?' Amma was enraged.

Sita, the epitome of silent suffering, while Surpanakha gave in to her wanton desires, both extreme characters in the epic Ramayana. I sometimes wished I were like Surpanakha, clearly stating my wish and going about it in a single-minded manner. I have always succumbed to pressure, always tried to please Amma, and now Varun. Creating chaos in the process, and finding myself always in the wrong.

Varun, you know is your illusive father, Paakhi. He was such fun to begin with. He would challenge me to do the wildest things possible. Setting me free, or was I just slowly yielding to his way of thinking? Whatever it was, it was intoxicating. I experimented first with alcohol, cigarettes and then gradually with drugs. It was my way of getting back at Amma. Who was she to tell me what I should do with my life? Did she ever explain why she came home so late at night? Her sudden absences? Amma never knew that I would be watching from my window, how she swayed and barely managed to get to her room. She would say work, political work, kept her out late. That she was providing us with an expensive education and trying her best, so that we would have every advantage in life which she didn't. How I hated her obvious lies.

Baba had died leaving her a young window. She got a job as a schoolteacher on compassionate grounds. Baba had been teaching in a government high school. Then her well-wishers persuaded her to contest the local municipality elections. Yes, we did lead a materially more comfortable life after that. But Paakhi, I just wanted those leering hangers-on to be thrown out of the house. There was a particularly crude, well-built one who always stared at me in an offensive way. One day he said, 'Ah, soon Vaidehi can also contest the State Assembly elections. We need some young people in the party.'

There was general laughter and smirking among the men seated in the room.

'I will never ever join politics. Politics is the last resort of the scoundrels,' I just flung open the door and walked out in a huff.

Later I could hear Amma's apologetic voice, 'She is still too young. Doesn't know how to talk to her elders . . .'

Oh, yes, we had fireworks, between Amma and me. Maybe the anger and rage brought me closer to Varun.

Amma wished me to portray the male Sita myth and then manoeuvre the men to get my way. Why? Because if you play the game by their rules you can still beat them (the men) and yet they will feel they have used you. It's a comfortable arrangement for everyone. Sita symbolizes sacrifice, a woman's greatest virtue according to patriarchal traditions. She has infinite forbearance. Justice remains a dream, equality an absurdity and suffering an everyday reality. But Amma, you would give speeches exhorting the poor and the downtrodden to demand equality. You espoused the cause of justice? Was it all a grand sham? Hypocrisy in its ultimate form? Amma, you never believed a word of what you stated so loudly and vehemently.

Oh, Varun, why did you do this to me? We had dreamt so many dreams together. What went wrong? You remember the V for victory? How that two-fingered symbol was a bond that separated us from the rest? V for Vaidehi and V for Varun. I would add V for Valentine. Amma blamed all my deviant behaviour on Varun. She disliked him intensely.

'That boy will lead you to your ruin,' she said more in anger than concern. 'He has no job, is just an average student. He comes from a family of petty shopkeepers. I could get you much better marriage proposals, if its marriage that you want,' Amma was coaxing, almost, as much as she was capable of.

'I can manage my life without your help, Amma,' I replied.

After that there was a general coolness between Amma and me. But I had Varun to turn to for solace. Amma, did you feel abandoned and neglected? Once I did hear you weep on the phone to Karan. But then I thought that it was a ploy you were using to turn even Karan away from me. I was surly and rude when Karan came home for his winter holidays. Not that Karan would ever touch on any contentious issue. He withdrew into his shell. Paakhi, we imprison ourselves in walls of our own making.

The delirious joy when I received the job offer from the *Times of India*.

The happiness was marred by Varun's constant rejections. All my energies went in trying to bolster his self-confidence. I was beginning to feel the strain, and felt that I couldn't carry on like this any longer. He had turned suspicious and possessive. It was difficult trying to prove my innocence again and again. After one such tumultuous fight he was overcome with remorse and started hitting his head on the wall. The thin stream of blood had me confused. Was I not capable of sustaining any relationship? First Amma, then Karan and now Varun were all drifting away from my life.

A quick marriage followed, with a promise that Varun would concentrate on running a car-rental service. Some uncle of his already had a successful venture and he would enter into a partnership by putting in a small capital. Borrowing from my savings and whatever Baba had left for me I raised the capital.

Paakhi, I did have a brief period of domestic bliss. Then the questions began, when would you have a baby? Initially all this amounted to an irritation and I would smilingly say, soon. My angel, why this agonizing wait? My fulfilment lay in being a mother. My mind and body hungered for the soft, cuddly touch of a baby. That special bond, which excludes the whole world, yes, even the father, exists only between a mother and her child. Then gradually not having a child became a matter of concern, so much so that I spent a fortune on medical investigations. The amounts spent on appeasing the gods remain unaccounted for. Paakhi, everyone plays on your fears. They hit you the hardest where it hurts most. Even Varun wouldn't spare me. I was taunted as a barren woman.

An incomplete life . . . A life without meaning . . . Meanwhile how I yearned for you, Paakhi. You were real; you existed. You understood my agony, but then you are so good at playing hide-and-seek. It was just that much more difficult to catch you, although I had caught a glimpse of you. I could hear your silvery laughter bouncing off me like moonbeams, but you would slip away.

Probably you couldn't bear my torment any longer, so you came. That was probably the happiest day of my life. The stars sparkled with a magical luminosity, sharing the mystery of the cosmos with me. Yes, the universe was hidden in me. How the world around me changed as well. I was complimented on my glowing complexion. But where was Varun? He appeared relieved and in between his drunken bouts, even concerned about my health. But once you were with me, darling, I needed no one. The whole world appeared vague and fuzzy. One heard and reacted to events of the day but it was like watching the horizon from the wrong end of the telescope.

Then, Paakhi, I was again rudely awakened from my reverie. You must take the 'test'. First from well-meaning relatives; then insistence from Varun. But why on earth? We want a son. A grim reminder of my role . . . Only the mother of a son has any meaning in this society. All my pleas fell on deaf ears. Paakhi, my darling, I tried to explain, my child, boy or girl, is precious to me. I have conceived after so many years. How can one, in this day and age, discriminate on the basis of gender? Varun very cunningly got my doctor to convince me of amniocentesis to detect possible genetic defects. To rule out 'Down's syndrome', specifically.

I felt hemmed in, Paakhi. I felt violated, but I bore up. I couldn't care less, even if they declared that my baby was suffering from Down's syndrome. I was confident that my angel would be perfect. Then the inevitable happened. The doctor came out with such a gloomy look that my heart lurched out.

'Tell me doctor what's wrong?' Was that my voice, so shrill and high-pitched?

'It's a girl.' He almost whispered it, as if he were pronouncing a death verdict.

'So?' I was bewildered. I was beginning to hear joyous songs of dance. The frowning and disapproving faces of Varun and his family started a roar . . .

'Drop it. A girl child, what will you get? At best she will turn out like you, an ingrate. Run away with some scoundrel. Better not to have any child than have a daughter.'

Like Sita I am all alone. My soul is in exile. Paakhi, you will not abandon me, will you? My angel, I write, so that someday you will understand the grief beneath the laughter. You are the reason of my existence, my sanity. With you holding my hands I also hope to touch the shimmering colours of the rainbow.

Why do you weep, my little angel? We will always be together. Won't we, Paakhi? What is it that distresses you? Paakhi, you are brave and strong, together we will conquer the world. No, no Paakhi, I will not let you go. The odds might be heavily stacked against us, but we will fight and survive. What is it that you say; you don't want to be another Sita? Abandoned by father, husband and family. No, Paakhi, listen, don't go . . .

Your Ever-Hopeful,
Ma

SITA: AN EXCERPT FROM A NOVEL

RAMNIKA GUPTA

RAMNIKA GUPTA'S NOVELLA in Hindi, *Sita*, recreates the hierarchical old order by designating it anew. This Sita is a Dalit woman, hardworking, robust and intelligent. When her husband and his second wife try to cheat her and even kill her, she proves stronger and more resourceful than them. The novella touches upon communal relations, class discriminations, labour laws and women's rights using the backdrop of the Ramayana but insisting upon the social change that has altered traditional values.

* * *

... The rice was turning green. Yaseen and his wife's wheatish complexions were also growing pale. The rice was dark green now. The pallor on the faces of Yaseen and his wife was washed by a certain inkiness. Sita, the rejected one, got up to eat. Yaseen's face turned yellow. He came out of the courtyard. A dog sat in the doorway, the one whom Sita fed every day before she herself ate. Yaseen kicked him aside and went and sat down on the parapet. Yaseen's wife's hand shook as she pushed the plate of rice in front of Sita. But Sita could gauge nothing. The dog came whining in. Sita saw something greenish in the rice. Then, like every other day she put a little rice in front of the dog. He cried out loudly as soon as he ate the rice and fell down stiffly. Sita's morsel hung in mid-air.

Seeing the dog fall down, Yaseen's wife ran nervously into an inner room. Taken aback, Sita went numb for a while. Then throwing aside the plate she got up. She tied the little child Sunil to her back and picked up a staff lying nearby. Sita bolted Yaseen's wife from the outside and coming out gave Yaseen a couple of sharp blows on his back.

'You pimp, be damned . . . go, take your wife away. Go, you rogue, get out of my house. I have thrown away my life's earnings on you and the two of you wanted to poison me? This is the price you pay for my lifetime's devotion!' Then she gave Yaseen a few hard ones on his head with a shoe. One wondered where she got the strength to do this. She threw Yaseen down from the platform. Those gathered around tried to hold her back, but to no avail. She went into the hut and clutching Yaseen's wife by the hair, brought her out as well. She pushed her towards Yaseen, and gave her a hard push.

She turned to the wife, 'I carried your belongings on my head and brought you here as my sister. I thought the two of us would make a living together—you would tend the land and look to things concerning its revenue and I would look to household chores. You bitch, mark my words! This husband of yours will not be able to do me any harm. The two of you planned to kill me? My son would have died without me, and my daughters, who knows what you would have done to them?'

Slapping them several times, Sita drove them away from the gathering crowd. Then settling down on the platform herself, she shot the choicest abuses at them for a long while. Then untying her son from her back, she hugged him hard and started crying. Other labourers gathered. Someone suggested that the rice be taken to the police station. Someone said it should be taken to the Panchayat. But Sita refused. She cried out loudly.

'Forget it! What are the police for . . . good for nothing. Now I will be my own defender. I have fed the bastard with my life's earnings. Had he been my son I would have frightened him into giving my share in the property. Had he been my daughter I would not have said a word. But now I will teach him what it means to rob an *adivasi* woman. If I go to court I will have to pay out every penny I own. Let my son grow up. I will then claim everything back from that man—my land, my truck. I will make his life hell on earth or don't call me Sita anymore! He will taste living death!'

'Don't you remember Sitaji had followed her husband to the forest?' someone from the crowd called out. Sita did not waste a split second. She jumped down and pounced on him, throwing him to the ground.

'You, son of a . . . you are teaching me the Ramayana! You call him Rama, this man Yaseen who has another wife? Ramji did not marry again. Get me right—I am no Sita to follow her man to the forest. I will instead send him there. I will see how you can hold a job and get married a second time, when your first wife is still there—wait and see!' Sita roared like an injured wrestler.

Her watchful men, her parents and others gathered around her. The labourers started telling her how to teach Yaseen a lesson. When Dr Mohanti—who had helped her give birth to her child—heard of it, he immediately came there with the union leader Godani. But by then Yaseen and his new wife had been driven out of the house.

Translated from the Hindi by
Rajul Bhargava

SITA IN MY DREAMS

ANAMIKA

Dasat hee gayi beet nisa sab,
Kaba-hun na nath, neend bhar soyo.
The night was whiled away in makeshift moves
When could I sleep a wink, O Lord!

THAT IS TO say, my life was spent preparing to live and life passed me by. When I got hold of a sheet, the mattress was missing and when I managed that, the sheet started playing tricks. At times I held one end and at times, the other. I occasionally sewed the seams or added a patch. But when I spread out the sheet, it wrinkled its brow and frowned at my useless life as a woman. As I stooped over to smoothen out the folds, the night went by. I tossed and turned, headrest to footrest, this way and that . . .

Dreams came and went, of Sita's discomforts, Sita's woes, her amazing resilience against the frowning folds of life in the court and the forest. She in her middle age, like me, would have spent hard nights too, on bramble beds in the forest, while Lord Rama must have had servants to the right of him, and servants to the left of him to make his bed—but he must have yearned for a wee bit of sleep, what with his king-sized bed and the guilt at having banished his queen . . .

My dreams tunnel into the womb of the earth that had burst open to gather the suffering of Sita. My journey is tortuous. A burrowing rabbit leads me to the epicentre where water and fire embrace each other, where *Sheshnag* lies somnolent. I spy Sita rubbing clean that very earthenware pitcher from which she was born. When I first heard this episode from the *Chandrawati Ramayana,* sweat broke out.

So Mother Earth was Vaidehi's (Sita's) surrogate mother, the real being Mandodari, King Ravana's wife? Mandodari had longed for her husband's attention and been denied. This injured vanity of a lonely woman caused her to drink from a forbidden receptacle of blood and she found herself with an unbidden child, immaculately conceived. Hiding the child in a pitcher, she prayed in anger and hope, 'Oh Ocean, carry this pitcher to a fertile bank where the daughter of this single woman may be incarnated. I invest my total being into this essence and pray to earth to give its womb to my daughter and so order the events of the future that she may, under some pretext, destroy my unjust, uncaring husband!'

Did Sita know her mother? Was this the same pitcher in her hand in the darkness of the earth's womb? I wonder, 'Is not Mandodari's pitcher a kind of metaphor?'

Pitcher in the water
Water in the pitcher
Water inside out
Break the pitcher and ease the water into water
So say the wise.

These traditional sayings make sense. The pitcher is like ego: fragile containers, artificial boundaries. That within, is without. The water is woman, fluid, lambent, taking whatever form of the pitcher she is poured into. That too is wisdom, said my grandmother. Mandodari's pitcher must have been very strong indeed that it weathered the waves and reached the Bay of Bengal. Perhaps that is why Sita's character is so fluid yet so strong.

Oh this bedsheet is now cold against my cheek, and I am tossing about again. Where was I—ah yes, Sita's strength. Ramaji is ready to leave for the forest. Bidding farewell to his mother, he goes to meet his wife and starts preaching to her about her rights and duties: 'I'm ready to go to the forest and have come here to see you. Remember, never praise me in the presence of Bharata—a prosperous man cannot stand comparison with another . . . Do not often speak about me to your friends, you can only win their companionship by behaving like them . . . The king has bestowed on Bharata the honour of being the heir apparent, so you should make efforts to keep him happy . . .'

The pitcher of male ego? A classic example of male logocentrism! Steeped in worldly wisdom, bereft of any streak of emotional agitation. Even if disturbance is within, it is not allowed to surface—for then it would be humiliating and demeaning to male propriety! Girls have less ego, they know they must obey the boundaries, like the water in the pitcher.

Sita might be their foremother. She tells Rama: 'Oh, my innocent Lord! You are asking me to be agreeable to someone who has taken away your right to be anointed the king? You are welcome to this obedience and ignominy, not me! How I should behave with whom, my parents have taught me well. You do not need to instruct me in this regard!'

Such direct talk I imagine in the privacy of home, if Rama and Sita enjoyed any privacy that is. There were problems being king and queen designate, I think. But later, in public, the chaste Sita is berated by Rama, questioned, tested, and turned away. How can I, Sita's legatee, forget those harsh words from a kingly husband: 'Ravana ran away with you in his arms and turned his lustful eyes at you—how can I, who belongs to an honourable family, then accept you?' Sita, aroused to defending her innocence and asserting her will, had invoked the gods of Fire and Earth to testify to her purity. And they had.

But a woman can keep proving her worth; does the power over her relent? This can go on forever! Many examples can be cited to prove Sita's self-respecting, compassionate and trusting nature. Honoured author Tulsidas, he was so embarrassed by the weakness of one whom he worshipped that like Hanuman, he preferred to overlook some episodes completely. However, women know that silence is often eloquent and suggestive. Mandodari's story came, remember, from a woman-inscribed Ramayana.

So, from my tunnelled space of inward journey I see Sita still cleaning the pitcher, snug at the epicentre of the earth. Speech eludes me. Those whom we hold in high esteem, our voices fail us in their presence. How do I begin addressing her? So many imaginary dialogues have already taken place that when we confront them we are like that child who has practised a lot but has a blackout when it comes to performing.

I take recourse to another memory of the strong Sita. I had heard the Tamil writer C.S. Lakshmi (Ambai) cite an episode from the *Sitayana* popular in the north-east of India. I will try to cast it through a fictitious dialogue. It is now over forty years since Sita came to the forest. (I am the same age, so the middle-aged Sita fascinates me, you see!) Rama has taken away Lava and Kusha—Sita spends her life eating fruits, talking to birds and animals, and practising her music on the *rudra veena*. In this version of the Ramayana, the defeat of Ravana is said to be merely an illusionary game. After the game was over, Ravana too came to the same forest as an ascetic. The melancholic strains of the rudra veena attracted him to the cottage. Sita is playing on the veena—her face towards the wall. Ravana stands enraptured. He does not try to distract her but awaits her attention. And when she does see him, she is shocked. (How does Sita recognize him, I wonder? In the traditional stories, Sita has never seen Ravana's face! But let us get on with this version.)

'You? How are you here?'

'O goddess! I have come here searching for you! I know that for Rama his duty towards his kingdom would be more important than towards his marriage; I also know that in order to appease a foolish whim of his people, he would leave you at the mercy of wild animals, all alone . . . This is what he said immediately after his victory over Lanka—that he had not fought in order to defeat me, but to protect the honour of his clan. Had he not said that you were free, you could go stay with Vibhishana or with any of his three brothers? I have, since then, been following your fate.

'When you had jumped into the fire to prove your chastity and when the Fire God came out bearing you in his arms, I burnt in another fire—the fire of repentance, and passion. At your swayamvar, Shiva was my adversary. I could not even move his bow. Ashamed, as I was returning, my eyes fell on your luminous face. After Rama had garlanded you, you stood by his side and you appeared like the full moon in a dark sky. A new emotion was born within me then, and was revived many times. I am a devotee of Shiva, Ganga is my mother, yet I did not ask for this moon but decided that when an eclipse darkens the light of the moon, or when stray tales malign it, I will stand up for it and be its champion.'

Sita was aghast: 'But you are the reason for this taint! If you loved me why is there such hypocrisy? Why did you come begging at my door? Why did you create an imaginary deer? And why did you surround me with all those sorrows?'

Ravana: 'It was only Maya, destined to be such. You are wholesome, unhurt, honoured by the gods. Even if you do not accept this theory, please think what could I have done? I had an only sister, immature. Had it been the modern times, Surpanakha would be taking her matric exams! How much does a young girl like her know? Infatuation at this age is not uncommon. In a mysterious jungle she comes across a glorious youth roaming fearlessly. A sixteen-year-old is bound to get enchanted! Surpanakha could have been sent home after being made to see reason, but why were her ears and nose cut off? What kind of valour is this? Don't you think that Lakshmana was following that baseless idea that in a male-dominated society a woman must not express desire or sexual need, and she must be punished if she does?'

Sita answered with aplomb: 'I had reproached Lakshmana for this but I was not his mother! I was not wholly responsible for his moral development. Then why did you drag me into the fray? And that too so cunningly? Why did you not directly attack Lakshmana?'

Ravana demurred: 'It is quite possible that my unrequited love made me don the garb of a beggar and come to your door. Well, that is all in the past. Now we are at that juncture in our lives when physical attraction matters little but deep affection and companionship become important. Rama has left you, taken your children away . . . I have wandered long and returned to your door once again. Will you teach me how to play the rudra veena?'

Sita sighed in relief: 'Look, my brother! The way you have been wandering in order to find me, I too have travelled to discover my inner self! . . . This rudra veena is actually my identity. How can someone appropriate another's identity? . . . You yourself are a great devotee of the gods. Cut your own wood, craft your own veena. The beats and rhythms of nature will teach you. Go, O Valiant One, once again I am asking you to leave my threshold. You will find your own safe shore. Pain is the road to salvation, friend, pain gives rise to the music in the rudra veena! Listen to the music within you and turn back.'

Then the aged Ravana went back and here, I too traced my steps back from the imaginary enactment in front of my eyes. Those who think Sita is a figure of mute obedience got her story wrong. How can they forget that her crossing the lakshmana rekha is an act of discretion in an emergency? She showed the courage to change the rules. What if the decision was wrong, was it not enough that a decision was taken? One out of ten decisions may go wrong, so what! According to her own thinking, Sita took the right steps—gave alms to a beggar, food to the hungry . . . and it was this so-called 'wrong decision' that became the reason of Ravana's defeat. Had she not chosen this way, how would Ravana have been killed, symbolic evil destroyed, lessons learnt for posterity? She was no mere puppet; Sita was an agent of change.

Let a few decisions in life be wrong—often they prove to be the impulse for some larger moves. My reverence for Sita is immense. I did not have the courage to impinge upon Sita's lonely meditation before the pitcher. Saluting her silently, I resolved to look again for my sleep in my troubled bed. Tulsi's words, '*Dasat hee gayi beet,*' resounded with a new meaning. The questions raised by Sita's tale will remain perennial. Each woman will answer them differently, but meaningfully, and with relevance to her time and place. Archana Verma, in her story *Tyohar*, writes of a young girl who is given the role of Sita to play in the local Ramlila. The girl argues with her brothers and friends that she wants to be Hanuman rather than Sita: 'To sit under a tree and cry the day out! Never!' she says.

This essay of mine is dedicated to that little artist of *Tyohar* and thousands of spirited girls like her with the hope that they will discover the strong Sita within them.

Translated from the Hindi by
Rajul Bhargava

LETTERS FROM THE PALACE

KUMUDINI

THIS LETTER IS to the beloved consort of Mithila's Lord Janaka from Sita Devi of Ayodhya.

I, Sita, prostrate prayerfully before Amma with a submission.

All is well here, and hope it is so with you too. The people and the chariot you sent have arrived. The messengers told us that you have instructed us to come to Mithila for Deepavali. Considering the state of affairs here, I am sure you will understand that it will be difficult for us to visit you now. My father-in-law is always at Mandavi's mother-in-law, Kaikeyi's house. My mother-in-law is furious. She conceals it well though, and is engrossed in prayer and serving food to Brahmins. I have to get up early in the morning, bathe and help her with chores. Work fills the day. There is not a moment's rest.

As soon as the wedding ceremonies were over, my brother-in-law Bharathan was taken away by his uncle. You know Shatrughna, he always tails his elder brother. Only after they return can we seek permission for the journey, and after all that, I don't know if we will be able to reach Mithila before Deepavali. I have great doubts about the whole thing.

After thinking it over, your son-in-law has decided that it is best we spend Deepavali in Ayodhya itself. Father will soon receive a letter about this from my father-in-law.

Do send the gift of silks to us. Your son-in-law likes only yellow silk. So, buy only that for him. Here, for Deepavali, a new design in gold bracelets is being fashioned for the son-in-law of the house,

Rishyasringan. It is lovely! Do make a similar one for your elder son-in-law and send it. Along with the people who bring this letter to you, I am sending a goldsmith who excels in that kind of workmanship. No one need know that I have written to you about this matter.

You wrote that a *sindoor*-coloured sari is being woven for me. Here in Ayodhya, people are very fastidious about the way they dress. I believe that their silks are brought by traders from foreign lands; those narrow borders look so elegant. My sister-in-law Shantha wore one such in blue. I long to have one like it! All the saris that you bought for my wedding have broad borders. I feel so embarrassed to wear them now. Everyone makes fun of me. Don't send me any more of that kind.

Salutations to my esteemed Father.

Ever your humble,

Sita

~

PRAYERFUL submission to mother.

All well here. After writing to you, I met my sister-in-law Shantha. It seems the blue colour is not fast. Fades soon. So, I don't want a silk of that colour. Send the sindoor-coloured silk as planned earlier. Or else, if you can find a copper-coloured one which is guaranteed to be fast, send that. It is boring to wear the same colour over and over again. Anyway, do what you feel is most convenient. I don't want to trouble you much. However, don't buy the blue shade.

Affectionately,

Sita

~

PRAYERFUL submission to mother.

All well here. Quite suddenly Father-in-law has had an idea. A plan to perform the coronation of your son-in-law! This means a sari—with your blessings—in the *pandal*! What kind of sari do you plan to send? Do you think the *navamallika* colour will be nice? Since it is going to be displayed in the pandal, it has to be a grand one. How quickly will you be able to get one with spots like a deer's worked all over it? Or will it be possible only if ordered well in advance? My mother-in-law does not like cuckoo- or peacock-colour. Tiger-stripes will look as if I'm in *puli-vesham*. I really don't know what you are going to do. My head is spinning thinking continuously about these saris. I simply cannot decide. Do as you think best.

Your loving Sita

P.S.—Or else, buy a very grand sari for both Deepavali and the Coronation Function combined.

~

MOTHER,

No need to send any sari. All is over. We are going away to the forest. The coronation—will now be for Bharatan. The person who is bringing this letter will tell you everything. I have only one dress made of bark-skin. If it rains in the forest and I get wet, I will have nothing else to wear. Therefore, if possible, send a bark-skin. Your son-in-law says that only your *appalams* taste heavenly. We are going to Chitrakoot. Nobody need know this.

Yours in haste.

Sita

P.S.—There is no need to worry any more about the colour of saris. Peace of mind is now mine. How helpful it would be if all women were to go to the forest! Half the worries would disappear.

Sita

Translated from the Tamil by
Ahana Lakshmi

POEMS

NISHI CHAWLA

SITA'S DIVINITY

That little one that I am,
I look quizzical and wonder
upon my divine essence.
The white potter takes
a lump of brown clay,
discretely molds and shapes
the pliable lump to a human
shade that he alone desires.

While firing the brown clay
in the gray kiln, he shapes it
black and then reshapes it blacker
until he meets his own black desires.
The image that he creates of me,
is firm now, centuries have eroded.
I remain fixed,
undressing me is only a ritual.

I grow into a colorful universe.
It is no treachery to show my
flesh in any color. I am incarnate
in the woman who bears a child
year after year, and one who never

will. I wear a red sari, my redness
bloody as sunken stars. The white
veil disappears in the black *burka*
I must wear all the time.

Since I cherished an ideal, I must
be the ideal one. I am the mother
and I am the daughter. I am the wife,
I am the one who cannot. The potter
stuck two mounds across me, and
then slit me up and down, so I must
embellish the truth about me.
The blood drops that I shed,
month after month, dry
my tears-driven ceremonies.

The voice that I have, he has
slaughtered into a thousand;
so I speak many languages, and am
known in many more. Someone sings
for me too; these songs have
a kindred tongue.
I, too sing, for I am Sita.

I am the victim
and I am the victimizer.
I am the earth goddess,
my healing reaches back to my self.
I am the earth woman,
my blood reaches back to my being.
I am your ancestor,
my being reaches back to you.

SITA IN HER EXILE

It may pay to make sense of the scene:
As the sun blankets the moon, its
spreading paint writing flaws
into the moon's bones, he gazes at her
with devotion deep in the forest,
sinking their feet together, she returns
to him the look of a Prometheus.
The stare does not suggest boundaries.

The peacocks hiss in wild ecstasy,
their notes quick gutting the forest's
sly silence. Doubling, then reversing,
peehaw, *peehuu*, they screech.
Their rumors drive the golden deer
crazy. Their tails spread wide, as
they would burn down the glory of
the trusted sun. Like the *madira* of their
long tails, dragging, then suggesting,
operatic masks, their ruling crowns tilt,
recklessly like petals, as it were.

There is a strange desire chanting,
a golden mask shakes the bough of
longing. She rides on it, then asks him
for a golden deer. As children plead,
possession possessed her, plucked
to the core. The lord of rebellion
wears a cleft crown. So her husband
lays down, a fine line drawn in
white around her cottage. She
insists, the fruit would fall to
the ground; she would not touch.

Meanwhile, the train of peacocks
does not relent. Their crowned heads
bob in relentless self-esteem. They
walk on the aroma of myrrh, a mesh
of white liquid blurring the sunken line,
its powdered remains on which, a lone
peahen reaps a tear; it rolls down
her cheek, then becoming smug,
begins its molting in degrees of comfort.

And yet she seems happy,
in the throes of her agni pareeksha.
Like an artist, in perfect alignment
with her chronicled exile.

AN INFATUATION

(FROM THE RAMAYANA)

AMIT CHAUDHURI

SHE'D BEEN WATCHING the two men for a while, and the pale, rather docile, wife with vermilion in her hair, who sometimes went inside the small house and came out again. She'd been watching from behind a bush, so they hadn't seen her; they had the air of being not quite travellers, not people who'd been settled for long; but they looked too composed to be fugitives. Sometimes the men went away into the forest while the woman attended to household chores—Surpanakha observed this interestedly from a distance—and then they'd return with something she'd chop and cook, releasing an aroma that hung incongruously around the small house.

She, when she considered herself, thought how much stronger and more capable she would be than that radiantly beautiful but more or less useless woman, how she'd not allow the men to work at all, and do everything for them herself. It was the taller one she'd come to prefer; the older one, whose every action had such authority. She liked to watch him bending, or brushing away a bit of dust from his dhoti, or straightening swiftly, with that mixture of adroitness and awkwardness that only human beings, however godly they are, have; he was so much more beautiful than she was. It was not his wife's beauty she feared and envied; it was his. Sighing, she looked at her own muscular arms, used to lifting heavy things and throwing them into the distance, somewhat hirsute and dark but undoubtedly efficient, and compared them to his, which glowed in the sunlight. Her face, which she'd begun to look in a pond nearby, had cavernous nostrils and tiny tusks that jutted out from beneath her lips; it was full of fierceness and candour, but, when she cried, it did not evoke pity, not even her own. The face reflected on the water filled her with displeasure. How lovely his features were in comparison!

After about six days had passed, and she'd gone unnoticed, hiding, frightened, and when she was glimpsed, frightening, behind the bush, she decided to approach him. She had grown tired of hovering there like an animal; even the animals had begun to watch her. Although she'd been taught to believe, since childhood, that rakkhoshes were better—braver, less selfish, more charitable, and better-natured—than human beings and gods, it was true that latter were prettier. They'd been blessed unfairly by creation; no one knew why. Long ago she'd been told that it was bad luck to fall in love with a god or a human being, but the possibility had seemed so remote that she'd never entertained it seriously. The feeling of longing, too, was relatively new for her, although she was in full maturity as a woman; but she was untried and untested, rakkhosh though she was, and uncourted; and this odd condition of restlessness was more solitary and inward, she found, than indigestion, and more painful.

She decided to change herself. She could take other forms at will, albeit temporarily; she decided to become someone else, at least for a while. She went to a clearing where she was sure no one would see her, where the only living things were some insects and a few birds on the trees, and the transformation took place. Now she went to the pond to look at the picture in the water. Her heart, like a girl's upon glimpsing a bride, beat faster at what she saw; a woman with large eyes and long hair coming down to her waist, her body pliant. She wasn't sure if this was her, or if the water was reflecting someone else.

Rama and his younger brother Lakshmana had gone out into the forest to collect some wood; she saw them from a distance. Her mouth went dry, and she snorted with nervousness; then she recalled how she'd become more beautiful than she'd imagined, and tried to control these noises she inadvertently made. She thought, looking at Rama, 'He is not a man; I'm sure he's a god,' and was filled with longing. When they came nearer her, she lost her shyness and came out into the clearing.

'What's this?' said Rama softly to his brother, pretending not to have seen her. Lakshmana glanced back quickly and whispered, as he bent to pick up his axe:

'I don't know—but this beautiful "maiden" smells of rakkhoshi; look at the gawky and clumsy way she carries her body, as if it were an ornament she'd recently acquired.'

'Let's have some fun with her,' whispered Rama. He'd been bored for days in the forest, and this overbearing, obstreperous creature of ethereal beauty, now approaching them with unusually heavy footsteps, promised entertainment.

'Lord . . .,' she stuttered, '. . . Lord . . . forgive me for intruding so shamelessly, but I saw you wandering alone and thought you might have lost your way.' Rama and Lakshmana looked at each other; their faces were grave, but a smile glinted in their eyes. They'd noticed she'd ignored Lakshmana altogether. It amused and flattered Rama to be on the receiving end of this attention, even if it came from a rakkhoshi who'd changed shape; and it also repelled him vaguely. He experienced, for the first time, the dubious and uncomfortable pleasure of being the object of pursuit. This didn't bother him unduly, though; he was, like all members of the male sex, slightly vain. Lakshmana cleared his throat and said:

'Who are you, maiden? Do you come from these parts?'

'Not far from here,' said the beautiful woman, while the covering on her bosom slipped a little without her noticing it. 'Lord,' she said, going up to Rama and touching his arm, 'let's go a little way from here. There's a place not far away where you can get some rest.' Within the beautiful body, the rakkhoshi's heart beat fiercely, but with trepidation.

'I don't mind,' said the godly one slowly. 'But what's a woman like you doing here alone? Aren't you afraid of thieves?'

'I know no fear, Lord,' she said. 'Besides, seeing you, whatever fear I might have had melts away.'

'Before I go with you,' conceded Rama, 'I must consult my brother—and tell him what to do when I've gone.' Surpanakha said: 'Whatever pleases you, Lord,' but thought, 'I've won him over; I can't believe it. My prayers are answered.'

Rama went to Lakshmana and said: 'This creature's beginning to tire me. Do something.'

'Like what?' said Lakshmana. He was sharpening the blade of his knife. Ram admired the back of his hand and said moodily:

'I don't know. Something she'll remember for days. Teach her a lesson for being so forward.' Lakshmana got up wearily with the knife still in one hand, and Rama said under his breath:

'Don't kill her, though.'

A little later, a howl was heard. Lakshmana came back; there was some blood on the blade. 'I cut her nose,' he said. 'It'—he gestured towards the knife—'went through her nostril as if it were silk. She immediately changed back into the horrible creature she really is. She's not worth describing,' he said, as he wiped his blade and Rama chuckled without smiling. 'She was in some pain. She flapped her arms and screamed in pain and ran off into the forest like some agitated beast.'

Crying and screaming, Surpanakha circled around the shrubs and trees, dripping blood. The blood was mingled with the snot that came from her weeping, and she wiped these away from her disfigured face without thinking. Even when the pain had subsided a little, the bewilderment remained, that the one she'd worshipped should be so without compassion, so unlike what he looked like. It was from here, in this state, she went looking for Ravana.

NOTES

SITA AND SOME OTHER WOMEN FROM THE EPICS

1. Sharma, Shastri Narahari Mangallal, *Shree Valmiki Ramayana: Shudhha Gujarati Bhashantar,* Sastu Sahitya Vardhak Karyalaya, Mumbai, 1999.

CHITRANGADA NOT SITA: JAWAHARLAL NEHRU'S MODEL FOR GENDER EQUATION

1. Gopal, S., *The Mind of Jawaharlal Nehru*, Orient Longman, Madras, 1980, p. 3.
2. Nehru, Jawaharlal, 'Women Should Not Be Weak', Gopal, S. (ed.), *Selected Works of Jawaharlal Nehru (SWJN)*, vol. 8, Orient Longman, New Delhi, 12 June 1937, p. 676.
3. See Bagchi, Jasodhara (ed.), *Indian Women: Myth and Reality*, Sangam Books, Hyderabad, 1995.
4. 'Bichitra', *Rabindra Rachanabali,* Birth Centenary edition, vol. 1, Government of West Bengal, 1961, p. 438.
5. Nehru, Jawaharlal, *The Discovery of India,* Jawaharlal Nehru Memorial Fund, New Delhi, 1982, p. 41.
6. Gandhi, M.K., *The Role of Women*, Hingorani (ed.), Bhartiya Vidya Bhavan, Bombay, 1964.
7. Quoted in Chattopadhyay, Kamaladevi, *Indian Women's Battle for Freedom*, Abhinav Publications, New Delhi, 1983.
8. Sangari, Kumkum and Vaid, Sudesh (eds), *Recasting Women: Essays in Colonial History*, Kali for Women, New Delhi, 1989.
9. Chatterjee, Partha, 'The Nationalist Resolution of the Women's Question', in Sangari, Kumkum and Vaid, Sudesh (eds), op. cit.
10. Jawaharlal Nehru to Frances Gunther, 5 May 1938, Frances Gunther MSS, file 190, acc. no. 691, Nehru Memorial Museum and Library (NMML).
11. 'Women and the Freedom Movement', *SWJN*, vol. 7, 6 October 1936, Madras, p. 479.

12. *Jawaharlal Nehru's Speeches*, 1953–57, vol. 3, The Publication's Division, Ministry of Information & Broadcasting, Government of India, New Delhi, 1958, p. 453.
13. Ibid.
14. Seton, Marie, *Panditji: A Portrait of Jawaharlal Nehru*, Rupa & Co., Calcutta, 1967, pp. 471–72.
15. *SWJN*, Second Series, vol. 10, p. 487.
16. Seton, Marie, op. cit., p. 92.
17. Ibid., vol. 10, p. 488.
18. Nehru's speech on the eve of departure of Mountbatten, *SWJN*, Second Series, vol. 6, 2O June 1948, p. 360.
19. Allahabad, *SWJN*, vol. 10, 28 February 1940, p. 529.
20. *SWJN*, vol. 2, p. 440.
21. *SWJN*, vol. 11, p. 646.
22. Jawaharlal Nehru to his mother, *SWJN*, vol. 1, 14 March 1912, pp. 96–97.
23. Jawaharlal Nehru to Indira, *SWJN*, vol. 6, 27 July 1934, p. 267.
24. *SWJN*, vol. 8, p. 676.
25. Ibid., p. 677.
26. Jawaharlal Nehru to Indira, *SWJN*, vol. 6, 15 June 1934, pp. 256–57.
27. *SWJN*, vol. 5, p. 292.
28. 'On the Treatment of Prostitutes', *SWJN*, vol. 2, 10 June 1923, p. 14.
29. Ibid.
30. Forbes, Geraldine, 'The Politics of Respectability: Indian Women and the Indian National Congress', in Low, D.A., *The Indian National Congress: Centenary Hindsights*, Oxford University Press, 1988, New Delhi.
31. Jawaharlal Nehru to Frances Gunther, op. cit.
32. *SWJN*, vol. 3, p. 362.
33. Speech at Mahila Vidyapith, Allahabad, *SWJN*, vol. 3, 31 March 1928, p. 361.
34. 'Jawaharlal Nehru to Gandhi', *SWJN*, vol. 11, 24 July 1941, pp. 658–59.
35. Quoted in Ali, Aruna Asaf, *The Private Face of a Public Person: A Study of Jawaharlal Nehru*, Radiant Publishers, New Delhi, 1989, p. 86.
36. Ibid.
37. Morgan, Janet, *Edwina Mountbatten: A Life of Her Own*, HarperCollins, London, 1991, p. 428.
38. Morgan, Janet, op. cit., p. 430.
39. Ibid., p. 471.
40. See Som, Reba, 'Jawaharlal Nehru and the Hindu Code: A Victory of Symbol over Substance', in *Modern Asian Studies Cambridge*, vol. 28, part 1, UK, February 1994.

41. Norman, Dorothy, *Nehru: The First Sixty Years,* vol. 1, Asia Publishing House, Bombay, 1965, p. 276.
42. Mehta, Ashok, 'Planning without Progress', in Zakaria, Rafiq, *A Study of Nehru,* Rupa & Co., New Delhi, 1989.
43. Amrit Kaur, 'A Friend without Friends', in Zakaria, Rafiq, op. cit.
44. *SWJN,* Second Series, vol. 2, pp. 426–27.
45. Gopal, S., op.cit., p. 8.

MATRILINEAL AND PATRILINEAL

1. Heimsath, Charles, 'Shakti: The Female Component of Indian Culture', *Illustrated Weekly of India,* 4 June 1972.
2. Ibid.
3. Kakar, Sudhir, *Intimate Relations: Exploring Indian Sexuality,* Penguin Viking, New Delhi, 1989.
4. Ibid.

DRAUPADI'S MOMENT IN SITA'S SYNTAX

1. Lakshmana rekha: In the Ramayana, during a hunt, Sita's brother-in-law Lakshmana, demarcates a circular space warning her against transgression. However, Sita crosses over when, caught as she is between refusing a Brahmin (actually the disguised Ravana) and being cursed, and violating her brother-in-law's injunction, she chooses the religious alternative of serving the Brahmin. The impossibility of Sita's position demonstrates the sheer perversity of patriarchal injunctions which seem to either invite transgression or make it inevitable, reducing Sita's agency to an option between punishments.
2. Draupadi's question to the messenger who brings the order for her to appear in the Kaurava court ('Go ascertain from the gambler if he lost himself, or me, first.'), is the 'sole and "unique" unanswered dilemma in the epic'. Rajeshwari, Rajan Sunder (ed.), 'The Story of Draupadi's Disrobing', *Signposts: Gender Issues in Post-Independence India,* Kali, New Delhi, 1999, p. 336. In this context it is necessary to note the elision of Sita as a goddess in the mode of shakti, her series of queries, anger, laments and finally her decision to abandon Rama that seriously critique the dharmic law he invokes to legitimize his actions. It is possible that the Hindu right's masculinist erasure of Sita from the conventional invocation (Siya–Rama to Sri Rama), is a sign of the continued ambiguous subjectivity of Sita, and the moral ambiguity of Rama especially within the context of the difficult questions and issues posed by feminist scholarship on the subject.
3. A similar logic is effected in the case of minorities where the mere fact

of not being Hindu—whether appropriately submissive or not—is sufficient reason for punishment.

4. Sudhir Kakar has tried to indicate the psycho-social implications of the social and cultural meanings of motherhood and the mother in the Indian context, indicating the substantial psychological influence of this figure. See Kakar, Sudhir, *Culture and Psyche: Selected Essays*, OUP, New Delhi, 1997; see also his *The Inner World: A Psycho-analytic Study of Childhood in India*, OUP, New Delhi, 1996, and *Intimate Relations*, Penguin, New Delhi, 1989.

TRIAL BY FIRE

1. *Manushi*, no. 98, Jan–Feb 1997.
2. *Manushi*, nos 50–52, Jan–June 1989.

SITA SINGS THE BLUES

1. Annette Hanshaw (1901–85) was one of the first great female jazz singers.

SITA IN PAHARI LOK RAMAIN

1. Published by Himachal Art, Culture, Language Academy, 2003.

REFERENCES

Bose, Mandrakanta (ed.), *Faces of the Feminine in Ancient, Medieval and Modern India*, Oxford University Press, New York, 2000.

Bose, Mandakranta (ed.), *The Ramayana Revisited*, Oxford University Press, New York, 2004.

Candravati, 'Ramayana' in Maulik, Kshitish Chandra (ed.), *Prachin Purbabanga Gitika*, Firma K.L. Mukhopadhyay, Calcutta, 1975.

Coburn, Thomas, 'Sita Fights While Rama Swoons', *Manushi*, no. 90, September–October, 1995.

Das, Balarama, *Jagamohan Ramayana*, Bhubaneswar, 1995.

Das, Siddheswar, *Vilanka Ramayana*, Ridge Printers and Publishers, Bhubaneswar, 1985.

Dev Sen, Nabaneeta, 'Candravati *Ramayana*: Feminizing the Rama-Tale', in Bhanja, Upendra M., *Vaidehishavilas*, 2000–04.

Dutt, Romesh C. (trans.), *The Great Epics of India: Ramayana*, Ess Ess Publications, New Delhi, 1992.

Hande, H.V., *Kamba Ramayanam: An English Prose Rendering*, Bharatiya Vidya Bhavan, Mumbai, 1996.

Krittivasa, *Ramayana*, second edition, Serampore.

Mahapatra, Sitakant, 'Jagamohan Ramayana Balrama Dasa: Inheritance and Innovations', in Singh, Avadesh Kumar (ed.), *Ramayana through the Ages*, D.K. Printers, New Delhi, 2007.

Meher, Gangadhar (ed.), *Granthabali*, Vidya Prakashan, Cuttack, 2006.

Ray, A. (ed.), *Dasharathi Rayer Panchali*, Mahesh Library, Calcutta, 1997.

Narayan, R.K., *Gods, Demons, and Others*, Viking, New York, 1964.

Narayan, R.K., *The Ramayana: A Shortened Modern Prose Version of the Indian Epic*, Indian Thought Publications, Chennai, 1973.

Narayan, R.K., *My Days*, Chatto & Windus, London, 1975.

Narayan, R.K., *My Dateless Diary: An American Journey*. Penguin Books India, New Delhi, 1991.

Rajagopalachari, C., *Ramayana Mumbai*, Bharatiya Vidya Bhavan, 2000.

Valmiki, *Adbhut Ramayana*, translated by Shantilal Nagar, B.R. Publishing Co., Delhi, 2001.

NOTES ON CONTRIBUTORS

A.K. Ashby learned about dance under the tutelage of eminent gurus Padma Shri Prahlada Vedantam, Padma Bhushan Vempati Chinna Satyam and Nilimma Devi. She is Associate Director of the Sutradhar Institute of Dance and Related Arts and a lead member of the Devi Dance Theatre. She was interviewed and filmed in 1995 for a BBC series on world dance. An avid writer of poetry and cultural ethnography, Anila penned the key poem for 'The Diary of Sita', a provocative choreographic work by Nilimma Devi.

Aman Nath is a historian, poet, graphic designer and copywriter. He has co-written award-winning illustrated books on art, history, architecture, corporate biography and photography. He is actively involved in the restoration of India's architectural ruins, run as the Neemrana 'non-hotel' Hotels, which have won awards from UNESCO as well as national awards from the Government of India.

Amit Chaudhuri is a novelist, critic, poet and musician. He has written, among others, *Freedom Song, Real Time: Stories and a Reminiscence, St. Cyril Road and Other Poems*; and edited the collection *Memory's Gold: Writings on Calcutta.* He is the recipient of several awards like the Commonwealth Writers' Prize, the *Los Angeles Times* Book Prize for Fiction and the Sahitya Akademi award. His acclaimed crossover project, *This Is Not Fusion,* is available on CD. He is Professor of Contemporary Literature at the University of East Anglia, UK, and was a judge of the Man Booker International Prize 2009.

Anamika teaches English Literature at Delhi University. She is a translator and an award-winning Hindi poet. She has written extensively on the myth of the fallen woman, including 'An STD Booth', 'A Hubble-Bubble Act', 'The Kotha of Dhela Bai', 'Pandita Ramabai's Copy of the New Testament' and 'The Diary of a Call-Girl-cum-Research Scholar'.

Arshia Sattar is a Ph.D from the Department of South Asian Languages and Civilizations at the University of Chicago. Her translations from Sanskrit of tales from the *Kathasaritsagara* and the *Valmiki Ramayana* have been published by Penguin Books.

Chandra Ghosh Jain has written short stories that have been published online as well as in print. An anthology of her short stories *Memsaheb and the Thief* has been published by Bumblebee Publishers, New Delhi. Her latest novel *Letters of a Silent Wife* has been published by www.4indianwomen.com.

D. Rama Raju is an acclaimed Telugu scholar and has contributed to the *Rama-Katha* in Tribal and Folk Traditions of India—Proceedings of a Seminar, ASI, Seagull Books. The Telugu version of Ramayana stories presented by Rama Raju contains elaborate accounts of various episodes in terms of folk perceptions.

Devdutt Pattanaik is trained in medicine and is Chief Belief Officer of the Future Group. He has spent the last twelve years of his life decoding sacred mythological stories, symbols and rituals and illustrating their relevance for modern times. He has fourteen books to his credit including *Myth = Mithya: A Handbook of Hindu Mythology*, *The Book of Ram* and *Seven Secrets of Hindu Calendar Art*.

G.K. Das received his education from Ravenshaw College, Cuttack, and the University of Cambridge, from where he obtained the Ph.D for his work on E.M. Forster. He was a professor of English at the University of Delhi and Vice Chancellor of Utkal University. His main publications are on Forster, D.H. Lawrence and Oriya literature and culture.

Indira Goswami is a Jnanpith awardee and is widely known for her literary writings and her research on the Ramayana. A prolific writer of novels and stories, her famous works include *Datal Hantir Une Khowa Howda* ('The Moth-Eaten Howdah'), *Mamore Dhara Taruwal* ('The Rusted Sword'), which won her the Sahitya Akademi award, 1982, and *Chinnamastar Mahuhtu* ('The Man from Chinnamasta'). Presently, she is completing her new novel *Thengfakhri*.

Karen Gabriel is a senior fellow with the Centre for Women's Development Studies (CWDS) and Reader in English at St. Stephen's College, Delhi University. She has worked and published widely on gender, sexuality, media, culture, nation and development. Her book on cinema, *The Sexual Economies of the Contemporary Mainstream Bombay Cinema (1970–2000)* is scheduled to be published this year.

Kumudini (Smt. Renganayaki Thatham) was one of the earliest women writers of twentieth-century Tamil literature. She translated Rabindranath Tagore's *Jogajog* from Hindi into Tamil. Kumudini also wrote the novel *Diwan-Magal* (1942), which advocated inter-caste marriages. A sincere

Gandhian, she corresponded with Gandhi, spent several months in Sewagram and founded the Seva Sangham in Tiruchi in 1948.

Madhu Kishwar is a senior fellow at the Centre for the Study of Developing Societies (CSDS). She is the founder editor of *Manushi*, a journal about women and society, being published since 1979, and the founder president of Manushi Sangathan, a forum for research-based activist interventions. Some of the books authored or edited by her are *Religion at the Service of Nationalism and Other Essays*, *Rashtriyata ki Chakri Mein Dharm*, *Off the Beaten Track: Rethinking Gender Justice for Indian Women* and *Deepening Democracy: Challenges of Governance and Globalization in India*.

Madhureeta Anand is Founder and Festival Director of the 0110 Digital Film Festival, and an award-winning filmmaker in her own right. She set up her own banner Ekaa Films, in 1995 and has directed many documentary films on culture, religion and anthropology which have been telecast on BBC, Channel 4, Discovery and National Geographic. Some have won awards, including the Royal Television Society Craft Award for her Kumbh Mela Series.

Malashri Lal is a professor in the Department of English, and the current joint director of the University of Delhi, South Campus. She has written and lectured extensively on women's socio-cultural positioning and women's writing. Her publications include *The Law of the Threshold: Women Writers in Indian English* and the co-edited volumes, *Interpreting Home in South Asian Literature* and *Speaking for Myself: An Anthology of Asian Women's Writing* (Penguin, 2009). Malashri Lal is presently exploring women's viewpoints in folk narratives of Rajasthan and Himachal Pradesh.

Mallika Sengupta is a poet and an important voice in contemporary Bengali literature. She has published eleven books of poetry, two novels and several essays, and edited an anthology of women's poetry from Bengal. She works as a lecturer of sociology in a Kolkata college. She is also the poetry editor of *Sananda*. Sengupta has won numerous awards, including the Sukanto Puraskar (1998) from the government of West Bengal.

Mandakranta Bose, FRSC, Professor Emerita at the University of British Columbia, has published extensively on Sanskrit texts on codes of conduct relating to women, as well as on the performing arts of India and the Ramayana, especially in relation to gender representation. Her many books include *Movement and Mimesis: The Idea of Dance in the Sanskritic Tradition*, *Faces of the Feminine in Ancient, Medieval and Modern India* and *The Ramayana Revisited*. Her forthcoming work is a critical edition of the eighteenth-century Sanskrit treatise on dance and music, the *Sangitanarayana*.

Manjeet Baruah is a lecturer in Translation Studies at the Indira Gandhi National Open University, New Delhi. His areas of research include Assamese literature, the Ramayana and folk culture. As a writer and translator, his books include *A Comedy of a Spark and Other Stories* and *Melodies and Guns*. His stories and research papers have appeared in journals such as *Indian Literature*. His most recent book is *Indira Goswami: A Compilation on Her Life, Works and Achievements*.

Meenakshi Faith Paul teaches English at the Himachal Pradesh University Centre for Evening Studies, Shimla. She is a poet and translator. As a researcher she focuses on the folk literature and culture of Himachal Pradesh, with special reference to narratives of women, ecology and temples as also to folk wisdom and traditional knowledge.

Meghnad Desai is an economist and a Labour Peer in the UK. He was made Lord Desai of St. Clement Danes in 1991, and was awarded the Bharatiya Pravasi Puraskar in 2004 and the Padma Bhushan in 2008. He has written books on Dilip Kumar's cinema, Ezra Pound's economic thinking, religion and ideology as the roots of terrorism, and development and nationhood, among other themes. He writes regularly for various publications including the *Times of India*, *DNA*, *Indian Express* and *Outlook*.

Namita Gokhale is a writer. She published the film magazine, *Super* from Bombay in the late 1970s. Her first novel was the critically acclaimed *Paro: Dreams of Passion* (1984), followed by *A Himalayan Love Story* and *Gods, Graves and Grandmother*. Her other works include *The Book of Shadows, The Book of Shiva* and *Shakuntala: The Play of Memory*. Most recently, she retold the epic *The Mahabharata* for young readers (Puffin, 2009). Namita Gokhale is a director of Yatra Books and one of the founder directors of the Jaipur Literature Festival.

Navaneeta Dev Sen is known for her sensitive portrayals of modern lives and her acute eye for issues of social justice. Her poems, short stories, novels, features and essays are marked by wit and humour. Among her well-known works are *Bama-Bodhini*, *Nati Nabanita*, *Srestha Kabita* and *Sita Theke Suru*. She is the founder secretary of the Indian National Comparative Literature Association and has received the Gouridevi Memorial Award; Mahadevi Verma Award, Celli Award from Rockefeller Foundation, Prasad Puraskar and Sahitya Akademi Award.

Nilimma Devi is a noted dancer and choreographer, who has devoted her life to the elegant art form of Kuchipudi. Her struggle against personal obstacles to master this art emerges as one of many strong metaphors in her work. A dancer of international repute who has garnered critical praise from India as well as the USA, where she is now based, Devi strives to transcend cultural boundaries and inform audiences.

Nina Paley is a long-time veteran of syndicated comic strips, creating 'Fluff', 'The Hots' and her own alternative weekly 'Nina's Adventures'. In 2002 Nina followed her then-husband to Trivandrum, India, where she read her first Ramayana. This inspired her first feature, 'Sita Sings the Blues' which she animated and produced single-handedly over the course of five years on a home computer. Nina teaches at Parsons School of Design in Manhattan.

Nishi Chawla holds a Ph.D from the George Washington University. She was born and raised in India where she taught for more than a decade at the University of Delhi as an associate professor. She writes and publishes fiction and poetry. Her books include *Samuel Beckett: Reading the Body in His Writings*, *Twist of Truth* and *A Human Silicon Chip*. She teaches courses in Literature and in Writing at UMUC and at UMD.

Ramnika Gupta is a devoted social worker and crusader for the cause of the downtrodden. The Ramnika Foundation that she set up several years ago seeks to bring upliftment for the *aam admi*. She has worked in Jharkhand with tribals, Dalits, women and minorities defying the mafia, and braved attacks on her life. She has also highlighted their plight through her literary works and brought Dalit writing to the attention of scholars and researchers.

Ranga Rao has published three novels: *Fowl-Filcher* (the first original novel published by Penguin Books India in their inaugural offering in 1987), *The Drunk Tantra* (Penguin, 1989), and *The River is Three-Quarters Full* (Penguin, 2001); a collection of short stories, *An Indian Idyll and Other Stories* (Ravi Dayal Publisher, 1989); two anthologies of translations: *Classic Telugu Short Stories* (Penguin, 1995) and *That Man on the Road* (Penguin, 2006); and a monograph, *R.K. Narayan* (Sahitya Akademi, Delhi, 2004).

Rashna Imhasly-Gandhy is a Delhi-based Jungian psychotherapist. Her speciality lies in family and partner therapy. She has conducted many lectures, workshops and training courses in Switzerland, Germany, Holland and Mexico. She is the author of the book, *The Psychology of Love: Wisdom of Indian Mythology* (Roli Books and Namita Gokhale Editions).

Ratna Lahiri is a freelance writer, editor and translator. In her various research projects she has focused on Indian and South-East Asian studies, specializing in Indian culture, religion, mythology and folk. She is the founder president of UJAAS, education for the girl child, and Stree Shakti, an organization devoted to empowering Indian women. She has written for the *Encyclopaedia of Indian Philosophy*, *Encyclopaedia of Hinduism* and for all volumes of the *Encyclopaedia of Indian Literature*.

Reba Som is Director of the Rabindranath Tagore Centre, ICCR, Kolkata. Graduating in history from Presidency College, she received her Ph.D from Calcutta University. Awarded the Jawaharlal Nehru Fellowship, she has several publications to her credit, which include *Gandhi, Bose, Nehru and the Making of the Modern Indian Mind* and *Rabindranath Tagore: The Singer and His Song.*

Rina Tripathi is a poet, writer and editor with a special interest in gender, ecology, environment and human rights. She has worked as a research assistant to well-known novelists and academics, and conducted indepth interviews with public figures. Her articles have appeared in *Life Positive* and in web magazines.

Shashi Deshpande has written nine novels and four children's books, and undertaken translations from Kannada and Marathi into English. She has several volumes of short stories and a collection of essays to her credit. She received the Sahitya Akademi award for her work, *That Long Silence*. Her works have been translated into various Indian and European languages.

Smita Tewari Jassal, an anthropologist by discipline, is a Madeleine Haas Russell Visiting Professor at Brandeis University, Boston. She has taught Gender and Development at Columbia University. Her works include *Daughters of the Earth: Women and Land* and *The Partition Motif in Contemporary Conflicts*. Her forthcoming volume is entitled *Unearthing Gender*.

Sonal Mansingh is one of the finest exponents of Odissi. Through her choreography and innovative techniques, she has brought the dimensions of social activism and contemporary relevance to traditional narratives from mythology. An extraordinary performer, teacher and scholar, she founded the Centre for Indian Classical Dances in New Delhi. Over the years, dance has brought her many awards, including the Padma Vibhushan in 2003, making her the first woman dancer in India to receive such an honour.

Tarun Vijay had written short stories and poems before working in a tribal area as an activist on environment and literacy. A columnist for major newspapers, he specializes in Chinese affairs and he initiated the Indus fest in Ladakh. A keen traveller and photographer, he has written a travelogue, *An Odyssey in Tibet*, besides several other books.

Vijay Lakshmi teaches at the Community College of Philadelphia. Her short stories, published in various journals have been gathered in a novella called *Pomegranate Dreams and Other Stories*. Author of *Virginia Woolf as Literary Critic* and several scholarly articles, she writes stories about the psychological conflicts and moral dilemmas of immigrant women settling in Western societies. Her stories have been translated into French and Chinese.

COPYRIGHT ACKNOWLEDGEMENTS

Grateful acknowledgement is made to the following for permission to reprint copyright material:

Penguin Viking for 'Introduction to Valmiki's Ramayana' and 'Women and Kingship in the Ramayana' by Arshia Sattar, originally published in *The Valmiki Ramayana*;

Karen Gabriel for 'Draupadi's Moment in Sita's Syntax', originally published as 'Draupadi's Moment in Sita's Syntax: Violations of the Past and the Construction of Community in Kamal Haasan's *Hey! Ram*', in Abraham, Taisha (ed.), *Women and the Politics of Violence*, Shakti;

The Little Magazine, Reprinted with permission from *The Little Magazine, vol vii: Sex Determination*;

Seagull Books and Anthropological Survey of India for D. Rama Raju's 'Versions of Ramayana Stories in Telugu Folk Literature', originally published in *Rama Katha in Tribal and Folk Traditions of India: Proceedings of a Seminar*;

Chandra Ghosh Jain for 'Sita's Letter to Her Unborn Daughter', originally published in *Memsaheb and the Thief: A Collection of Short Stories*;

Ramnika Gupta for 'Sita: An Excerpt from a Novel', originally published in *Sita*, Anurag Prakashan;

Ahana Lakshmi for Kumudini's 'Letters from a Palace', originally published in *The Hindu*, Sunday Literary Review, 3 April 2005;

Nishi Chawla for 'Sita's Divinity' and 'Sita in Her Exile', originally published in *Confluences: Indian Women, Indian Goddesses*, Indialog;

Amit Chaudhuri for 'An Infatuation (from the Ramayana)', originally published in *Real Time Stories and A Reminiscence*, Picador.

While every effort has been made to trace copyright holders and obtain permissions, this has not been possible in all cases; any omissions brought to our attention will be remedied in future editions.

INDEX